"Take the Witness!"

"Take the Witness!"

ALFRED COHN

AND

JOE CHISHOLM

GARDEN CITY PUBLISHING COMPANY, INC.

Garden City, New York

PRINTED IN THE UNITED STATES OF AMERICA

FOREWORD

My father, whose life story is told in "Take the Witness!" was a criminal lawyer.

When I was a little girl, we used to go out to the ball games and when a player got mad at the umpire and started after him with a bat, the bleachers would rise and shout, "Go ahead and kill him, we'll get Earl Rogers to defend you."

And Dad would chuckle and roll himself a cigarette with one elegant gesture and beam, for he loved crowds.

The murder cases he tried, almost a hundred of them, were as thrilling as any stage or screen or detective fiction have ever offered.

California still held traces of the picturesque West, the glamorous West, when Dad was headlining. Moreover, he believed implicitly in showmanship. And no matter who was on trial—whether it was Clarence Darrow huddled in his chair beneath an accusation of jury bribery, or the suave, silver-haired McComas who had made good his title of lady-killer by shooting his mistress, or the beautiful Gabrielle Darley, in a real-life "Frankie and Johnnie" murder case, or Patrick Calhoun, fearless and aristocratic in the famous San Francisco graft cases—no matter whom he was defending, Dad always held the center of the stage himself.

His fireworks were always more impressive, because he himself belonged to the John Drew school. No one ever had such beautiful manners as Dad, when he was cross-examining a female witness for the prosecution or dodging ink-wells thrown by some district attorney whom he had baited beyond human endurance.

[v]

FOREWORD

John Barrymore, when he played a stock season in California as a young leading man, used to spend his spare time in the courtroom watching Dad. He once told me that Dad was the best actor he had ever seen. "And he writes his own lines as he goes along, too!" said Jack.

When I was covering the Hickman case a few years ago, I spent a lot of time around the new courthouse. And though Dad had been gone for years, I was stopped over and over again by dignified judges and well-known lawyers, by bailiffs and under-sheriffs, by newspaper reporters and politicians, and they all said the same thing, "There's no one around now like your Dad."

And then they would tell me their favorite story about Earl Rogers. Wherever in California to this day old-timers gather, they tell tales of the things Dad did, in courtrooms and out.

Most of those tales are in this book by Al Cohn and Joe Chisholm, both of whom knew him well, for Al was an Associated Press reporter on some of Dad's best cases and Joe Chisholm studied law under him. And I find that the tales make even better reading than they have made conversation.

Once in a while comes a man who intrigues and fascinates public imagination, who dazzles his associates, who gains a hold upon the memory of all who knew him. Such a man is nearly always worth reading about, and my Dad was such a man.

I know, and as proof of that, in California I was, am, and no matter what I might do always will be, "Earl Rogers' daughter." If I happen now and again to write something that isn't too bad, my mail brings hundreds of letters which frankly state that the highest compliment they can pay me is that I inherited a little something from my father.

One came this morning. It says, "Many years ago your brilliant, perfectly adorable, pitiful Dad was my patient for a short time. Were he alive today he would be proud of the defense you wrote for that trained nurse. What higher compliment can I, also a trained nurse, pay you than to say that the little girl he never forgot, even in his most obscure moments, has grown up to carry on as he would have wished?"

Yes, the obscure moments came.

If he had been anything but a great criminal lawyer I believe he would be alive today. In his prime. For he was only fifty-two when he died. And we would have been spared those last days when his pride and his love sent him to die alone.

I wanted to be a criminal lawyer. "I'd rather see you dead," said my Dad.

For he believed by that time, as I came to believe, that no one could survive the strain, the pressure, the strange immoral mesmerism, of criminal law as it is practiced in America.

Certainly he did not survive it. He was a man of great strength, of enormous brain power, but too much imagination.

"Take the Witness!" will make you understand the great game of criminal law as it was played a generation ago— before it became a racket, when it was really exciting and vital. It was the greatest of all games, for it was played with a human life as the stake. And in Dad's day it was played on the level. He was no one's "mouthpiece." He was a *lawyer*.

Once in a case, all Dad saw was his goal: "Not Guilty."

How many nights I have seen Dad pace the floor all night long, strained and desperate, searching for some way to save the life of his client. (I have always thought it was lack of sleep which drove him to seek relief in alcoholic stimulants. Literally, he *never* slept when he was trying a tough case. In the end that will break any man.) His client! No matter who he was, no matter if Dad knew him to be guilty, that client's life was in Dad's hands and he must preserve it.

And he poured himself out, his talents and his personality, at top speed and white heat. Many a time I have taken his coat, after a tough cross-examination, and wrung it out as though he had been swimming.

FOREWORD

No man ever worked harder—and it sometimes comes to me now as a tragedy that he worked as he did for such ends. He was worthy of greater causes.

Yet into each fantastic, thrilling case he put the best that was in him. I can see him, as he sat robed in the elegant wine-red velvet dressing gowns he affected, actually memorizing a witness's direct examination, while I cued him on it, so that when it came time to cross-examine he knew every word the witness had spoken.

"Take the Witness!"

The district attorney is through. He turns from his star witness—it may be that dark-eyed girl who had such a good memory for dates; it may be a cold, impressive medico, or a bull-necked, dogged, shrewd politician. Glancing about the courtroom, he says, "Take the Witness!"

You can feel the stir. The whispering, the rustling, the craning of necks. Now the drama is about to begin. The witness shifts nervously, or glares defiantly, or sits stolidly under control.

A tall, theatrically groomed figure, with heavy shoulders and a slim waist, rises and walks around the end of the long table. His black hair shining, his Irish-blue eyes intent, he stands in front of the witness.

Sometimes he smiles, in a pitying way. Sometimes he grins, nastily. Sometimes his jaw shoots forward and his heavy black brows come down menacingly. Sometimes his voice is like oil, sometimes it is like a charged electric wire.

Something vibrates through that courtroom. The plump little girl in the front row gasps, "Oh gee, ain't he handsome!" The row of law students jammed along the back cranes forward. His Honor ceases to read extraneous papers and looks down from the bench.

Earl Rogers is about to cross-examine.

I never knew quite how he did it, but that is the way it was.

FOREWORD

Once, in a certain case, before he took over the chief witness for the prosecution, he handed me a little slip of paper upon which were written eight questions. "That's all I really want to ask him," he said.

It took him four days to ask those eight questions—four days to slip them in so that the clever witness—he *was* clever —would not know where they were leading. When the eighth one came, the witness saw the noose he had made for himself and collapsed.

That was cross-examination. They use different methods now. I preferred the old ones.

In time he came to have a great reputation.

One day I was sitting in my Dad's office when a well-dressed, high-bred old Chinaman entered. (Dad for many years represented most of the high class Chinamen in California, and once at least his arbitration settled a tong war. He was a great favorite with the California Chinese and on their holidays our house was always full of lilies and strangely flavored nuts, of magnificent jade and rich embroideries which had come as presents to "Mr. Rogers.")

This Chinaman wanted to know how much Dad would charge to defend him for murder. Dad told him. He sat down, began pulling little bags out of his voluminous garments and finally counted out the money in gold. Then he arose and with a deep bow started out.

"Hey!" said Dad, "come back here. What's all this? Where are you going?"

"I go kill the man now," said the Chinaman. "Then I be back."

That is a true story. I was there.

In the summer of 1921 we stood, my father and I, upon the wide crescent of the beach at Del Mar, looking not at each other but at the giant combers that broke along the Pacific. For he had just told me that he knew his hold upon life was loosening fast and that he wished it so.

I had spent hours trying to make him come home and live
with me again. But he said that he knew how he had disap-
pointed me and that above all things he could not bear to see
the sadness upon my face.

"It will not be for long," he said, "and you must let me
go and hide away and live out these days as best I can. It is
easier for me when I am alone, for then sometimes I can forget. Forget what I have been, what I should be—and what
I am.

"And when I am gone, which I pray may be soon, I don't
want you to grieve, because all that is best of me will remain
with you. You know what I think, you know my mind, and
the blessed gift of memory will keep me close to you. When
you read again the books we have read together, it will be as
though we met once more, and when you read a new book
you will know what I would think of it, as well as though
I spoke to you. You will remember the times we have spent
together; and your love for me, which has survived so much
else, will survive death. You will lose nothing but this broken-
down, burned-out material shadow, which has become a burden to us both."

So he prepared me for his death, as he had prepared me for
everything else in life. That very day, standing shoulder to
shoulder with him, his hand in mine to comfort me, I suffered the real pangs of parting and when at last his heart
failed beneath the strain he had willfully put upon it, my
grief had grown strong in the conviction that I would never
lose him.

I never have.

Yet never has he been so much with me as when I first
read "Take the Witness!"

There are things in the book with which I do not altogether agree. That is bound to be. There are things I wish
need not have been told. But, after all, a man must stand
upon his life as a whole, he must be judged by the entire span

[x]

of his existence. And since the story of his life was to be told, it seemed necessary that I should explain to you the reason for that collapse which brought to so untimely an end his swift and flashing career.

He was a great man and we, my brothers and I, are proud of him and willing that Earl Rogers should stand upon his record. His weaknesses were weaknesses of the flesh which could not endure the super-strain he put upon it.

I believe he was the greatest criminal lawyer who ever lived. That may, at first glance, sound fantastic. True, the stage upon which he played was not as large nor the audience as great as for some others. But I defy you to put any other man's record beside his, case for case, verdict for verdict, and then disagree with me. And I care not whether it be the record of Sir Edward Marshall Hall, who lost many more cases, or Bill Fallon, the "mouthpiece," or Clarence Darrow. One thing I would stake my life on—Dad wouldn't have lost the Massie case. That would have been considered a mere warm-up, in *our* office.

When you have read this book you will not, of course, know the Dad I knew. He is peculiarly my own. That is why you must forgive me if I have spoken proudly of him. You see, that's the way I felt about him.

But within this book you will know the Earl Rogers who made courtroom history, who was the idol of the crowds and the bewilderment of his own profession. You will see the best courtroom lawyer of them all in action.

And you will read that for which, it seems to me, it is worth while to tell the story: his own amazing prophecy concerning the law, lawyers and their future in our country—a prophecy which has already come to pass. If this awakens your thought to some of the dangers around us, his message will have achieved a great purpose.

For this record of the things he did, I thank those two loyal friends, who have thought his memory and his achievements great enough to stand the truth, the whole truth, and nothing but the truth.

That he never in his life bribed a juror or corrupted a witness, *I know*. That he was ever suspected of such tactics was due only to the jealousy of those who could not get his results by playing the game on the level in the courtroom.

He had a touch of genius. And though perhaps we could not love him without pain, we could and did love him without reservation. Someone may question his pre-eminence as a lawyer. But no one can ever question that as a Dad he was supreme.

ADELA ROGERS ST. JOHNS.

"TAKE THE WITNESS!"

CHAPTER I

"IF you are guilty, hire Earl Rogers!"

Such advice would quite naturally bear the inference that Mr. Rogers had a way of getting murderers out of trouble that was not exactly ethical, to say the least. It might have been construed also as the possession of certain attributes that were not contained in the repertoire of other lawyers.

Regardless of the interpretation placed upon the oft quoted saying—and it was quoted scores of times in the course of a quarter century—the records show that close to a hundred slayers escaped the gallows through the efforts of Earl Rogers; and there is little doubt that most of them were guilty enough to have merited the extreme penalty.

Of course there will always be those who will say that Earl Rogers was a crooked lawyer. That is said about every success-ful defender. As long as any of his contemporaries—his pro-fessional brethren—are alive, there will be voices to speak in derogation of his ethical righteousness, to flout any defense of his honesty. Some of his detractors obviously were, and are still, inspired by jealousy because of his almost infallible habit of freeing persons charged with capital crimes. A considerable section of the American bar has always looked askance at those who choose to follow the criminal side of the law. No doubt such viewpoint has had great justification.

Such crookedness as jury tampering and the manufacture of evidence has been associated with the practice of criminal law for the last few generations. Almost every successful jury lawyer of recent years has been more or less openly charged with overstepping the bounds of ethical propriety, if not of actually violating the laws governing criminal procedure. Earl Rogers may have transgressed also but he was never called upon to clear his professional reputation of any such stigma. Of course there were suggestive hints on many occasions. If it happened to be a shooting, officers and police reporters were wont to ask facetiously: "Has Earl found the second gun yet?" In more than one case where the only possible plea could be self-defense, another gun was actually discovered, but not in a single instance was it ever disclosed that the newly discovered weapon had been planted by anyone connected with the defense.

Time after time a prosecutor brooding over an unexpected, undeserved verdict of acquittal would growl that "Rogers must have bought the whole damned twelve this time." Yet in the course of more than twenty years no accusation of corrupting a juror was ever laid at his door. To this it might be argued that he was too clever to be caught at anything questionable. But during his vivid career, whether one considered him genius or charlatan, super-pleader or shyster, none could say that he had a peer for resourcefulness in tight places or an equal as a cross-examiner.

If one were to claim for Earl Rogers title as the most brilliant and resourceful criminal lawyer of all time, it would perhaps be branded as a bit of modesty typical of Los Angeles, where Earl Rogers began, and ended, his meteoric career. There is no question as to the presumptuousness of any such claim in behalf of a small town Western counsellor. It would seem almost as ridiculous to mention any self-educated attorney practicing in an obscure corner of the world in the same breath with a Choate, a Russell or even a Darrow; yet it was Clarence Darrow himself who once declared that Rogers was the greatest jury lawyer of his time. Darrow should have been competent to judge. The Chicago attorney was looked upon at the time as the nation's foremost criminal pleader. Moreover Darrow had engaged Rogers to defend him on a charge of having bribed members of a jury in the celebrated case of the McNamara brothers, dynamiters of the *Los Angeles Times*. Rogers became "the man who defended Clarence Darrow," which served to classify him among the great of the bar. To him it was the supreme accolade of his profession.

Those who knew him best have always maintained that Rogers considered himself above questionable tactics. He was too sure of his own ability, knowledge of law and resourcefulness to admit the necessity of improper methods. On the other hand, he is credited today with the creation of new courtroom tactics, of revolutionizing the procedure of criminal law in several important instances, of founding a new school of trial behavior. And, although there may always be more or less controversy as to his full right to these credits, Earl Rogers, to the great majority of those familiar with his record, was a wizard of the legal profession. Even to the later generation of attorneys, his name remains synonymous with almost unbelievable forensic adventures.

The only son of a Methodist minister, raised in austere and highly intellectual surroundings, with an ambition to become a jurist of the highest tribunals, Rogers became a criminal lawyer practically against his will. And, once thrust into this exciting vocation, he decided to go all the way and become the foremost in that strenuous line of advocacy.

In a comparatively few years he had gained the reputation of never losing a case, which is the chief stock-in-trade of the criminal lawyer. The technique of the young attorney was as changeable as his own kaleidoscopic personality. He suited his methods to the needs of his case. His daring and boldness in court were at times breath-taking and he had an almost supernatural divination of human thought, impulses and frailties. Occasionally his daring would get him into trouble, but his lightning wit would invariably come to the rescue. Despite this, however, he never relied upon chance. He was painstaking in his preparation of cases and in addition to getting his law and his testimony set in advance he gave even more time to the study of the jury—the twelve human beings who held the fate of his client in their hands.

He accepted seemingly hopeless cases and won them against overwhelming odds. He became a foremost figure on the Western Slope and died in obscurity and poverty, literally within the shadow of the scene of his greatest triumphs. He died alone in a bare little hotel room, a stone's throw from the Los Angeles courthouse, his once buoyant frame little more than an empty hull, his once brilliant mind dulled with the ravages of drink.

At the peak of his career Earl Rogers was one of the best known men on the Pacific Coast and his fame as a lawyer was nation wide. In dress a Brummell, in manners a Chesterfield, he had the pride of a conqueror and the vanity of a matinee idol. He loved adulation whether it was the backslapping of fellow drinkers at the Alexandria bar, the rather awed worship to be had in a New High Street parlor house, or the sanctimonious hand clasps of Christ's Episcopal vestry, of which he was an intermittent member. He was equally at home in all of them—bar, brothel or church.

From the time of Earl's birth at Perry, a little town fifty miles East of Buffalo, N. Y., in 1870, his father, Reverend Lowell L. Rogers, had planned a career in the ministry for his only son. Frustrated in his own desire to become a great evangelist, he hoped to transmit his ambitions to his first-born. With his histrionic artistry, his fervor and his hypnotic control of audiences, young Rogers doubtless would have become a national figure in the evangelical field. But he had little liking for the church.

The elder Rogers, although a minister of the Gospel and a college professor, was something of an adventurer himself. He brought his family West in the early Seventies, preached in Oregon and Northern California and was president of two Methodist colleges on the Coast in the early Eighties. His wife was also a member of the college faculties. Coming to Southern California the minister-educator indulged his adventurous spirit by plunging into the current craze of real estate development. Everyone else was doing it in the Eighties and it was not regarded as undignified for a preacher to promote real estate ventures between sermons. Earl's first earnings came from employment helping a surveyor who was laying out a subdivision which was being promoted by his father near Colton in Riverside County.

The real estate boom did not extend quite as far as the Rogers development however, and it was a failure. Earl had been attending college at Syracuse University of which his father was a graduate and the failure of the realty venture caused his withdrawal from college before graduation. His entire preparation for the university had been directed by his father and mother. Earl, like his two sisters, read Latin and Greek and spoke several modern languages. The two girls became excellent musicians and although he never put it to practical use, Earl's knowledge of music was far greater than that of the average musician.

It was while he was a student at his father's alma mater that young Rogers had his first adventure in love. It resulted in his marriage to Hazel Belle Green and he brought his bride back to California with no very definite plans for a future except that included in an ambition to be a newspaperman. He worked for a while in San Diego and did desultory writing for Los Angeles papers. But there was no money in newspaper work. He wistfully thought of the career in medicine and surgery, for which he had indulged an early passion, but that meant years of college. There was a baby now and a definite income was required.

In getting news stories the young reporter had come in contact with the courts and the lawyers. He met the town's leading attorneys and was attracted by their problems. The drama of the court room appealed to him. The life of the prosperous lawyer of that day was free and easy but pleasantly flavored with dignity and adulation.

Entering the office of Judge W. P. Gardiner, one of the learned lawyers of the Coast, Earl took up the study of law with the eagerness and zeal of a fanatic. He wanted to learn all about legal science without loss of time. He became entranced with its various phases. According to his early mentors, he could assimilate more law than any student in their experience. He spent his nights as well as days in law libraries, pondering principles and decisions. And what he read he retained in his remarkable memory.

In the middle Nineties it was the ambition of every young law student of the Southwest to study in the office of Senator Stephen M. White, then regarded as California's greatest lawyer and most brilliant statesman. Earl mustered up all the influence available, but it was his own personal application, couched in language that the senator himself affected and with the same emotional appeal, that won the opportunity for him. He became the favorite pupil of Stephen M. White.

During this period Rogers took his first interest in politics. Perhaps it was because of the fact that Democrats were so scarce in Southern California that the party of Jefferson appealed to him, but more likely it was the influence of White, who was one of the few Democrats ever to represent California in the United States Senate.

It was also during this period that the young law student became intimate with Bacchus. And strangely enough his first recorded inebriety was a result of the visit of William Jennings Bryan to Los Angeles on his first campaign for the presidency in 1896. Of course the famous apostle of cold water and grape juice had nothing to do with it and, if necessary, could have proved himself blameless. Nevertheless it is a matter of record that following the banquet to the "boy orator of the Platte," Earl Rogers staggered home under the influence of liquor for the first time.

The old Los Angeles of the Nineties was as different from the present bustling metropolis as day is from night. It was an easy-going, joyous community, a municipal good fellow. The playground for miners and cattlemen from Nevada, Arizona and the interior of California, it had color and glamor. Saturated with the bland and indulgent spirit of the carelessly joyful Spanish-American and the happy-go-lucky gringo pioneer, there was no thought of a future in which its climate would be glorified; no hint of the coming hordes of invaders from Iowa and Illinois, Nebraska and the Dakotas, who were to change everything there but that self-same famous climate.

Though deeds of violence were common, there was no underworld there in the modern sense. There was a gradual gradation of social planes from the proudest families down through the higher-caste gamblers, the saloon-keeping politicians, to the redlight habitués of both sexes; but those at the top were never afflicted with desire to start crusading against vice conditions. Each individual was too engrossed in his own vocation and enjoyment to annoy his fellows with reforms.

The better families, descendants of the Dons as well as the many aristocratic Southerners who had come West with successive tides of adventurous souls, were as proud as any belted earl, although never exclusive. The upper-class native Californian and early pioneers were hospitable, large-hearted and unsuspicious. They were more than charitable in their judgment of their fellow men, overlooking anything and everything that did not concern themselves or the public safety.

Such an easy-going attitude was natural in Los Angeles then. Social life was full of what would be today startling uncertainties. The man with whom you were doing business every day might be anything from a defeated Mexican or South American revolutionist, with a price on his head, to an ex-convict. The pleasant neighbors who had bought the house across the street might be married—or they might have neglected that formality because of marital entanglements back East. Back in the early days a man who came within one vote of being elected Los Angeles' chief of police went to the California penitentiary soon after for some old score.

There was nothing cold or discriminating about those genial old-time Angelenos.

Instead of there being a single organized political group, powerful through graft and control of officials, everybody in Los Angeles with the inclination played politics, impelled by the excitement of the game, much as men now play polo or women play bridge. Fire Chief Moore and the descendants of some of the old Spanish families composed the upper stratum of political activities. Below them were the Manning brothers who ran a saloon on Aliso Street; Felix Clevier, whose bar on Commercial was patronized equally by politicians, gamblers, and prostitutes of the prouder class —parlor house madames; Tom Savage, who also dispensed liquor, and fixed the police when necessary for his redlight district patrons; and the Gallagher boys, who also combined booze and polemics.

But among these active politicians there was nothing in the nature of big graft. The so-called "big shots" interested themselves in the game for the love of it and the satisfaction of getting a friend a public job when needed. The saloon keepers in return for the votes they delivered on election day were satisfied with pull enough to keep their patrons out of jail and thereby secure their gratitude and steady patronage.

And even the lowest order of gamblers (known among

their kind as "tin horns"), the pimps, and even the free lance hold-up thugs of that younger Los Angeles were respectable soldiers of fortune when compared with the modern gangster. They had the saving grace of being fellows who were willing to take a chance—at cards, at sticking up a train, or in open gun fight between themselves.

There was one other strong man of politics in the Los Angeles of thirty-odd years ago, but because of his line of business he was not considered a member of the inner circle, for Ballerino was made a rich man by the rent from cribs strung for blocks along Alameda Street. Inmates of cribs ranked at the bottom of the redlight's social scale, just as the most fashionable class of that scarlet realm were the proud inmates of the parlor houses. For in Los Angeles' redlight sphere caste held its rigid way as completely as elsewhere. But Ballerino, although tainted with the social obscurity of his tenants, was nevertheless accorded his due amount of influence.

When the boys were flush with recent payrolls or winning streaks at poker or faro they sought the sumptuous parlor houses of Commercial, New High, or Marchessault streets; but when their pockets were light they had to be content with such feminine society as might be encountered in the cribs. While visitors at the parlor houses were admitted only after a considerable wait at the outer portal, and were then ushered into a parlor—whence the name of the institution— that served as a place of reception, selection and dance hall, the cribs were far more accessible, in fact completely democratic.

The cribs of Alameda Street were narrow rooms, not much wider than their front doors, each one exactly the image of its neighbors, numbering perhaps forty to a short block of one-story brick. The hustlers of the cribs were anything but haughty. They stood in the doors of their narrow cubicles, when not entertaining visitors, or lolled on the sidewalks, displaying their charms to as great an expanse of cuticle as the benign laws and humorously tolerant policemen of the day allowed. "Come on in, boys, and I'll show you a good time," was the stereotyped chant of the crib siren.

Such was the bizarre environment in which Earl Rogers began his amazing career. The Los Angeles of that day formed a perfect background. It was large enough to center attention of the outside world; but not so large as to smother the exploits of any young individual setting out to carve himself a name.

CHAPTER II

WHEN young Rogers entered the office of Stephen M. White, he was a pale, rather anemic young student. His somewhat diffident demeanor gave no hint of the consuming ambition that burned within his breast, nor of the colossal egotism behind his glooming eyes.

Young Rogers had at that time no thought of taking up the practice of criminal law. True, White was a great criminal pleader who had saved from the gallows many a seemingly certain victim, but he was also a leader among civil lawyers, a brilliant orator, and had a personality of rare charm. Furthermore, he was still wearing his laurels as a United States Senator. He had made a great reputation at the national capital. By his colleagues of both parties he was regarded as the best constitutional lawyer of his time. Hard-drinking, poker-playing "Steve" White added immeasurably to California's favorable regard by the rest of the nation during his term in the Senate and his fame still lingers. He left a record of integrity and public service seldom equaled.

It was not easy in those days of corporation-controlled politics to be an honest representative of the people. In California, Collis P. Huntington, with his Southern Pacific railroad, was all powerful. The S. P. machine controlled city councils, county boards, the state legislature, the delegation to the national capital. It even had an important voice in the selection of Presidents.

The story is told that White was offered a fortune not to oppose Huntington's pet scheme to have Santa Monica, sixteen miles away, made the official seaport of Los Angeles.

Long before boom times in that city, the railroad builder foresaw its future. San Pedro was farther distant than Santa Monica but White felt that San Pedro harbor was the natural port and should be developed by the government.

Huntington owned thousands of acres in the Santa Monica Bay district. He had never before been thwarted in a legislature, state or national, and when his lobbyists reported that White could not be moved, the railroad magnate rushed to Washington. White's memoirs, corroborated by voluminous documentary evidence, indicate that Huntington offered him property even then worth a half million dollars—if he would just go away on a vacation until Congress passed the bill to spend millions on a harbor at Santa Monica.

But White remained and defeated the bill and the people of Los Angeles erected a huge bronze statue to him in the courthouse yard in appreciation of his honesty and courage.

Stephen White was almost as famous for his drinking prowess as his forensic skill, and in those days it was possible to aspire to public office without fear as to what the Anti-Saloon League or the W. C. T. U. would think or do. A man's personal habits were his own private business. Many were the soul-stirring and vote-getting orations that White delivered when he had to gauge his equilibrium by the feel of the speaker's table beside him.

And if ever a man was justified in reasonable indulgence in alcoholic stimulant, that man was White. Judges and attorneys familiar with his courtroom deportment always knew if "Little Steve" was cold sober, or had taken a couple of drinks before going into action. If abstemious, his intellectual faculties were apt to be heavy, his delivery ponderous. But when slightly energized by whisky his fine brain functioned with a machinelike precision that was fascinating; whether in dramatic appeal to his auditors' emotions or coldly telepathic analysis of the inner thoughts of hostile witnesses, his performance was replete with artistry and skill.

Returning from his term in the Senate, White resumed his place as the foremost member of the Los Angeles bar and the foremost patron of its bars.

This was about the time when Earl Rogers entered White's office to complete his course in law. A few years later his erstwhile pupil displaced White as the outstanding criminal lawyer of the state, winning his first important murder case against his former mentor in a notable trial.

"Steve White is his own worst enemy," his friends were wont to say when strong drink was gradually exerting its mastery over him. Not so many years later they were saying the same thing about Earl Rogers. White died at forty-seven, a victim of alcohol. That was in 1901.

Rogers had no thought at that time of succeeding White either as a criminal pleader or a superior drinking man. At the time he was admitted to the bar, in 1897, he had certain definite ideas as to the practice of criminal law. He believed that there was too much trickery and dishonesty in saving criminals from the punishment they deserved; that the ordinary practice of criminal law was a prostitution of the second greatest profession—the first always being medicine.

Like many another beginner, he opened his own office and took such cases as came his way, mostly minor civil actions. His chief income came from the collection of bad debts.

When Rogers started out on his own he was associated with Telfair Creighton, but the firm of Creighton & Rogers lasted only a year. Creighton was a Southern Democrat of high social standing in Los Angeles, who was at one time editor of the *Los Angeles Herald*. He was in no sense a criminal lawyer, and Earl's alliance with him indicates that at that time he cherished no ambition to follow the practice of defending criminals.

But cases were cases and paid fees. Living was getting more

expensive. Eggs had gone up to fifteen cents a dozen and there was a baby girl who required clothes. So when a few police court cases came his way Rogers would accept them even when Creighton turned up his aristocratic nose at the idea of an appearance in a police judge's court.

Then came Earl's first criminal cases in the higher court and in quick succession he appeared for the defendants in a murder case, an adultery trial and an embezzlement charge. There were interesting features in each of them.

"Doc" Crandall, a more or less notorious character, was the leading actor in the murder case. "Doc" got his title as a veterinary, but he was more prominently identified with the social activities of the city's redlight district than in professional equine circles. During the trial, his avocation was designated by the prosecution as that of pimp or mac.

There had been a week-end party at Ballona Beach, those present being "Doc" and Jack Bowman, another habitué of the restricted district, and their lady friends. There was a row between the two men and Jack's career was ended by a bullet. Crandall was brought to trial and defended by Lawyer W. H. Shinn. He was convicted of manslaughter on the testimony of Ruby Gaines, one of the women on the party, and the only witness to the shooting. "Doc" was sentenced to ten years, but Shinn, who was an adept at getting reversals, won a new trial on appeal and promptly turned over the case to Rogers. Whatever the reason, it is not in the court files.

The record does show, however, that Crandall was found not guilty and set at liberty. The transcript shows no sign of any testimony by Miss Ruby Gaines. The reason is clear. The district attorney's office could not find Ruby and the story was widely circulated that she had been virtually abducted at the beginning of the trial and kept in a highly inebriated condition until the jury had returned its verdict.

The prosecution made desperate efforts to locate Ruby but they could not discover her.

Whether or not the sedate young attorney for the defense had anything to do with Ruby's disappearance was never clearly disclosed, but Ruby told everyone who would listen to her that "that goddamn Rogers was at the bottom of it."

With most of the criminal cases coming out of the red-light district, a charge of immorality originating in the better residence section attracted much attention during that period. It was considered quite a social error for a gentleman to reside with a lady who was not his legal wife. In this case a Mrs. Luther Bethel had her husband and a woman named Peaslee arrested on a charge of adultery. Luther had, it seems, been dissatisfied with his wife's cooking—or something—and was taking his meals at Miss Peaslee's. The complaint also averred that he was sleeping there also.

Much evidence was introduced to prove that Bethel and the Peaslee woman were living together as man and wife. Rogers, to the surprise of everyone in the court room, did not combat this testimony. He even encouraged the state's witnesses to elaborate on the representations of the offenders that they were husband and wife.

Instead of introducing witnesses for the defense, Rogers rested his case and then sprang the big surprise. First he read the law under which the defendants were being tried: "If two persons, either being married to another, live together in a state of open and notorious adultery, each is guilty of a felony." Rogers took the firm position that as the couple had lived as husband and wife, therefore the cohabitation and adultery were *not* open and notorious, but were entirely latent and concealed, and that therefore there was no crime under the wording of the statute. The clear-cut logic of the young barrister's argument resulted in a dismissal of the charges.

Not only were the defendants freed, solely upon the wording of the statute and not because of any doubt of their guilt, but the California legislature changed the statute after the Bethel case, eliminating the words "open and notorious." And the courts now hold it not necessary to show some assumption publicly of adulterous cohabitation before such offenders may be prosecuted. Nor does the present law regard adultery as a felony.

Rogers' handling of the Bethel trial attracted considerable attention, mostly from members of the bar; but it was not until the Blackman case was virtually forced upon the new law firm that public interest in the slim young Rogers was aroused.

W. R. Blackman, secretary-treasurer of the city's chief public utility corporation, was indicted for embezzlement of his company's funds. It caused a sensation. Dr. Bryson, close friend of both Rogers and Blackman, induced Earl to take the case after several prominent lawyers had rejected it as hopeless.

Blackman and a retired English army officer, Captain Bolton, had kept the corporation's books, all entries in those days being made in handwriting. Just after the trial started Bolton committed suicide with his army revolver. Earl would not allow his client to take the stand and strenuously objected to introduction of the company's books in evidence.

The jury found Blackman guilty of embezzlement and he was sentenced to ten years in the penitentiary. This Rogers had foreseen and had conducted his whole case with a view to its appeal, a method of legal procedure he learned to abhor and rarely resorted to thereafter throughout his career as a lawyer.

But the California Supreme Court bore out his contention that, inasmuch as it had not been established which handwriting in the ledger was that of the accused man, the books should not have been admitted as evidence, and Blackman was set at liberty.

There was nothing spectacular about the trial, but the fact that Earl had freed his client after several of Los Angeles' leading attorneys had refused to defend Blackman because they regarded his case as hopeless greatly enhanced the growing reputation of the young lawyer.

After the Blackman trial came the dissolution of the firm of Creighton & Rogers. When Rogers hung out his own individual shingle more business came to him. He was beginning to cut a considerable figure as a defender of those charged with felonies, but it remained for the Alford trial to establish him among the leaders of the Los Angeles bar.

CHAPTER III

JAY E. HUNTER was an outstanding figure of Los Angeles in the latter Nineties, charming days of transition in the old Pueblo of the Angels. The sway of the Dons still tinctured with its warm romance the social life of the city. Spanish grandees had not yet ceased to entertain with baronial splendor, and many of the city's haughtiest families blended in their veins the proud blood of the *conquistadores* with that of those invaders who were of gentle birth and culture.

In this alluring environment Attorney Hunter shone as could only a man of old family traditions and rare personal charm. He was a scion of Southern aristocrats, brilliantly educated, tall and handsome. As he strode jauntily along Spring Street swinging his heavy cane, his garb the ultimate word in fashionable apparel, tipping his hat to acquaintances of either sex as was still the gracious California custom, his was the most distinguished figure in a town of gallant men.

Hunter was a member of the exclusive California Club in a day when "exclusive" connoted something other than a present day tabloid reporter's label for everything from a popular downtown hotel to the stockyards district. Moreover, he was a lawyer of distinction, rich, single; the city's most eligible bachelor. He was the beau ideal of the community's social life, its cotillion leader. Los Angeles knew no more popular man.

So when Jay E. Hunter was killed by William Alford in 1899, Los Angeles stood aghast. Business and professional men were profoundly shocked. The whole city hotly demanded that Hunter's killer be brought to full and speedy justice. There was even talk of summary punishment for the slayer.

Hunter's slayer was an obscure member of the community, a lowly mechanic, unknown beyond his few humble acquaintances. He had obtained a judgment against Hunter for a debt which the latter denied owing. It was for a trivial plumbing job. On numerous occasions Hunter declined to pay the bill. Then, as was one of the quaint customs in the South whence the slayer also hailed, Alford had a printer run off a few dodgers whose text was headed by the line, "Jay E. Hunter Does Not Pay His Debts." With a sample copy in his hand he went to the Stimson building on Spring Street on February 18, 1899, declaring he would get the money due him.

Being of hot Southern blood, Alford used no restraint in telling those he encountered on his way to Hunter's office just what he intended to do to the attorney if the latter did not pay him. These intemperate remarks, added to other evidences of the mechanic's violent state of mind, supplied damaging proof against him later, as showing probable murderous intent when he had sought out Hunter.

Alford encountered Hunter outside the latter's office on the third floor of the building, waved the printed slip before the attorney's eyes and declared that if the debt were not immediately paid he would cover the city's streets with the typed denunciation. Several tenants of the office building heard Alford's loud declarations that he would "fix" Hunter if he didn't pay up. There followed a physical encounter during which Alford shot and fatally wounded Hunter. Auditors of the quarrel and friends of the dying man claimed he had been shot down in cold blood. Alford was indicted for murder in the first degree.

The first move of the slain Hunter's host of friends was to retain Stephen M. White to act as special prosecutor. With the district attorney aided by California's greatest pleader and every person of social and business standing in the city demanding speedy conviction of the accused, the obscure mechanic who had committed the faux pas of snuffing out Jay E. Hunter seemed doomed. Even without White's great ability on the side of the prosecution Alford would have had but a ghost of a chance, for the evidence against him was seemingly conclusive.

The killer's only possible defense was the one which he advanced: That Hunter had knocked him down with a heavy cane, that he continued to beat him over the head with the big stick when he was prone; that then, but not till then, did he draw his gun and fire.

But Coroner Holland's findings at the inquest just about put the halter around Alford's neck. They were to the effect that the lethal slug had perforated the intestines five times, had amputated the appendix—*and had ranged downward*. How could a bullet range downward through a standing man when fired by one who lay on the ground? No California attorney cared to represent Alford. He had little, if any money. His case seemed hopeless.

There were no witnesses to the actual shooting, which occurred just outside Hunter's office. However, an attorney named Stephenson, occupying the suite adjoining that of Hunter, testified at the coroner's inquest that the wounded man had run into Stephenson's office closely pursued by Alford, and that the latter was aiming a gun at Hunter and trying to shoot him again, but that Stephenson disarmed Alford.

With this damning physical and oral evidence against Alford and with White as the chief prosecutor, it was no wonder that all leading attorneys considered the accused man already convicted and declined to defend him.

It was into this spot that the debonair young Rogers chose to step. Perhaps the hopelessness of the case attracted him; perhaps the opportunity for widespread publicity. But, whatever urge other elements may have held for him, Rogers

would never have taken over such a tough case were it not
for a bit of sentiment. The accused man had told Earl, who
was a young father, that Mrs. Alford was about to become
a mother and that his conviction would almost certainly result
in further tragedy. Again Earl went carefully over Alford's
story of the killing of Hunter. He sat silent for many minutes
after his searching questions had all been answered. He must
have sensed some shadowy chance for the prisoner, for when
he left the jail he had agreed to take Alford's desperate case.

When it was announced next morning that Earl Rogers
had undertaken to defend the accused man, members of the
bar grinned pityingly or sardonically, according to their
natures.

On the opening day of the trial the social prominence of
the murder victim and the eminence of the special prosecutor
assured a capacity audience in which the bar was almost
as well represented as was the social register—if the City
of the Angels had such a volume at the time.

The counsel for the defense was befittingly garbed in a
new suit from the town's leading tailor, having expended
$40 of his $100 retainer for that purpose. His young wife accompanied him as he took his place inside the rail; and attracted no little attention. It was her first appearance as a
spectator in a trial in which her husband participated. Her
fame as a beauty quickly spread and for years she was known
as one of California's most beautiful women. Whenever a list
was made of the beauties of the Pacific Coast, the dark and
stunning Mrs. Earl Rogers was always included.

Little trouble was experienced in getting the jury and the
taking of testimony was begun. Coroner Holland was the
first witness. He testified to the condition of the body and
his opinion as to the position of the decedent when shot.
Cross-examination failed to change his testimony, but Rogers
managed to extract sufficient comedy relief out of the quizzing of the coroner to take the minds of the jurors off the

grimness of the evidence. He created laughter by making Holland admit that he would not perform the autopsy upon the body of Hunter until it had been removed from a rival undertaking establishment to the mortuary conducted by a friend of the coroner's office.

A few moments later, following the same tactics, the young attorney brought a burst of grim laughter—and a reprimand from the court. A damaging bit of evidence had just been presented, and, to offset its effect, Rogers ventured the comment that he asked no special consideration for his client because of the fact that Alford's bullet had, without any expectation of a surgical fee, amputated the appendix of the decedent.

This apparent levity did not do the counsel for the defense any good, so far as a superficial observer might suppose, but the resulting objections from the prosecution's side of the table and the court's stern reprimand drove out of the jurors' minds the telling point which had been made against the defendant.

It was the inception of a technique new to Los Angeles courts and one that played a highly important part in the career of the young lawyer.

In the beginning of the case Rogers was painstaking in his effort to establish two things in the jurors' minds: that Hunter had beaten Alford over the head with a heavy cane, and that all bullet wounds inflicted upon the slain man had struck him from in front. He had feared an attempt by White to confuse the minds of the jurors concerning these vital points, and that was exactly what the prosecutor proceeded to do.

When White had finished his direct examination of the chief autopsy surgeon, Dr. Carl Khurtz, the prosecution had left an impression that Hunter had used his cane only to repel his assailant. Rogers launched his attack at that point as follows:

ROGERS: With respect to the wounds upon the person of Mr. Alford, when you made the examination of them did you request that a written description, illustrated by a diagram, be made?

DR. KHURTZ: Yes, sir.

ROGERS: Will you read that description carefully and see if it is a correct copy of what you had taken down? (*Handing the witness a paper.*)

DR. KHURTZ: That is the description; yes, sir.   . . . .

ROGERS: From that you are able to give a good description of the wounds you found upon the person of the defendant?

DR. KHURTZ: Yes. (*The witness proceeded to describe the head wounds in detail in reply to an exhaustive series of questions by defense counsel.*)

ROGERS: Could those wounds be inflicted by the *end* of this cane?

DR. KHURTZ: Most of them are too long for that.

ROGERS: By what part of this cane were these scalp wounds likely made, Doctor Khurtz?

DR. KHURTZ: By this part, lengthwise. (*Pointing to side of cane.*)

Rogers glanced significantly at the jury. He excused the witness. He had demonstrated by a state witness that the cane had not been used defensively.

Attorney F. A. Stephenson, who occupied the office adjoining Hunter's, and had disarmed Alford after the shooting, was questioned by a veteran of the district attorney's office, General Johnstone Jones. White was absent at the time. Rogers asked but a few questions.

ROGERS: You knew Hunter carried a heavy cane, didn't you?

STEPHENSON: I guess it was heavy. I think he always carried one.

ROGERS: Do you know anything about Mr. Hunter hitting people over the head with his heavy walking stick?

STEPHENSON: I never heard of it before he struck Alford.

ROGERS: But have you heard since then about his striking people with it?

STEPHENSON: Yes.

At this point, too late to undo the damage to his side, the veteran Jones burst into a storm of objections that halted any further questioning along that line; but Earl had obtained the desired evidence of Hunter's former violent use of his cane. Had White been present, he would have squelched such cross-examination at its beginning.

Dr. C. W. Pierce, who had assisted at the operation performed at the California Hospital in an attempt to save Hunter's life, was carefully questioned by the prosecution as to the course of the fatal bullet, and testified that it had ranged downward. This testimony, fatal as it seemed to Alford's defense, did not perturb Rogers in the slightest degree. His first question when he took over the witness for cross-examination was disturbing to the prosecution.

ROGERS: Doctor, you will observe that on the front of the left leg of these trousers, which you have identified as Hunter's, the edges of the anterior hole are somewhat discolored, as if by powder marks.

DR. PIERCE: Yes, sir.

ROGERS: And the edges of the hole in the posterior part of the trousers are everted, as you medical men express it; that is, turned out; the hole is not discolored. And you will note that the fiber on the edges of the hole in front are not everted, but evidently were carried into the leg.

DR. PIERCE: I don't know whether they were carried into the leg or not.

ROGERS: But you do know from examination of these two holes that the bullet entered from the front and passed out at the rear of the trousers, do you not?

DR. PIERCE: Yes.

Rogers waved a hand. He was through with the witness.

CHAPTER IV

ALTHOUGH Senator White was regarded as the mainstay of the prosecution, the nominal chief of the state's forces was Johnstone Jones, usually referred to as General Jones. He was a deputy in the district attorney's office, a rather pompous individual who took himself very seriously. With him as a victim Earl Rogers started during the Alford trial on a career of prosecutor-baiting that was an interesting and entertaining phase of his trial procedure, as well as a highly useful one.

Earl seized every opportunity of embarrassing the General who was immediately confused by satirical asides or veiled ridicule, provided it was not too well veiled. It provided diversion for the jurors and at the same time belittled the prosecutor in their eyes. Much of Senator White's time was consumed in protecting his confrere from the shafts of ridicule which Rogers aimed at him on the slightest provocation. It might be stated parenthetically that it was his expertness at baiting the opposition which brought Rogers ten years later into the famous San Francisco graft prosecutions.

Dr. Ralph Hagan was one of the witnesses for the state and Jones was assigned to get his testimony. The prosecutor asked him during the course of his examination for an exact description of the spot where one of the fatal bullets had entered the body of the slain man. Slightly nettled by his questioner's apparent inability to understand his previous replies, the doctor asked:

"Do you want the exact measurements?"

"Yes, the exact measurements," instructed Jones.

"On a level with, and four inches from the anterior superior spinous process of the ilium," was the reply.

"If you can find that long thing on me," declared Jones, "I wish you would point it out."

Before the doctor could leave the stand for the purpose of demonstrating the location of the "long thing" on the body of the prosecutor, Rogers leaned over and jabbed his finger into the General's paunch hard enough to make him grunt. The surprised prosecutor turned upon counsel for the defense.

"Here, I didn't ask you," he remonstrated. "Besides, what do you know about anatomy?"

"He indicated the spot exactly," declared Dr. Hagan.

Rogers directed an ingenuous smile at the prosecutor. "Aren't you going to thank me, General?"

Several of the jurors laughed audibly, Judge Smith grinned and the representative of the district attorney growled as he rubbed the sore spot.

Rogers realized his predicament when it was announced that the state rested. The defense had but few witnesses, other than the defendant himself, and Rogers frankly expressed his dread of what White would do to the accused man on cross-examination, for White was scheduled for that task.

When the noon recess provided a respite, Rogers went immediately into a conference with his client for a last rehearsal of the defendant's testimony. Then Alford was taken back to his cell and Rogers made a dash for a nearby saloon which specialized in a good lunch to be had with a glass of beer. There he found White at the bar drinking his favorite brand of Kentucky whisky. His former mentor congratulated Earl on his showing thus far and slyly hinted at what he was going to do to the defendant who was scheduled to take the stand late in the afternoon. It is the custom of defending lawyers to call their client to the stand as the closing witness of the defense. The reason for such a custom is obvious. Other witnesses for the defense will have been heard and if there has been any variation in their testimony or any unexpected damage done the defendant, opportunity will be given to readjust his own story to the best advantage. Rogers had planned to call a number of character witnesses and also to introduce medical testimony.

While they were drinking, Rogers suddenly became deeply interested in White's maneuvers with the bourbon bottle. The senator had been drinking throughout the trial. He would get a good start before the morning session. During the noon recess he would eat a sandwich and take three or four drinks. Before returning to the court room he would go to his office and lie down for a brief nap to get in shape for the afternoon session. This had resulted in occasional tardiness. At first he was a few minutes late, and the court usually waited for his return. But more recently he had been as late as ten or fifteen minutes and the judge, becoming impatient at his continued delays, ceased to extend this courtesy, starting the session promptly at two o'clock.

"Have another, Earl," smilingly invited the Senator, "you'll need it for this afternoon."

"No, thanks, Senator, got to get back to the office to meet somebody," declared his former pupil.

The Senator reached for the bottle and Earl left the saloon quickly.

Earl was in his seat when Judge Smith nodded for the trial to resume. Senator White was not present.

"Call William Alford," said the counsel for the defense.

General Jones gasped and started to remonstrate but caught himself before he could voice any protest.

In quick, incisive tones Rogers shot his questions at the defendant. The accused man told his version of the killing in a series of well-rehearsed replies. He told how Jay Hunter had attacked him with the loaded cane and how when he was prone on the floor in the hall of the office building and

[27]

fearful that Hunter would kill him, he drew his gun and shot upward into the body of his assailant.

Rogers turned sharply to the space occupied by the prosecutors at the old, long mahogany table.

"Take the witness!" he barked.

General Jones looked frantically toward the doors of the court room in the hope that he would see the alert little figure of Senator White. All of the state's plans had been founded upon White's grilling of Alford. Admonished by the court, Jones began questioning the defendant in perfunctory manner, as Rogers grinned sardonically at the prosecutor's obvious uneasiness. The General stumbled through a series of interrogations that strengthened rather than weak‚ened the story of the defendant.

As Jones was bringing his examination to a halting conclu‚sion, there was a sudden commotion at the doors. A glance in the direction of the railed enclosure was sufficient for the "little giant" to size up the situation. The harassed Jones mumbled: "No more questions" as White forced his way through the crowd.

"No redirect examination," rapped out Rogers as he waved Alford from the witness stand.

Senator White raged and stormed but realized himself that there was nothing to be done. As he grew calmer, he turned reproachfully to Rogers.

"That was a dirty trick, Earl," he declared more in sorrow than in anger.

Earl professed innocence. But after court had adjourned he defended his course by calling attention to the fact that his first duty was to his client. The man's life was at stake, he protested, and it was his solemn moral obligation to overlook nothing that would aid the defendant's cause.

But Rogers had an even greater sensation with which to climax his defense. Old-time lawyers on the Coast still talk about it. It completely overshadowed the trick he had played on White and even the latter forgot all about the alleged breach of custom in his efforts to trump the ace which his young adversary pulled from his sleeve a short time later.

There were a few character witnesses to testify to the good reputation of the defendant and then the attorney for the defense rose to his slim height. Pausing long enough to get the complete attention of the court, jury and spectators, he dramatically demanded that the coroner be instructed to bring into court the intestines of the late Jay Hunter.

The horrified spectators gasped. The judge, the district attorney and the special prosecutor were astounded. Instantly White was on his feet, smothering the court with a barrage of objections. He did not sense Earl's object in making such a ghoulish request, but he was as suspicious as he was bewildered. He feared some mystic trick that might confuse the jurors' reason. He had good reason to know that the youngster who had studied law under him was far beyond average men in his knowledge of many psychological reactions of the human mind.

"There has been no foundation laid for such a request!" declared the bewildered Senator.

"I must beg the pardon of eminent special counsel for the prosecution," drawled Rogers; "but the prosecution itself has laid such foundation. Coroner Holland has testified that the fatal bullet ranged downward through the intestines."

"And I suppose," scoffed White, "the defense maintains it ranged upward."

"*Exactly!*"

At his astonishing declaration everyone in the court room gasped. The coroner and autopsy surgeon gaped at Rogers incredulously.

Despite the fervid objections of Prosecutor Jones and Senator White, Judge Smith ruled that while it might be in bad taste it was perfectly legal to have the bowels of the slain man produced forthwith.

Then occurred a scene which had no precedent in a criminal trial in the West. A large glass jar was brought into court with its gruesome contents preserved in alcohol. But before it could be admitted as evidence, White made a last desperate effort to prevent introduction of this confusing thing into the case.

"How do we know this proposed exhibit is the viscera of the late Jay E. Hunter?" demanded White. "How does anyone know it is a part of any human being's anatomy?"

Whereupon Rogers placed the coroner and autopsy surgeon on the stand and made them testify that the jar's contents were part of Hunter's remains. The two witnesses readily identified them by the unbroken seal that had been placed upon the jar, and in reply to Earl's questions the coroner further testified that the jar had not been out of his possession since it had been sealed by him.

Then Rogers called to the stand as an expert witness Dr. Edward M. Pallette, twenty-five years of age and in practice only a year.

With the coroner and autopsy surgeon to aid him, White tried all of his wily arts in an attempt to discredit Pallette, but the young defense attorney had coached his youthful friend so thoroughly that Pallette's testimony stood solid as a rock. With a large colored picture of the human viscera, Earl calmly proceeded to prove beyond any doubt that the bullet had proceeded upward through the intestines instead of downward. And by the admissions he drew from the chagrined coroner and autopsy surgeon he made of them witnesses as valuable to the defense as Pallette.

He explained in minute detail, using the picture of a man's bowels in normal position to illustrate his anatomical lecture, that if Hunter had been standing erect the bullet could not possibly have followed the course shown in the jar's contents; that only because of a stooping position upon the part of the dead man, one where the bowels had been folded over upon themselves by a doubled-up posture, could the bullet have punctured the intestines as revealed by the glass-enclosed exhibit.

There could be no doubt, pointed out young Rogers in summing up, that Hunter had been bending over his victim in the act of caning him, as testified by the defendant, when the latter drew his gun and fired. So, although the bullet had entered above the navel and lodged in Hunter's posterior, it had literally been *traveling upward* from where Alford shot from the floor, for at that instant Hunter's shoulders were lower than his hips as he struck at the man beneath him.

The jury retired and speedily brought in a verdict that the defendant had acted in self-defense and therefore was not guilty.

The verdict created a sensation. Jay Hunter's slayer had been freed and Stephen M. White had been beaten in court for the first time, and by his erstwhile pupil, a more or less obscure beginner. Earl Rogers had blasted the theretofore impregnable "little giant" and upon his ruins rose to glory.

CHAPTER V

THE verdict in the Alford case was the talk of Los Angeles for some time and the town also noted the effect on young Earl Rogers. It was quite natural that there should be an immediate change in his professional status; that it should mark the turning point in his career.

Prior to accepting the Alford defense Rogers had been only lukewarm towards the criminal side of the law. He had had an exalted idea of the profession. High judicial honors were the ultimate goal of every young lawyer and such honor seldom came to the defenders of those charged with criminal offenses. But now Earl was determined to abandon any judicial aspirations and become instead the greatest criminal lawyer in the West.

The practice of civil law was more dignified and there was more money in it, but it was in the criminal courts that drama reigned supreme. The conduct of a civil suit had none of the glamor of an exciting murder trial, none of the opportunities for personal aggrandizement in the way of newspaper notoriety or public adulation. There might be a big fee in winning a suit to quiet title where an important corporation was concerned but such a case provided no opportunity for histrionics, or the performance of sensational stunts.

Although some of the veteran members of the bar did not hesitate to criticize Rogers for the trick he had played on Stephen White, the general attitude of the Los Angeles lawyers was one of acclaim. The winning of a case was the important thing and Earl was accepted as one of the elect. This meant a greater volume of business, so Earl rented a better suite of offices. He moved his family into a more desirable residential section.

Not content with forcing the veteran White off his pedestal, the victor even went so far as to assume some of the personal mannerisms of the vanquished. He also dabbled in Democratic politics and gave a little more serious attention to his drinking. His self-esteem, never of low degree, showed its sudden growth in overweening confidence. He became more fastidious in his dress. In a very short time he was being pressed for money by the city's leading tailors.

The great bulk of Earl's practice in the next year or two came from the lower social strata of the city, the gamblers, saloon people and denizens of the redlight district, and there was plenty of business. Much of it was ordinary police court traffic but most of the capital offenses were committed by those affiliated with the businesses of prostitution and gambling. Practically all of the offenders found their way to the Rogers office.

Earl's chief standby during this period was a unique character called Bill Jory. Bill would have fought to the death in resentment of classification as a pimp, although he boasted of his intimacy with Big May, a person of considerable importance in her social circle. It was Bill, however, who brought in most of the cases to Earl Rogers.

At that time the Rogers offices were described by a rival attorney as the strangest legal menagerie in the country. The location was on the second floor of the Redick Block opposite the plant of the *Los Angeles Times* and a block away from the court house. The staff included a number of young beginners in the law, several legal derelicts, Bill Jory and an occasional ex-policeman or detective who had influence in the underworld. No one received any regular salary. Each was content to take whatever Earl passed out and not infrequently the office served as sleeping quarters for members of the staff.

There were times when there was a complete dearth of funds and on these occasions Bill Jory was wont to negotiate a loan from Big May, usually in what was designated as the "rush act," in behalf of Rogers himself. Bill had for Earl a doglike affection that never wavered. He rated his hero as the greatest of all lawyers; and, in fact, looked upon him as nothing short of a demi-god.

Jory knew all of the intimate gossip of redlight and gambling circles and more than once he had steered into the Redick Block offices a slayer whose gun was still warm even before the police were aware of his identity as the killer. A gambler who had drawn his weapon in the heat of an argument, or a sporting house madame who had cancelled her current love with a lethal bullet, felt no qualms as to their future provided Earl Rogers appeared in their behalf.

Most of the dignity of the Rogers staff was provided for some time by Judge Gooding, who had served under President Benjamin Harrison as chief justice of Arizona Territory's supreme court. He came to Los Angeles in comfortable financial circumstances with a desire to continue the practice of law with as little wear and tear as possible. He had seen Rogers in action during the Alford trial and had chosen Earl as a sort of associate. From him Rogers gained considerable knowledge of the inner complexities of the higher politico-judicial angles of the game.

One of the younger members of the staff was Frederick Spencer, who gained admittance because of his knowledge of shorthand. In later years he became a prominent figure in the practice of civil law. Spencer in turn brought into the "menagerie" a chance acquaintance down on his luck, John Davis, who at one time had been secretary to United States Senator Arthur Pue Gorman of Maryland. Davis was addicted to strong drink, but he was a fellow of gentlemanly deportment and was allowed to sleep in the office in return for cleaning it in the mornings.

Davis, encouraged by Rogers, managed to rehabilitate himself. He quit drinking and secured a remunerative position; strangely enough, as a wine salesman. But the nature of his work was such that after a time he fell into his old habits again. One day he called upon Earl and told him that he could see nothing in the future that bore any resemblance to happiness. Earl argued with him and succeeded in restoring something of his former courage.

A few hours later, word came from the receiving hospital at the police station that Davis had shot himself in the head. Rogers and Spencer called at once. Davis was lying on a cot in the police hospital and as the two lawyers approached him, the wounded man seemed to be looking at Earl. There was a slight sound as his lips seemed to move. "He's trying to speak to you, Earl," whispered Spencer. Earl shook his head and said dramatically, "No, it's all over; that's the death rattle." He was right. Davis' head fell over and he died.

Perhaps the most colorful figure associated with Rogers during a period of ten or more years was Luther Brown. Young Brown came to Earl in the Nineties. He was a politician of great ability and resourcefulness as well as an able lawyer. He was an important cog in the Southern Pacific political machine and had much to say as to the nominees to office selected by the Republicans. Brown, as time went on, won a reputation as the most expert fixer operating in California courts as well as in politics. He remained with Rogers longer than any of his early associates and became a prominent figure in the celebrated San Francisco graft prosecution.

Just across Broadway from the Redick Block, George Simpson had a saloon on the corner of that thoroughfare and First Street, which was much frequented by the alert young disciples of the law. Neither Earl nor the younger members of his entourage were given to overplaying their hands at the drinking business in those earliest days, but the nearby oasis was a fertile source of news of political and criminal activities, and also served as a meeting place with those queer folk whom Rogers did not care to have appear in his office.

But their selection of the corner barroom was not in any degree influenced by esteem for its proprietor. They considered Simpson, despite his prominence as a political boss, even lower in the moral scale than Landlord Ballerino of the cribs. This was because of a lowdown trick he had played on his trusting mother-in-law.

For some unfathomable reason this estimable woman's daughter fell in love with the drunken Simpson and married him. The mother was heartbroken over the marriage, but she was a woman of resource and bought him the saloon, trusting he would speedily drink himself to death. The ungrateful wretch, however, immediately quit using alcoholic beverages and waxed healthy and prosperous. For this inexcusable act the young lawyers regarded George Simpson as wholly unethical.

Anyone who joined the Rogers criminal law-collection agency-detective bureau institution was flirting with destruction because of the human dynamite which formed a considerable part of his clientele during his legal adolescence. Dignified and erudite ex-Chief Justice Gooding was one of the group who found that out.

In the late Nineties there was a period of several months when citizens were held up and robbed with such regularity that the newspapers referred to it as The Reign of Terror. Not only were the highwaymen robbers, but they were so vicious that they shot several men, some fatally, who failed to stick up their hands quickly enough.

Two men, Watson and Dixon, were arrested as suspects. As long as they remained in jail the robberies stopped. Earl was retained by the accused pair. He got them out on bail and immediately the reign of violence was resumed. Rogers claimed it was a trick of the police, who arrested Watson and Dixon again, declaring they were responsible for the new holdups. He succeeded in getting them out on bail a second time.

Shortly after they were released, Judge Gooding was strolling up and down in front of his residence one evening, placidly smoking his after-dinner cigar, when two men stepped out from the shadow of a pepper tree and with levelled pistols told him to throw up his hands.

The Judge couldn't imagine anyone bold enough to rob an ex-chief justice and proceeded to parley with them in his haughty manner; whereupon one of them shot Gooding and emptied his pockets. The Judge recovered from his wound, but he had no hesitancy in voicing his suspicions that the pair of alleged robbers were the clients of his young associate.

The Rogers office was the stage for what may be termed a continuous performance. Something exciting was occurring there all the time.

One day a client of Earl's, George Clayton by name, burst into the suite in the Redick Block with murderous intent. He was full of bad whisky and carried a six-shooter in his hand. No one was in the office at the time but Bill Jory. Clayton immediately covered Bill where he sat in a chair and ordered him to elevate his hands.

As Jory held his arms aloft the red-eyed intruder told him he had come there to kill Rogers, and that if he had to wait for him very long he would kill Jory "just for luck." As he expounded his intent to the deeply interested Mr. Jory another attaché, Fred Thompson, entered and was profanely instructed to sit beside Bill and emulate the latter's pose.

At this stage of the lecture Earl came into the room and, instantly grasping the meaning of the scene, seized the barrel of the gun in one hand and locked his other arm around Clayton's waist. But the latter was a powerful man and he began to force the gun slowly downward to bring its muzzle against the body of his slighter antagonist. Realizing he was no match in strength for the other man, Rogers shoved

Clayton backward off his balance by a quick heave of his shoulder, sprang into the next room and slammed the door.

Asking Clayton through the door what he wanted, Earl was informed that the gunman had come after six dollars he claimed the lawyer owed him in settlement of a civil case which Rogers had won for him. Opening the door slightly, Earl handed Jory a ten-dollar bill and told him to go downstairs, get it changed, and hand Clayton six dollars.

Clayton was gathered in half way down the stairway by an officer from the nearby police station, for between sentences of his conversation through the closed door the lawyer had telephoned in a low voice to the police.

When Rogers was summoned to the police station to place a charge against Clayton, the latter, taking advantage of a moment when the arresting officer was making an inventory of the gun and other personal effects of the prisoner, swung suddenly and unexpectedly on the lawyer's jaw and knocked him cold. Earl regained consciousness on a cot in the emergency ward. Clayton got a year in San Quentin to meditate upon possible flaws in his bill-collecting methods.

So keen was Rogers' appraisal of the chances of any case that he often accepted legal fights which would have seemed hopeless to a man of less adroit mentality. His resourceful brain and profound self-esteem made him regard any court fight as certain of success if he could see in it the slightest balance in his favor.

Many of the cases he took after all other attorneys had turned them down as certain victories for the prosecution, turned out to be ridiculously easy for the defense when Earl had applied his many-faceted mind to their solution.

One of his earliest efforts along these lines illustrates his unusual fertility in expedients. It was that of a clever hotel thief accused of stealing a ring, greatly valued by its owner for purely sentimental reasons, but it was actually worth only three dollars. The case against him was circumstantially strong. Earl decided upon a defense of mistaken identity.

When the defendant appeared in court he was seen to be a quiet-mannered and well-garbed man of middle age. On one of his fingers was a ring set with a fine diamond of two-carat size. His cravat bore a scintillating pin whose large white stone was flanked by two pigeon-blood rubies.

A heavy gold chain of the ship's cable style affected by prosperous citizens of those days was draped across his embroidered vest, and when occasionally he drew out his watch to note the time of day, it was disclosed to the jurors as a solid gold hunting-case timepiece that must have cost a tidy sum.

During cross-examination of witnesses for the prosecution and in his argument to the jury Rogers made no direct allusion to the defendant's fine raiment and costly jewelry, although he did pass an occasional abstract remark about the looseness of accusers generally, and the district attorney's office in particular, in causing needless shame and expense to people whom sane folk obviously would not suspect of petty thievery.

As they sized up the well-to-do gentleman who was accused of risking his liberty by purloining a three-dollar trinket, the jurors could not suppress their amused smiles at the absurdity of the whole proceedings, and when the evidence was all in they voted "not guilty," after only a short discussion.

When the released man had finished shaking hands with the last of the jurors, who told him they felt as if they should apologize to him for the embarrassment he had suffered, he strode away with head erect, between his admiring friends, Rogers and Jory. In fact the attorney and his factotum walked affectionately close to the recent defendant, and another anxious-visaged man kept just three paces to their rear, until, beyond sight of the courtroom attachés and jurymen, the quartet halted.

Then Earl and Bill stripped the acquitted man of his jewelry and satin vest and handed them over to the pawnbroker from whom the valuables had been rented for the occasion. The owner of the gems and waistcoat had constituted himself an extra guard because the young attorney, who always spent his fees as fast as he got them, had been unable to put up a cash deposit large enough to cover the lender's estimate of what the articles were worth.

Another case which illustrated his prolific command of shifty devices when in tight corners occurred only a few weeks later. He accepted, after considerable deliberation, the defense of a man accused of stealing a horse from a prosperous German farmer. The complaining witness was a man of integrity, well liked by a wide circle of acquaintances, and he was positive in his identification of the thief.

As the trial opened, the defendant, dressed in worn overalls, a week's stubble on his chin, sat beside the immaculately garbed Rogers. The accused kept nervously twirling his oddly shaped green hat, apparently to his attorney's annoyance, for two or three times when Earl, his brows puckered in an irritated frown, whispered to his client the hat-twirling for a time ceased. This byplay had served to bring the hat-juggling to the attention of court, jurors and spectators.

When Rogers took over the old farmer's cross-examination he seemed more inclined to engage him in friendly conversation about crops, cattle raising, and the general condition of agriculture than to subject him to any court routine. But finally, having exhausted the subject of farming, he pleasantly asked:

"Can you identify the man who stole your horse, Mr. Schultz?"

"Sure I can, Mr. Rogers," the witness assured him.

"Will you mind pointing him out, if he is in this court-room?"

Mr. Schultz gazed at the man with the green hat and said, "That's the feller; the one with the green hat."

But while the attorney had engaged the farmer in gossip about crops and cattle, Bill Jory, arrayed in worn overalls and with a stubble grown for the occasion, had exchanged seats with the real defendant and was nervously twirling the latter's green hat when Mr. Schultz identified him as a horse thief. Schultz insisted that he could not be mistaken. As Bill was known to almost every person in the room the case was literally laughed out of court.

After his rout in the Alford murder trial by his former pupil, the once invincible Senator White appeared in but few other cases of great importance. Into a comparatively short public life he had compressed such an immense aggregate of work as criminal pleader and civil lawyer, prosecutor and United States Senator, that, between his intense labors and the constant stream of hard liquor he consumed, he was burned out mentally and physically when he had reached the age of forty-five.

After Rogers' rapid ascent to the heights he was occasionally associated in legal battles with his quondam teacher and opponent. Their last case together was memorable only for the pathos it involved. They were defending one Ygnacio Vilderain in a negligible misdemeanor trial, their client having been charged with attempt to bribe a humane officer in an effort to avoid the law in connection with some dog racing he was promoting.

Earl's usual dexterous attack upon the prosecution cleared the defendant of the charge, and after the verdict in their favor had been rendered, White, his once magnificent mind now only a fitful glow, eyes dull from drink, turned to Rogers and said:

"Earl, this case will be the making of us."

That was more than even the habitual immobile composure of Rogers could bear. Suddenly it brought back to him the record of splendid achievement of the man beside him, memory of what had perhaps been the ablest mind California ever produced. And here was the little giant of court and forum boasting with maudlin seriousness of the winning of a measly misdemeanor case.

"Yes, it will be the making of us, Senator," agreed Earl, putting his arm about White's burly shoulders as he glared savagely at a grinning court bailiff.

CHAPTER VI

In the year or two prior to the advent of the new century, Rogers devoted himself to study with all the ardor of a religious zealot. He now had a clear conception of his goal and he plunged ahead under full steam, adding to his rapidly growing fund of knowledge. He slighted no subject that had to do with the practice of criminal law, giving especial attention to medical jurisprudence.

Of course it was more or less necessary to obtain a steady income, small as were his requirements and those of his family. Likewise his aides in the office had to be kept in eating- and drinking-funds. And, hard as he studied, he seemed to regard his research as something to be kept from even his associates. He wanted them to feel that Earl Rogers did not have to look into books for knowledge.

There was a succession of murder cases, most of which were won with ease; but in each trial he learned something new and in almost every one he introduced some interesting innovation in criminal practice.

It was at this stage of his career that Earl made an important decision. It was never to take a case that was absolutely hopeless, no matter how much in money it would bring to him. Many of his early associates still argue that he had determined upon this course because he felt that success was a criminal lawyer's chief asset and that a losing case would impede his rise to the top. Yet all agree that, contradictory and complex as was his nature, it was always clear that money never entered into his calculations. Money, to him, was invented only to be spent.

There was yet a deeper psychological angle to this phase

of the Rogers philosophy. Since boyhood Earl had been accustomed to dramatizing whatever he thought or did. Now as a climber on the ladder of fame this trait was accentuated to a remarkable degree. He had developed an ego that could not bear the thought of defeat in any field. He tried valiantly to conceal this complex from his closest associates and was generally successful. If he turned down a case, usually some reason other than its hopelessness was given; but the few who could look deep into his carefully concealed mental processes were convinced that he had only one reason for not tackling a losing case. A defeat would violate that secretly guarded complex.

In every trial Earl Rogers was the hero of the play, and the curtain cannot go down on an unsuccessful hero.

As with the passing of time the defense of criminals came to occupy most of his life, his avidity for the limelight increased steadily. Self-exploitation became a passion with him. He assumed a rôle from the moment he entered the courtroom until he left it. Often he resumed his posturing among his intimates. It became a moot question among his friends whether his genius—or weakness—for self-dramatization was being employed as a means to an end: whether it was a device to enhance his criminal pleading and further his career; or whether his ambition to become a celebrated criminal lawyer was itself born of the overwhelming, all-consuming passion for occupying the center of the stage.

That flair for expressing everything in terms of drama would have made him today a great actor on the stage or the screen, perhaps both, for his towering ego even in the beginning was equipped with a rich imagination and an exquisite sense of form. All modern authorities insist that a successful trial lawyer must be a good actor.

Strangely enough, Earl Rogers was brought to the stage and the screen some years after his death in the character of Stephen Ashe in the dramatization and picturization of "A

Free Soul," written by his daughter, Adela Rogers St. Johns. But, excellent as book and play and picture were, the real Earl Rogers was far more dramatic than his fictional counterpart. No writer, no matter how gifted, no actor, be his talents ever so great, could resurrect the brilliant but baffling character whom many observed and none ever really knew.

How Earl would have enjoyed his daughter's word portrait of his many-phased mind! How intense would have been his egoistic enjoyment of his life action on the screen! And without a possible doubt he would have left the theater with the sardonic reflection that the actor who portrayed his own character was neither the type, nor a true interpreter of his superior mentality.

But Earl Rogers did not fit into the rôle of a modern gang lawyer, as depicted in the motion picture. His career and personality were firmly rooted in another period, an era when a criminal lawyer was still an unfettered adventurer, a buccaneer identified with the lives and exploits of the ready gun-toters and nervy highwayman. He would not have functioned as the fetch-and-carry legal clerk of the modern assassin-sneak, the messenger of a gang leader assigned to call upon a complaisant judge for a writ of habeas corpus.

The western criminal was a joyous free-booter up to the beginning of the post-war period when crime underwent modern organization development. Following the trend of everything else, crime then became a closed monopoly highly organized and centrally controlled. Its usually colorless, salaried mouthpieces are called in to perform their duties much the same as the leaders call in a chauffeur or machine-gun operator. No one who knew him could conceive of Earl Rogers ordered here and there like a glorified trouble-shooter.

Rogers' love of dramatics which he capitalized so effectively in court was often carried to his domestic life. After a particularly arduous ordeal in court he went on a drunk which lasted several days. Winding up as usual in a Turkish bath for the inevitable boiling out, he bethought himself of the good wife. He feared the reception that would be awaiting him. Perhaps he had exhausted the stock of time-worn alibis.

At any rate he had an inspiration. He sent to the office for one of the embryonic legal lights who frequented that interesting place. Before the arrival of the young lawyer he had one of the rubbers lay him out on a cot. In a whisper barely to be heard he confided to the messenger that he was dying and wanted Mrs. Rogers brought immediately. There was no suspicion in the mind of the speeding messenger that the end of the brilliant young attorney was not in sight.

Admitted to the home, the breathless carrier of tragic tidings blurted out his awesome message.

"He said that you must hurry to his bedside before it's too late. He has a last message for you about the children. He—"

But that was as far as the message ever got.

The messenger of woe wended his way back slowly to the bath place, his ears burning.

As he approached the bedside of the stricken man, the latter raised his head slightly and whispered: "Is she coming?"

"She says if she does come down here, you'll be sorry."

The supposedly dying man dropped back wearily. Then he calmly got off the cot and yelled to the negro rubber: "Boy, bring me my pants!"

He staged other fake deathbed scenes in later years, some of them funny, others tragic; the principal character, of course, always being Earl, the actor. But although much of his dramatization occurred out of court it was in the conduct of an important trial that his real artistry scintillated.

As has been intimated, this predominating phase of his life was, strangely enough, never discussed by Rogers even as a bit of court technique.

Although he talked freely to everyone concerned about his methods and inventions, he was never known to discuss, even as an abstract dissertation, the use of drama either for the winning of lawsuits or the achievement of a personal career. To those close enough to him to study his fascinating mentality, this secretiveness concerning the subject was deemed proof that his histrionic passion was founded deeply in a complex which he thought was a most sedulously guarded secret.

According to psychologists, most individuals of exaggerated ego and craving for self-dramatization are of shallow intellect. But Earl was an outstanding exception to that human rule, for behind all his self-love and play-acting there loomed a mentality of unusual force, a perfectly balanced sense of artistry, and a realization that unremitting work is the parent of all knowledge. So, notwithstanding his overweening self-conceit and consuming desire to bask in the adulation of his fellow men, he never relaxed—except during occasional sprees—from his intensive study of the law, never neglected his ingenious creation of new methods by which he could apply that law to his own ends.

CHAPTER VII

LITTLE had been written, until recently, in laudation of the criminal lawyer of a generation ago. The few masters of that branch of the legal profession were still an unknown quantity, even to the average member of the bar. The textbooks available to the young pleader ambitious to shine in criminal law contained only the conventional tools of their trade—rules of evidence, statutes and their interpretation, the precedents built up by judicial decisions. There were no printed volumes to inform the student of the many tricks and devices, circumlocutions, and evasions of criminal defense.

Rogers seemed to sense these things by some sort of intuition, a sixth sense that stood him in good stead many a time and saved scores of his guilty clients from the gallows. The inventions and contrivances handed down to him by such mentors as Stephen M. White were constantly improved upon and perfected by Earl.

That many regarded him as a jury fixer is not strange, for jury tampering was not uncommon in criminal and damage suits in those days. The California railroads, for instance, were conceded to have nearly all damage suits against them fixed in advance because of precedent—judges' decisions—lawsuits decided during two score years of domination by the Southern Pacific's powerful political machine, when many of the state's judges could not be elected to office without the assent of the masterful president of that railroad, Collis P. Huntington.

There are always controversies about the great. To many of his lawyer contemporaries Rogers was a charlatan with little knowledge of the law and the reputation of never preparing a case. Yet Earl was perhaps the most indefatigable worker in preparation of criminal cases who ever lived. He regarded the practice of criminal law as a science, studying and developing it as painstakingly as any savant ever delved into the mysteries of geology or astronomy.

And his knowledge of criminal law, the aid to criminal practice accruing to him from his proficiency in other learned professions, his diamondlike clarity of intellect, his never-failing resourcefulness under fire, gave him advantages so far beyond those of the average criminal lawyer that he scorned all such clumsy devices as packing juries. Instead he derived an exquisite exaltation from outthinking his opponents. His lightning wit was a lance dipped in divine flame. His fine perception of the psychology of jurors and witnesses made him seem clairvoyant; and perhaps he was.

It is virtually impossible to confirm many of the stories which have Earl Rogers as the protagonist. The mere fact, however, that such tales are attached to his name is more or less proof of his high place in the legal profession.

Perhaps most of the myths about Earl Rogers are due to the keenly evolved technology that much of his audience never wholly sensed, so elusive were his methods.

For instance, late in the Nineties he perfected a system of jury investigation that later became universal practice in all criminal trials. This courtroom strategy was based mainly upon ascertaining the life history of each prospective juror. Earl would learn, as minutely as could be, the story of every talesman, and once the jury had been selected his research would be continued so intensively that when the trial was well under way counsel for the defense would know the family history of each of the twelve men, his religion and politics, his virtues and frailties; and, quite often, carefully-guarded facts not known to the community at large.

He was also a past-master at handling judges, and at playing upon their weaknesses just as he did upon the jurors'.

He realized that one of the first essentials in criminal practice is to get before the jury things that are not admissible under what many regard as ridiculous laws governing the admissibility of evidence. So with specious cleverness he paid open homage to Greenleaf and the other authorities on evidence while he really side-stepped those hindering formulas as he kept the learned judges charmed by his many delightful sophistries.

In Earl's carefully conceived analysis of jurors—or those whom he almost infallibly realized would become jurors—he in the beginning relied almost altogether on Bill Jory as his investigator. As his practice increased, however, he added a former policeman named Hawley, who had quit the department under a cloud. But Luther Brown usually had charge of this phase of his practice. Every night, during the preparation of a case, Rogers would go over with Brown, Hawley and Jory the results of their day's work. When the impaneling of the jurors began he knew exactly which twelve men he wanted on the jury. Of course he could not get them all, but his average was usually high. And when time came for argument he knew just how to appeal to each man in the box.

Such methods are no longer possible in California. The rapid growth in population and the tremendous increase in litigation have brought about new laws governing jury selections.

Perhaps the best illustration of Earl's manner of securing and handling a jury is provided in the Mootry case, a celebrated murder trial of the Nineties. It was one of the first opportunities for trying out his theories.

Charles F. Mootry was brought to trial in December, 1899, for the slaying of his wife, Martha. The murder attracted intense attention from members of the bar and entertained a host of sensational-minded and morbid members of the lay community. Generally there was little doubt that Mootry had killed his wife. The romance of the Mootrys, if such it might be termed, was a sordid affair of the tenderloin's mean purlieus. The slain woman had been a performer at the Club Theater, a leg show on Main Street, the lofty moral plane of which may be estimated from the fact it was frequently closed by the police.

Mrs. Mootry's maiden name of Martha Hoff she had changed to Minnie Huff when she resorted to the stage for a livelihood. But despite her work at the shady Main Street show shop she must have retained some of the wholesome qualities of her girlhood, for her professional associates had derisively nicknamed her "Virtuous Minnie."

Mootry had been a pimp all his life—or at least since he had been old enough to carve out a career. He had never submitted to the curse of honest toil, preferring to spend his shiftless days as a mac, living a life of ease off the money of redlight women who were love-hungry enough, in their soul-starved lives, to pay for a man's companionship even if they had to buy it with the money earned by their weary nights of shame.

That Mootry was an efficient *palo blanco,* as the Mexicans scornfully call fellows of his trade, is certain. Other moron males of the redlight district admired him immensely. In their cynical wisdom they predicted that he would make good at "putting Virtuous Minnie to work," with which intent they knew he had married her. Her paltry wages as an actress of her type had been no inducement for Mootry to wed her. That he had considered it necessary to marry her at all indicated that she must have been ethically above her environment, unless her possession of a house and lot had moved him to his unusual condescension toward a member of the other sex. Or perhaps the fact that Martha had remained anatomically virtuous had stirred Mootry's biological curiosity to unprecedented recklessness. Anyhow, he had startled the whole reservation by leading her to the altar—a justice of the peace's office.

In their cottage on Julian Street, with none there except Mootry and his wife, Minnie was shot in the breast by a .22 calibre revolver. When a neighbor rushed in at the sound of the gunshot she was lying in a crumpled heap on the floor of the living room, blood gushing from her lips. Mootry came in from the kitchen, blood on his hands, saying his wife had shot herself. The visitor suggested that Mootry run to a telephone and summon a doctor, but when the physician arrived she was dead.

The bullet had severed an artery, the blood rushing into her lungs and suffocating her. Near her on the floor lay the pistol which had caused her death. On a table beside which she had sat when the wound was inflicted rested an old Danish Bible with worn binding, which, it developed, had lain at the bottom of her trunk for years until the day of her death.

Mootry's story was that he had been in the kitchen when he heard the shot and had rushed into the living room as his wife toppled off the chair. He said that her dress was afire where the bullet had entered and that he had put it out. His explanation of the blood on his hands was that he had tried to stanch the bleeding from her mouth with a towel. He testified that her last words were: "I did it myself," and "I still love you."

The evidence against Mootry, however, seemed irrefutable. There were no powder burns on the girl's breast around the bullet hole, and the coroner and the doctor who had first examined her declared there was no evidence of her dress having been afire. Obviously, if she had pressed the gun against her bosom, or held it within a few inches of her body when it was discharged, the black powder used in those days would have ignited the cloth.

At the preliminary hearing the testimony of acquaintances

of the two was that Mrs. Mootry owned the house in which
they lived and that many of their bitter quarrels resulted
from her husband's requests that she deed the property to
him. One of the girls who had worked with Mrs. Mootry at
the Club Theater said that Mootry, since his marriage, had
been familiar with another woman, and that on more than
one occasion he had declared he would like to get rid of his
spouse. The girl's lover corroborated this testimony.

A negress who lived at the rear of the Mootry's cottage and
sometimes did their washing said she had seen Mootry slap
his wife's face and turn the hose on her when she had gone
into the backyard to help him at work in the garden there.

A few weeks before her death Mrs. Mootry had gone to
a rooming house on Court Street, telling the landlady that
she had been put out of their home by her husband, that
he had threatened to kill her, and that she was in fear of her
life because of his violent temper. While in the lodging house
she was visited several times by Mootry, who, according to
witnesses, used abusive language to her. A policeman who
resided there testified that during some of Mootry's visits to
the lodging house he had prevented him from treating his
wife with physical violence.

As this seemingly hopeless case went to trial, Rogers had
decided upon his course. He felt that, keen as he was at
cross-examination, any attempt to break down the prosecution witnesses' testimony would only result in making their
evidence stronger in the eyes of court and jury. So he determined to ignore all the testimony, and to rely wholly upon
his own keen psychology and persuasiveness when it came
time to select the jury and argue the case before those twelve
men. Naturally, he seemed desirous of getting on the jury
fellows of the same moral stripe as the defendant, but the
watchful prosecutor, C. C. McComas, a veteran of the district attorney's office, balked all such apparent attempts upon
the part of his opponent. After some skirmishing along that

line Rogers seemed resigned to letting McComas have his own way and the jury box was soon filled with a lugubrious invoice of churchmen.

When the selection of the jury had been completed Mc-Comas turned to one of his associates and said in Earl's hearing: "If that isn't a hanging jury I never saw one."

Rogers smiled cryptically and observed, "Then you should be thankful to me, Mac, for I certainly helped you pick that collection of Sunday school teachers."

Thinking this over, the prosecutor recalled that Earl really had been as insistent as himself upon a sanctimonious spirit on the part of those chosen, after his first ostensible attempts to put over a couple of rounders. But if the crafty assistant district attorney for a fleeting moment suspected any fell design upon his adversary's part, he at once dismissed the thought. Considering the moral status of the defendant, a straight-laced jury was the very thing the prosecution most desired.

From the opening of the case the heaviest handicap which the defense suffered was the attitude of Mootry himself. His long, unprepossessing face was unmistakably marked with the lines that come from dissipation. All his actions were trivial and coarse, his every effort bent upon attracting attention. He was bold to the point of effrontery. His curly hair always had the appearance of having constant attention. His immaculate white hands proclaimed as much as his brazen visage that he was of the tenderloin.

He chewed gum constantly, or ate fruit and candy, smacking his lips loudly as he leered about the courtroom. Once when he recognized two tawdry, overdressed women as they entered the room, he clapped his hand to his grinning mouth and ejaculated, "Oh, Mamma!"

Whenever it occurred to the defendant that he was not occupying all the attention that should be accorded a person on trial for murder, he would suddenly jump up and change his seat, or motion wildly for the bailiff to attend to some of his petty wants. He wearied his disgusted attorney by constantly whispering instructions. All that was gruesome and horrible about his poor wife's passing brought a smile to his lips. It was reported that he was studiously avoided by all his associates in the county jail.

He was also avoided as much as possible by Earl Rogers, who sat as far away from his client as possible without making it noticeable, brooding, no doubt, upon the added burden this oaf's behavior was piling upon a defense already half sunk. Only the lure that such a hopeless case held for this super-gambler with the law could have overcome his repugnance for the human pawn he was using in his fascinating game of criminal pleading.

When the testimony was all in, Charles Mootry was a ten-to-one bet to have his unlovely neck stretched. In his opening argument Prosecutor McComas called attention to the fact that the defense had not advanced a single worthwhile item of evidence. But because of the hint of a suicide defense contained in a deposition from a St. Louis actress, to the effect that Minnie Huff had once said she would rather kill herself than become deaf, the prosecutor devoted much of his address to attacking that supposed motive.

McComas told the jurors that they must work on the presumption that Mrs. Mootry would not have committed suicide, that the love of life—of mere physical existence—alone would have prevented her from resorting to self-destruction.

To this contention Rogers interposed a vigorous objection. He held that in law only one presumption was admissible, and that was the preëminent one, always recognized, that the accused is innocent until he is proved guilty.

When Earl began pacing gracefully before the twelve men, his musical voice lulling their taut nerves after the tiresome wrangling of days spent in examining witnesses, he held in his shapely head the biography of every man before him.

Starting with juror number one, he addressed him in confidential tones. "John Burbank," said he, "you will ever remember those unforgettable days when you courted your girl in that little Illinois town. Of course she is still your sweetheart, always will be; but the thrill of that moonlit Sunday night when you sat holding hands on the steps of the First Methodist Church of Chillicothe will never be forgotten.

"That blessed period of our lives is as holy as the sacrament of matrimony itself, those days when we laid siege to a sweet maid's heart. It is the hallowed era which sanctifies our lives and sheds a ray of heavenly light throughout all our years until the very end."

With softly-modulated accents he rendered his moral discourse upon the surpassing sweetness of courting days, drew charming word-pictures of the peace and content which follow the mating of those fortunate ones who are united forever by the magic of pure love.

As he enlarged upon his enthralling theme he illustrated it with the love stories, one by one, of others of his rapt listeners. He did not make the mistake of being too definite as to detail as he sketched their probable romances. Earl was too much the artist for that. But so close did he come to the actual facts of every juror's days of wooing that each thought the graceful and sentimental fellow before him had accidentally happened to describe his own days of tender emotions almost exactly as they had been.

"But," exclaimed Rogers with swift transition to sternness, "Charles Mootry had no such blissful background for his romance. No church steps were his to sit upon as he held his sweetheart's hand. No; when he met his fate, when he realized that he cared for Martha with a love that surpasseth understanding, she was an actress in the tawdry Club Theater, resort of only dissipated and immoral men.

"But he took her away from her sordid surroundings, gave

[56]

her his name, and brought into her loveless life the only happiness she had ever known.

"Which of us, had we suddenly found ourselves loving a girl in such an environment, would have ignored her past, would have taken her to the altar and there entered with her into the holy bonds of matrimony?

"And he had not our moral concept to guide him. The men with whom his lot had been cast sneered at him for his weakness in wedding a girl of a social plane where none of them marry women, but only live off their wages of sin. So, my brethren, contrasting his perverted viewpoint with our more fortunate one, he was really nobler in his act than even we would have been had Fate put us in his place.

"What greater proof could we ask of his love for the girl he wed? And, brethren, men who love greatly, no matter what their moral or social degree, do not slay those they love."

As Earl swung partly away from the jurors in his involuntary gesture toward Mootry, the latter simpered in an expression which he probably considered the effect required of him at this phase of his story, and spectators on the opposite side of the room from the twelve men in the box noted that the deep disgust of Rogers at sight of his client made the lawyer grimace.

Had the jury seen that glance of loathing, the pleader's soul-stirring exhortation would have gone glimmering. But Earl, with a sweeping gesture as rapid as his thought, interposed his own immaculate form between the jury and the accused man as he turned back to the rapt dozen he was hypnotizing, his austere features again displaying a mask of mournful sincerity.

The Mootrys had not quarreled on the day of her death, declared Rogers. And Mrs. Mootry had long been worried, fearful, because of her gradually increasing deafness. Had she not declared to her actress chum years before that she would end her life before she would lose her hearing? Obviously, he maintained, she had killed herself in a fit of despondency. Why else, he solemnly demanded of the jurors, should she have delved into the bottom of her trunk and got out her old family Bible, printed in her native Danish language, which she had not perused in many years? Was not that long-neglected reading of the Word of God the act of a woman contemplating the approach of death?

For hours he built up his thesis, adroitly concealing the fact that he was keenly observing the jurors' psychic reactions to his churchlike exhortation, artfully adapting his plea to their mental changes as his keen intuition told him the nature of his hearers' slightest emotional response.

At this point in his argument Earl reverted to the testimony of the policeman who had sworn he had prevented Mootry from beating his wife, and to the stories of the Club Theater girl and her sweetheart. They had been the chief witnesses for the state and had withstood Earl's grilling. He ridiculed the possibility of such testimony being seriously considered by intelligent jurors. Then came the finish.

"My friends," he intoned sepulchrally, "has it come to such a pass in this unregenerate day and generation that your brother or my brother may be sent to the penitentiary, ay, even hanged, solely upon the testimony of *a pimp, a prostitute, and a policeman?*"

That protest against the evidence of at least two of the three witnesses who were the very moral antitheses of the God-fearing jurors, plus apt alliteration's archaic aid, had the desired effect. The jury retired and brought in a verdict of not guilty—voted on the first ballot.

As Earl paused outside the courtroom for a moment's raillery at the expense of the still astonished and glowering prosecutor, Mootry swaggered up to his liberator, mouthing a speech of thanks that was palpably rehearsed, glancing about from the corners of his eyes to note if his action were being

observed by everyone present. It was obvious that his coarse
vanity and not any impulse of gratitude moved him as he
extended his flabby white hand to Rogers.

"The truth will prevail, Earl—" he began grandiloquently.

But the barrister turned upon his recent client eyes whose
disdain burned all the insolent affectation out of Mootry as a
white-hot flame sears the wings off a moth. Then as the other
recoiled from that look of withering repugnance, Rogers
turned away like one smitten with nausea, brushing the
skirts of his cutaway coat as if freeing it of dirt.

"Get away from me!" he snarled harshly, "you slimy pimp,
you know you're as guilty as hell!"

CHAPTER VIII

It was long before the day of intensified publicity and the stimulation of public opinion through the services of the press agent. In recognizing the value of this medium as an adjunct to a growing practice and a boundless ambition, Earl Rogers was far ahead of his times.

Trials were handled by the local press as mere items of news. That so little drama crept into the reports of court incidents was perhaps due to the fact that this element was ordinarily lacking.

A daily visitor to the Rogers offices at that period was a young reporter who had a somewhat different slant on the handling of a crime story or trial. His name was Harry Carr and he has since become famous as a columnist, war correspondent, and commentator on important public matters. Harry was the first Los Angeles reporter to sense the fact that Rogers was creating history in criminal procedure; that he was lifting court trials out of their former dead level of monotony; that he was transmuting humdrum legal procedures into fascinating shows. And he played them up; greatly, of course, to the advantage of Rogers. The two became close friends and whenever possible the lawyer saw to it that Harry got all the breaks. If he had something sensational to reveal in a trial and his friend was working on a morning paper, he would wait until it was too late for the afternoon papers. If Carr were employed on an afternoon paper, as he was early in his career, Earl manipulated things so that Harry alone got the story for his newspaper.

Throughout his career, Rogers never neglected the reporters. Rather he cultivated them and his office was good for at least one story a day even to the greenest cub reporter.

The Mootry case was given wider mention in the local newspapers than even the Alford case, solely because of the unprecedented manner in which Rogers conducted the defense.

Another rather colorless murder case at about the same time was dramatized into first-page prominence. It was the trial of a prospector named Chaudefosse, a Basque, charged with the slaying of a Frenchman named Delbasty, also a prospector. The alleged murder was committed after a drunken party in Dead Man's Canyon, north of Los Angeles.

According to Harry Carr's description in the *Los Angeles Times*, Chaudefosse, fifty years old, "was the height of a hitching post and about as round as a barrel and exuded much Gallic temperament and the odor of garlic mingled with that of Dago red."

The prosecution maintained that the Basque had deliberately shot the deceased through the femoral artery with a load of buck-shot and that when his victim lay bleeding to death from the wound in his thigh, the defendant had kicked him.

"Did you do that?" sternly demanded Earl when he had placed the defendant on the stand.

"No, sir," exclaimed Chaudefosse, as tears streamed down his homely face. "I am not a barbarian."

The jury believed that he wasn't. Also that he was telling the truth when he declared that the gun was discharged during a struggle between the two men. He was liberated.

Among his trials of that period Rogers lost just one, and although it was a more or less obscure case it had one interesting angle.

Rogers had been summoned to San Bernardino to aid a former boyhood friend, Lawyer Benjamin F. Bledsoe. Bledsoe cared little for criminal practice but had been importuned to take the case of a deputy sheriff who had been indicted for the theft of some $10,000 of the sheriff's funds.

It seemed to be a pretty clear case against the defendant and Bledsoe wanted him placed on the stand as the only possible means of creating that highly necessary reasonable doubt in the minds of the jurors that the money was taken with criminal intent. Rogers was convinced that it would be fatal to put the man on the stand. Bledsoe was as insistent that he should be permitted to testify in his own behalf. A deadlock ensued and Bledsoe finally suggested that the matter be arbitrated by the defendant himself. The latter was called in and the question placed before him. He made the decision to take the stand.

The jury brought in a verdict of guilty and the convicted man was sentenced to ten years in San Quentin. "It was an error by the home team," explained Rogers to his associates upon his return to Los Angeles. He refused to admit that it was *his* case that had been lost.

At about this time the entire Pacific Coast was revolted by the most brutal murder of a decade. A shoemaker named Methever, seventy-three years of age, hacked ten-year-old Dorothy McKee to death with an ax one night on the ocean's strand at Long Beach.

And, to render more awful the ghoulish character of this shocking piece of butchery, Methever, after chopping the life out of his little victim, had strolled leisurely to his room back of the shoe shop and gone to bed. But later, when the officers of the law came to arrest him, Methever shot himself in an attempt to commit suicide, blowing one of his eyes out of its socket. The killer was immediately rushed to the Los Angeles jail to save him from the fury of a Long Beach mob.

News of the thing of horror on the beach of the Los Angeles suburb was spread far and wide even before the newspaper headlines were screaming it along the streets next morning. At once the sensation crowded all other news off the front pages of the Southwest.

On the second day after the crime Earl Rogers and his staff were discussing the murder and what defense other than the vague plea of insanity could possibly be offered for Methever. That is, the others were discussing it while Earl, with his feet cocked up on the desk, lay back in his chair and listened with half-closed eyes.

"We ought to be able to land this one, Earl," said young Fred Spencer as he watched his chief questioningly. But Rogers maintained his attitude of gloomy contemplation.

"Hell, yes," urged Jim Hawley, Earl's jury investigator. "Look at your record to date. Doc Crandall, Alford, Chaudefosse, Mootry, and the rest. Not a damn' one hung. Not even one sent to the pen."

The junior member of another law firm breezed in. From his guarded observations the object of his visit was soon apparent. His firm would like to get the case, but until they learned if Rogers might be in touch with Methever they would make no overtures toward securing it. Earl's reputation as a defender of killers was already that potent.

Finally Rogers spoke. "We've just been talking about the Methever case," he drawled non-committally. "It's a tough one," he added.

"Yes, I know," sparred the visitor; "but we poor lawyers can't pick and choose. The main questions are: Has Methever any money, and which of us is going to get it—I mean the case, of course."

Earl brought his feet to the floor. From the upper left-hand drawer of his desk he took a brown cigarette paper and tobacco and deftly rolled a cigarette. His gray eyes shot a sudden look at his questioner. He drew the cigarette along his tongue to complete the building of a smoke. As he reached for a match his teeth clinched and the muscles on either side of his jaw bulged slightly, the only sure index to his emotions. After he had inhaled deeply and sent twin streams of blue smoke trickling through his nostrils, he spoke again.

"Do you boys want it?" he asked.

"Well, Earl," replied the other, still essaying to be non-committal, "there's going to be a big pile of newspaper stuff, a lot of talk and excitement, a heap of advertising for Meth-ever's lawyers."

"I wouldn't be surprised," was Roger's cryptic observation, and the other attorney departed without learning anything from the occupant of the Redick suite.

None realized better than Earl that there would be im-mense public advertising for the man who handled the case.

Methever did want Earl to defend him. He had sent word by one of the attorney's staff that he wished Rogers would take his case. He had over $700 in cash, he told the messenger, and could raise as much more on his Long Beach property.

And $1400 was a huge sum to the improvident young law-yer just then. He was broke, as usual. But up until then he had not lost a murder case. His score was perfect, and his overpowering vanity flinched at the bare thought of risking his reputation on this unusually knotty case of the murderous shoemaker. But then—$1400 was terribly needed.

Public sentiment, too, would be against him if he defended this fiendish murderer, but he dismissed that thought dis-dainfully. "No lawyer ever got anywhere by taking popular cases, nice ones," he ruminated aloud, as one of his youthful associates listened expectantly. "Bucking public sentiment makes no difference *if you win*. There's only one test of a lawyer with the public: That's his record for winning cases. People forgive everything but failure."

As the attorney spoke the group in the office heard the tattoo of light feet on the wooden stairs. The door was flung wide open. Little five-year-old Adela Rogers marched confi-dently up to her father's desk.

"Oh, hello there, sweetheart!" greeted Earl as his eyes lighted up with affection; "what brings you here?"

"Daddy," she announced, "mother's downstairs in a store. She sent me up to get three dollars."

"Oh, is that so? Well, I'm afraid that's too much."

He searched himself thoroughly and brought forth a lone silver dollar from a pocket. He laid it on the edge of the desk. The little girl gave a disdainful look and stepped back.

"Mother wants *three* dollars," she reiterated firmly.

"Well, that's all I can spare, dearie."

The child made no move. She stood there looking defiantly at her father. Her father looked at her, his eyes again somber.

"Mother—wants—three—dollars," she again repeated, deliberately, meaningly.

"Well, you tell mother," he said with a troubled frown, "I've got just exactly two dollars in my pocket, and I'm sending her half of it. Do you understand that? Now, you take that dollar and go—"

Miss Adela Rogers reached for the coin, turned about, banged the door. Then they heard the stamp of her little feet receding down the stairway.

"Well, are you going to take that $1400 and defend Methever?" anxiously asked Earl's youthful associate.

"No! I've never lost a case and I'm never going to lose one, either! And—

"Why, man," he suddenly burst out, "that might have been my own little daughter lying there hacked to death on the beach!"

But no one, not even members of his own family, have ever known whether it was his dread of losing a case, or sentiment inspired by little Adela's sudden visit, that moved Earl Rogers to turn down the Methever case with its boundless possibilities of dramatization and the sorely needed fee of $1400. Another lawyer defended Methever, who was speedily tried, quickly convicted and expeditiously hanged.

[65]

CHAPTER IX

DURING these hustling early days Rogers somehow or other found time to indulge his passion for anatomical and surgical lore. It had become more than a hobby with him, more than a furtherance of a youthful dream. Each case he handled brought a more complete realization of the value of such knowledge in his profession. He thrilled with delight at opportunities to impress the court, jurors, rival counsel, and courtroom habitués with his knowledge of things medical.

Doubt was frequently cast upon the depth of that knowledge. Enemies declared that it was purely superficial; part of a poseur's act. Yet time after time Rogers would astonish state medical experts on the stand with his questions and confound them with his oral reactions to their replies. He delighted in propounding extended hypothetical questions, long before this form of interrogation was made famous in the Harry Thaw trial. He loved the sound of those lengthy Latin medical terms and they rolled off his eloquent tongue with the rhythm of classical poetry.

Rival members of the bar sourly declared during discussions of the subject that Earl obtained his effects by intensive memorizing of technical terms under the careful coaching of one of his doctor friends. They couldn't believe that an attorney who was so constantly in court and so sedulously engaged in drinking could acquire any fundamental knowledge of the highly technical medical profession.

Yet, not many years later, Rogers was made a professor of medical jurisprudence at one of the Los Angeles colleges. And many an expert medical witness who ran afoul of Earl on the stand was convinced that the lawyer knew as much as any doctor.

His proficiency was undoubtedly due in a great measure to that deep-rooted boyhood desire to study surgery. His expertness was credited largely to the aid of three young physicians. They were Dr. Edward M. Pallette, who had aided the defense in the Alford trial and had successfully withstood Senator White's scathing cross-examination; Dr. Claire Murphy, who was regarded by members of his profession as one of the best informed of men on anatomy; and Dr. Robert V. Day. Murphy, most brilliant of the trio, has long since passed away.

All three were under thirty and despite their youth they were dynamic members of their profession in Los Angeles, far keener mentally than the average young doctor, and filled with enthusiasm for whatever was new and progressive in the broad realm of medical science. All of them were the young attorney's social intimates, Pallette having been the Rogers family physician since his first acquaintance with Earl.

Eagerly aided by these well-informed and sympathetic instructors, he applied himself to the study of medicine with all the intensity of his assiduous and receptive nature. And, as soon as he had gained a general knowledge, he began paying particular attention to those branches of the profession which have special application to forensic medicine, legal practice.

Gunshot wounds; incised lesions, or stab wounds; all phases of insanity from sheer madness down through the many functional disorders to mere mental defects that cause inclination to perverse actions; the study of psychiatry, or treatment of those mental diseases; the intricate subject of poisons and narcotics and their effect upon the human organism—all these special branches of medicine which are included in medical jurisprudence Rogers absorbed with an avidity inspired by ambition to become eventually superior in such knowledge to any medical practitioner.

He haunted hospitals, operating rooms, morgues. Wherever a difficult operation was to be performed or a mysteriously slain body examined, Earl Rogers was one of the interested and expert investigators present. He was especially fascinated by the emotional effects of alcohol.

Earl even went beyond the purely medical phase of mental phenomena, studied James and all other authorities on those obscure mental manifestations which are not even treated by ordinary psychologists. He delved into thought reading, and those phases of our psychic life which consist of premonitory thought schemes not yet articulate. This knowledge of the borderline of everyday mental processes and vague subconscious activities he felt would greatly add to his already uncanny reading of others' minds when they were on the witness stand.

Before Earl had been at his medical studies much more than a year his rapidly growing knowledge of anatomy and surgery produced striking results in the Mellus case. In this remarkable instance a man already convicted and sentenced for murder was the beneficiary of Rogers' medico-legal skill. The case was unique and unprecedented in criminal jurisprudence.

The defendant in the case, D. E. Mellus, was a conductor on the Santa Fé railroad and he was accused of the murder of H. A. Landon, another employee of the railroad company.

The killing of Landon by Mellus came as the climax of a series of labor disputes that threatened to tie up the railroad company in a general strike. In an effort to settle the differences between the company and its disgruntled employees, an agreement was reached to leave the disputed points to arbitration. Mellus, a freight conductor, was chosen as the representative of the workers, a second arbitrator was appointed by the company and the third man selected by the other two.

After lengthy sessions of the board of arbitration, a decision was handed down which favored the company.

Mellus' run brought him into Colton, a railroad town a short distance from San Bernardino. There was considerable feeling against him among the railroaders there and the conductor was accused of having sold out his fellow workers.

When his train reached Colton on its next run the yards were spotted with ominous groups of men. None spoke to the freight conductor as he went to the trainmaster's office to report.

As he shouldered his way back to the train some of the men muttered savage insults intended for his hearing, but he ignored the jibes and climbed aboard the caboose. He had hardly entered the car when Landon, one of the disgruntled railroad workers, leaped upon the caboose steps and rushed inside to attack Mellus. In the desperate fight which followed Landon was killed.

The survivor of the battle of the caboose surrendered to the authorities. He was indicted and tried for murder. In his defense Melus testified that as he and Landon swung about the caboose, locked together in a desperate struggle, they fell heavily against the cast-iron stove which is anchored in the middle of every railroader's rolling home, and that Landon's head struck the top of the heater with such force as to fracture his skull and kill him.

But the autopsy's results were all against Mellus. After the coroner's surgeon had cut off the top of the dead man's skull the state's attorney showed the court and jury how a piece of bone had been broken loose from one side of Landon's skull. This, he testified, could have been caused only by an unusually heavy blow against the opposite side of the victim's head.

In surgical terminology such a head fracture is called a

contre coup, and anatomists hold it to be indisputable that an injury of that kind may be caused only by the heaviest sort of physical impact, such as might have been delivered in the Mellus case by a full-arm swing of a brakeman's crook or pick-handle used for setting hand brakes, or the heavy iron poker always used in the caboose of a freight train.

Playing cleverly upon this testimony of the state's autopsy surgeon the district attorney succeeded in convincing the jury that Mellus had murdered Landon. They brought in a verdict of guilty and the defendant was sentenced to life imprisonment.

After Mellus' sentence his relatives went to Earl Rogers. They knew him because he had lived in Colton as a boy. Now he was a reputed worker of legal miracles, and they begged him to do something for the condemned man. Earl agreed to look into the convicted man's chances, visited him in his cell and had a long interview with him. Mellus stood up under a searching examination by the attorney, adhering to his original story of the fatal battle in the caboose. Earl was sufficiently convinced of the prisoner's innocence to undertake his defense.

After weeks of investigation of every person and circumstance connected with Mellus before and during the trial, Earl's minute research had convinced him that he had found the weak spot in the prosecution's case. Then it took another two weeks of his time and all the influence he could bring to bear to get a court order allowing him to exhume Landon's body.

After that Rogers speedily convinced the court that he had unearthed new evidence of sufficient weight to justify another trial. At the second trial he had present not only the autopsy surgeon upon whose testimony Mellus had been convicted, but facing that expert across the table were Doctors Day and Murphy for the defense. And in the center of the table rested a grisly witness—the grinning skull of H. A. Landon.

With the dead man's skull on the table before the judge and jury Rogers started to disclose his novel defense—that what had appeared to be a fractured skull due to a violent blow was the result of carelessness by the autopsy surgeon.

With the skull in his hands and the eyes of each juror glued on it, Rogers explained how in performing that autopsy a hole had been drilled into the skull and from that a saw-cut made around its circumference so that the top of it could be removed. But in sawing around the skull the surgeon had not cut evenly, reaching the place of beginning at a point above the drill hole and thereby allowing a triangular piece of bone between the saw cuts and the suture (natural crack or seam in the skull) to fall out.

The defense surgeons, Day and Murphy, testified that this faulty work, and not an unusually heavy blow, had been the real cause of the piece of bone becoming separated from the skull. Earl also showed—what had been completely overlooked in the first trial—that the skull of the deceased was abnormal in that it was almost as thin as an egg shell. Under the cross-fire of the two medical experts' testimony and Rogers' withering cross-examination the state's surgeon finally broke down and admitted he had been at fault. The defendant was found not guilty.

Although he used the two able young surgeons in that trial, before enlisting their services as expert witnesses he had carried out, unaided, a minute investigation and learned how the inefficiency of the prosecution's autopsy surgeon, and the frailness of Landon's skull, had caused the jury to bring in a verdict of guilty against an innocent man.

CHAPTER X

MORE than thirty years have passed since the Catalina Island Murder, yet there is hardly a gathering of reminiscing lawyers in Southern California today at which mention of that case is not made. It is cited by professors of advocacy in the classes of the various Coast law schools and, as is so often the case in many-told tales, various versions have resulted, in all of which Earl Rogers is the outstanding hero.

At Avalon, the sole town of Catalina Island, three men went into a room to play poker. Two of them were mere boys in years. The third was a professional gamester—a short card man. The boys emerged from the room alive, each accusing the other of having slain the gambler who was known to the profession as the "Louisville Sport."

The Avalon of those pre-Wrigley days was as fascinating as it was anomalous. Although nominally a part of the State of California, Catalina Island and its beautiful resort of Avalon were really a principality, owned by the Bannings, an old California family, and ruled by them as absolutely as any prince or potentate who ever reigned. But their sway was pleasant. No one was ever punished by fine or imprisonment for infraction of any of the island's rules, unless banishment might be considered punishment.

In a pleasant cove on the mainland side of Catalina Island the town rested like a gem in its setting of blue ocean before it and green hills above. No surf rolled against its strand, for it is on the lee side of the island, where the water laps gently at its gravelly beach like the soft movement of an inland lake.

In those still waters nature had made a marvelous garden

of many-colored marine growth through which fishes of all imaginable species, tinted with every hue of the rainbow, flashed constantly in and out of the prismatic forest along the ocean floor. Through glass-bottomed boats divers could be viewed against the vivid background wrenching loose from deep rocks the iridescent abalone shells picked out by watching purchasers above.

To seaward flying fish whirred above the waters as finny hunters pursued them. Anglers fought yellow-tail and tuna until their arms ached from the spring of the big rods. Enthusiasts hurried to those waters from as far away as London when cabled that the mighty tuna were running. It was a fisherman's paradise.

Gambling was illegal in California even then, but, by some strange indirection of applied law, gaming at Avalon was never interfered with. At the rambling Metropole Hotel, as respectable a hostelry as ever served a mess of sand dabs, gambling was always in progress, as it was at Dan Jerrue's nearby resort.

Every evening a brass band played at a beautifully landscaped cleft in the hillside at which gathered most of Avalon's gay population. And that concert was held to be the most sacred of all Avalon's delightful institutions, despite the mediocrity of the band, which played for free dancing at the Pavilion after the concert.

A stone's throw away drinking and gambling were wide open; but if you spoke out loud during the band concert one of the Bannings' minions stepped up to you and handed you a yellow ticket. It was a one-way trip to the mainland and you took the next boat leaving Avalon.

Such was the colorful background of a remarkable murder trial, the mystery of which to this day remains deeper than the blue Pacific waters which lave the late Chewing Gum King's famed isle.

Who killed W. A. Yeager, the Louisville Sport?

Harry Johnson?

Or Alfred Boyd, the boy who was placed on trial?

No man knew, except the twain who accused each other. Earl Rogers never told. Perhaps he never knew. So profound was the riddle that it has remained a matter of baffling speculation for thirty years among the elders of the courts.

The story that is most frequently related is that Rogers brought about the acquittal of each defendant by having him place the blame on the other. The first one having been once in jeopardy could not be tried again no matter how conclusive the evidence produced by the second during *his* trial. This is one of the fictional or legendary versions, as only young Boyd was ever tried.

At midnight of August 12, 1902, Yeager and the two young fellows began their fatal game. About daylight two shots roared in the room. Johnson emerged in the Metropole barroom with smoking revolver in hand, saying that Boyd had sent two bullets crashing through Yeager's brain when the gambler had refused the boy's request to advance him fifty dollars on a watch.

At the time, Boyd made neither admission nor denial of guilt; but upon the other survivor's accusation the former was placed on trial for his life two months later.

The accused boy came of a distinguished Southern family. His step-father with whom he lived had one time held a high position in the national government at Atlanta. Oscar Lawler, now one of the West's leading corporation lawyers, was well acquainted with the boy's family. He asked Earl Rogers to join him in the defense and Earl, already greatly interested in the case, readily assented.

Young Boyd was crippled as the result of an injury sustained at school. He was a handsome little fellow with pathetic eyes; something of a contrast to young Johnson, who was a dapper, flashily dressed and self-contained youth. Both had worked as clerks at cigar counters and had become acquainted in this way.

Handling the prosecution were District Attorney Rives and his deputy, C. C. McComas, who had opposed Rogers in the Mootry trial. McComas was a brilliant prosecutor and a picturesque character. His partially bald head was covered by a large lock of black hair which he wore draped across the bare top of his forehead. He chewed tobacco constantly during trials, and to protect his expansive starched shirt front from his sharp-shooting at courtroom spittoons, he wore a handkerchief hanging bib-fashion from the front of his collar. Often during bursts of emotion his raven forelock would fall in front of his eyes and then he would drop his handkerchief, although only upon rare occasions would he miss the cuspidor with his javelin of brown saliva.

District Attorney Rives, although lacking his assistant's colorful make-up, was an attorney of sound legal training, vast experience, and an alert mind.

To the newspaper reporters McComas confided just before the trial opened that it was not at all going to be a question of veracity alone between the defendant and Johnson, as the prosecution possessed strong corroborative evidence by which they were confident of fastening the guilt upon Boyd. As the trial proceeded, it turned out that he was not exaggerating the state's case.

With the jury box finally filled, the real show started on October twenty-fifth. There was the usual dull routine which attends the openings of such public spectacles. A county surveyor confirmed the accuracy of a map depicting the scene of the Avalon killing. He was asked a few perfunctory questions by McComas to fix in the jurors' minds the main points of interest. The prosecutor was notoriously good-tempered, hard to roil. Rogers was the only attorney who ever caused McComas to lose his temper, and even Earl accomplished that result only upon rare occasions. But he was always trying.

"Where was the lunch counter located?" the assistant prosecutor asked the county surveyor, as they discussed the various features of the barroom of the Metropole.

Rogers began his work of getting the jury amused, equable. He turned to an attorney sitting beside him and in a loud stage whisper remarked, "I should have thought Mac would have asked for that the first thing." McComas was noted as a great trencherman.

McComas looked at his young adversary reproachfully, gave a long meditative spit at the nearest cuspidor and called for Harry Johnson. The trial was on.

Johnson gave his occupation as that of cigar-stand clerk. The witness said that he and Boyd and Yeager had begun playing poker about midnight; that Yeager and Boyd started with fifty dollars' worth of chips each, himself with twenty dollars' worth; that the game lasted until about five in the morning; that by then the professional gambler had won all of the boys' money, including a second fifty dollars advanced by Yeager to Boyd upon the latter's diamond stud, and that then Boyd asked the Louisville Sport to lend him a second fifty dollars on a watch.

When Yeager refused Boyd drew a pistol, testified Johnson, and shot the gambler through the head twice, and as the bullets crashed through Yeager's skull the latter nodded twice spookily as he sat upright, his hands resting upon the table's edge amidst the money and poker chips which he had been counting. After shooting the gambler, according to the witness, Boyd pointed the muzzle of the smoking gun at him, held it leveled in Johnson's direction for a moment, then tossed it beneath the latter's chair. Johnson then picked up the gun, he said, because he felt that was the safer course.

When Johnson had concluded this narrative of the fatal poker game he paused.

Then McComas brought the defense attorneys to their feet with the question, "Did you have any arrangement with Yeager about the game?"

In a few terse sentences Johnson said that he had been in collusion with Yeager to fleece Boyd through the ruse of marked cards. For luring Boyd into the game, Johnson was to receive half of Yeager's winnings.

This was a bombshell thrown into the camp of the defense. It wrecked their whole case, for Rogers had expected to show that Johnson, having lost to Yeager, would have possessed a motive equal to that of Boyd to kill the gambler.

Forced upon a moment's notice to conceive a new plan of battle, Rogers was equal to it.

"Why did you pick up Boyd's pistol when, according to your testimony, he threw it under your chair?" asked Rogers.

Again Johnson said that his act was inspired by his estimate of the state of Boyd's mind at that moment.

"But you have already said that Boyd pointed his gun at you after he had shot Yeager, yet you were not afraid."

Johnson said that was right. He had not been afraid when Boyd pointed the gun at him nor after he had thrown it on the floor.

Earl asked him if he hadn't jumped when Boyd pointed the gun at him, or at least flinched; but Johnson maintained that he had not been scared by the other's threatening action.

Then Rogers deliberately abandoned that line of questioning. "Did you mention at the preliminary hearing that you and Yeager were playing partnership?" Rogers asked.

"No, sir."

"Why not?"

"Well, I didn't care to."

Earl was silent, looking at Johnson contemptuously. Soon the witness, for all his coolness, began to fidget under the steady scornful gaze of the stone-still attorney. "Well, I wasn't asked," he finally said.

Still Earl regarded him disdainfully.

"I wasn't asked that," floundered Johnson.

Now Rogers' eyes were boring into the witness's brain.

"The question wasn't asked me," blurted Johnson. It seemed as though Earl's somber, penetrating orbs were stifling the witness.

McComas realized that Earl had something up his sleeve, but despite his apprehension he was powerless to prevent whatever was coming. Knowing now that Johnson was almost hypnotized, completely off his guard, Rogers shoved his index finger almost into the witness's face and barked out like a pistol shot:

"Didn't you step into a wash room at the Metropole to wash the powder stains off your hands?"

"Why, no," stammered the rattled Johnson, "I don't think I did."

Rogers smiled at McComas with saturnine satisfaction. He had scored his first point in his suddenly conceived plan to discredit the whole prosecution, witness and all. He gesticulated to McComas,

"Take the witness!"

The usually wary McComas fell into the trap. He felt his witness would surely be discredited in the jury's eyes if the unanswered question were allowed to hang in the air.

"Isn't it a fact," he asked Johnson, "that you had no powder stains on your hands?"

Instantly Rogers was boiling over with fury, denouncing the prosecutor for asking the witness a leading question, upbraiding him bitterly as a legal trickster. But his rage was all assumed for its effect on the jury. Had McComas taken a second thought he would have realized that Earl had purposely withheld from adding, "Oh, you don't *think* you did?" to Johnson's rattled answer, "Why, no, I don't think I did."

That was one of Rogers' favored subtleties: not bringing a serious cross-question or an argument to a verbal conclusion, although making that inference apparent. Leaving the obvious deduction to the jury would lead them to believe that they had ferreted out the unavoidable construction from the premises themselves, and so result in their being subconsciously aligned with the defender.

In this particular instance he had calculated upon the additional advantage of luring the prosecutor into prompting the witness in his anxiety and thus giving an unfavorable impression of the prosecutor's tactics.

Again Earl turned his glooming eyes upon the crestfallen McComas. But through their inscrutable regard there flashed a glint of humor. He had scored upon his adversary and was accomplishing the almost impossible feat of rattling that affable personage.

A few moments later Rogers, resuming cross-examination, sat down at the death poker table, which had been brought to the courtroom from Catalina Island. He slammed Yeager's bloody hat down over his own head and began asking Johnson to explain certain points about Yeager's position when shot. Purposely his questions were vague and asked in such a low tone that McComas again did just what Rogers was playing for. Naturally wishing to hear what was being said he strolled over, glasses on the end of his nose, to be near the table and the witness.

"Oh, here's Mac," exclaimed Earl in an aside which was audible to nearly everyone in the courtroom. *"He'll* tell you what to say!"

Before the enraged McComas could retort or appeal to the court Rogers had resumed his questioning of the witness.

Again and again he queried, "And you say you were not at all alarmed when Boyd pointed his pistol at you after he had just killed Yeager?" Johnson continued to reply that he had not been in the least frightened.

District Attorney Rives finally complained:

"Why waste the court's time with silly, useless repetition?

You have already asked the witness that same question at least twenty times and he has always given you the same answer."

At this Earl seemed vastly amused. He glanced at the jurors as if to make certain that they had taken in the complaint of the prosecutor, and then repeated the question to the witness, who once again said he had not been in the least afraid. By this time the jurors and all of Los Angeles were convinced that Johnson was not alarmed when Boyd pointed the gun at him. He left the stand and others followed. Then the defense began, but made little headway. There was only one witness of importance for the defense, the accused youth himself. His story of the game was much the same as Johnson's. They had played with the Louisville Sport before and had won. During the game which ended in tragedy he had been drinking throughout and losing. He admitted trying to borrow additional money on his watch but stated that at this time he was too befuddled with drink to realize what was going on. He testified that he tipped back his chair and started dozing, to be awakened by the sound of two shots. He admitted ownership of the weapon, but declared stoutly that he had not brought it from the room which he and Johnson occupied. Then came the day for addressing the jury.

Rogers, always the fastidious dresser, appeared in frock coat and white waistcoat. As he began his argument to the jury the real show was on. There was a charm not only in his pleasant voice, but the alert precision of his addresses, the lambent wit that enlivened his discourse, were always the feature of those entertaining performances which had been only tame every-day court trials until his graceful advent on the legal stage.

Rogers reviewed the evidence quietly and without passion. He spoke of the youth of the defendant and his family. He deplored the obvious fact that the boy had taken up with bad companions. He made it evident that Johnson was one of them. He argued that any intelligent person if asked to choose between the stories of both lads would unhesitatingly say that it was Boyd who was telling the truth. He ridiculed the argument of McComas, who had opened for the prosecution, that Boyd was the only one of the two who had a motive for killing the gambler. But there was little excitement in his manner or voice and lawyers within the rail were beginning to whisper to each other that Earl wasn't at his best. But Rogers was merely setting the stage.

Suddenly pausing in the smooth flow of his argument, Earl's calm manner underwent a quick transition. Those within the rail and the spectators without sensed that something dramatic was about to happen. It did. Earl backed to a position alongside counsel's table. With an inarticulate cry he stooped over and in the fraction of a second rose to his full height, brandishing a huge Colt's .45. Several women screamed. Earl turned and pointed the murderous-looking blue barrel directly at the district attorney and his veteran assistant. McComas dodged behind a chair and Rives ducked under the table.

The entire court-room was in an uproar. Panic-stricken attorneys who were well acquainted with Rogers thought that he had suddenly become insane from the strain of the trial. Bailiffs rushed towards him. He waved them away. By now he was grinning.

District Attorney Rives appeared from the shelter of the table.

"Hey, Earl," he yelled. "Is it loaded?"

"Sure, it's loaded," was the response.

"Well then, don't point it this way," roared the district attorney.

"Put it up, Mr. Rogers! Put it up!" pleaded Judge Smith from the bench.

Then Earl began to laugh at the men at whose heads but

an instant before he had been pointing his gun with a murderous gesture.

He turned to the jury and told them impressively that what they had just witnessed was the only possible reaction of normal human intelligence to sudden fear of death.

Then half pityingly, half ironically, counsel for the defense gazed upon Rives and McComas as he asked the twelve jurors if they felt like believing anything Johnson had said during the course of the trial, after having heard him declare twenty or thirty times that when, "according to his worthless testimony," Boyd had threatened him with a smoking revolver, a gun that had just slain a man—with the echoes of the fatal shots still reverberating in the death room—Johnson had not only been unafraid, but had not even flinched.

When District Attorney Rives closed for the prosecution he delivered a masterly address, summed up the great weight of circumstantial evidence against the defendant, ridiculed what he referred to as Earl Rogers' "play acting"; but the testimony of the state's only direct witness had been so completely discredited by Earl Rogers' dramatic gun play that the defendant Boyd was acquitted on the first ballot.

CHAPTER XI

About this time appeared one of the first best sellers of the new century, "The Right of Way," by Gilbert Parker. It was regarded as something of a sensation by the reading public and was rated by reviewers an outstanding novel. But nowhere did it have the startling effect it exercised upon the life of Earl Rogers.

The hero of the book, Charlie Steele, was a young lawyer of aristocratic mien, endowed with remarkable intelligence, brilliantly educated—and a slave to liquor. He was a Chesterfield in deportment, an esthete in dress, and a dazzling figure in the courtroom. Women were fascinated by him.

Steele's superlative mentality was that of a sophisticate, with cynicism predominating. He freed a murderer in a vivid court trial while the aristocratic young lady to whom he was engaged watched with fascinated attention. Then when his client sought to express his gratitude Steele rebuffed him dramatically. "Get away from me!" he ordered. "You're as guilty as hell!" Almost the very words which Earl Rogers used to repulse Mootry several years previously.

"Beauty" Steele, the Canadian aristocrat, held for the young western attorney an overwhelming fascination. Gilbert Parker's romantic hero completely bewitched him. The appeal of this wholly fictitious but extremely dramatic character was more real to him than his own flesh-and-blood associates. He became "Beauty" Steele.

Though the effect of the book upon him was definite, the transition in his mannerisms and customs was too gradual and subtle to be wholly realized in the beginning. Perhaps he was already an embryonic Charlie Steele and his transformation but a natural development.

At any rate, there was at first no startling reaction when Earl began appearing at the office in a series of new suits. In a very short time he had the most elaborate wardrobe and the most voluminous tailor bill in Los Angeles. The latter bothered him less than the matutinal decision as to what he would wear.

If an important trial was in progress he made it a rule to make a complete change at the noon recess. He was the first lawyer in the town with sufficient courage to wear spats before a jury. That took nerve in those days. Often an important point made by the opposition was completely overshadowed by the sartorial display flashed at the afternoon session by counsel for the defense.

Rogers was seldom called upon to defend his fastidiousness in dress, but when some intimate rallied him upon his elegance he invariably denied that it was a manifestation of vanity. His explanation was that it was good business to keep his personality impressed upon the jury or upon the public.

No better word portrait of him can be drawn than that of Stephen Ashe, Earl's prototype, in his daughter Adela's novel:

"A pale gray suit. That blue shirt, with such a fitting collar as a man may dream of his whole life and never possess. That tie, combining the elements of dignity and daring that alone can go to make a tie what it should be. The faultless gardenia. They made him stand out from the crowd. No chance for the jury to lose sight of him. He did not intend that they should. For there was no movement, no expression, no act of his but would have some meaning." That was Earl Rogers.

His variations of taste in dress soon were being followed by all smartly-garbed males of Los Angeles. Members of his professional circle, social climbers among the city's business men, bartenders, gay dogs and rounders generally—every male with any pretense to correct attire followed Earl Rogers' lead in haberdashery as completely as income, or taste, or courage permitted. He became the Beau Brummell of the Southern Californian metropolis.

From earliest youth Earl's deportment had been that of a well-bred gentleman, especially as to his mode of speech. But from the day when he came under the spell of "Beauty" Steele he became more precise than ever in diction; elegant, at times almost pedantic. He adopted the broad Anglican "A" and affected other stagey accents, perhaps from familiarity with current vocal mannerisms of the American stage.

But the very flower of this rapid growth of estheticism was the dainty conceit which replaced Earl's former pince-nez —a bejeweled lorgnette. Until that time the lorgnette had been regarded solely as the visual adjunct of dowagers.

Before he introduced this ultra-fashionable bauble to marveling judges and others of the courts, however, Rogers had become so expert at its manipulation that the first few times he folded it and tossed it into the breast pocket of his coat with one deft motion, they imagined it had disappeared through sleight-of-hand and waited in breathless anticipation for him to produce it from the disdainful district attorney's ear or the learned judge's whiskers.

But the lorgnette also had a utilitarian function. Once his scornful legal rivals and delighted courtroom spectators had got over their first astonishment at this unique instrument, they began to note that Earl had a way of disconcerting hostile witnesses by peering at them through his de luxe glasses, making them feel as if they were bugs being examined through a microscope.

But, notwithstanding his vain attention to personal adornment and elegant posing, and even despite his addiction to drink, Rogers' study of the science of law and the art of pleading never flagged. He possessed a phenomenal capacity for grueling work, and his naturally retentive memory continued to develop remarkably as he called on it for ever-increasing service.

Lawyers who were associated with Earl during his days of greatest renown still declare their belief that never has another attorney prepared his cases with such painstaking care. If need for such research was imperative, he would work not only all day but most of the night. Flogging his leaping brain with coffee and brandy, he would read unceasingly, make reams of notes, cram his wonderful memory throughout the silent watches with a wealth of detail that was amazing.

But when he entered the courtroom next morning, debonair through ministrations of Turkish bath and barber, he would not only have his defense worked out to perfection—he would also have a better case prepared *against* his client than that built up by the district attorney. Not a single authority, never a decision, which could possibly be cited by the prosecution, that Earl had not already run down, whose weak points he had not ferreted out to crack like a whip about the ears of the prosecution should they quote it against him.

Yet so great was his artistry that everything he did in the courtroom smacked of spontaneity. Often the presentation of one of his carefully worked-out periods was regarded as extemporaneous by members of his profession, even by his own legal associates. The public always looked upon him as just a marvelously clever fellow showing off in court and making all his telling points on the spur of the moment, when the breaks came his way.

One of the innumerable illustrations of Earl's memory was given in his cross-examination of a physician in one of his minor criminal cases. The doctor was well informed on his subject, and it was obvious that he had been thoroughly coached by the district attorney's office as to Rogers' reputation for confusing medical witnesses.

Although the expert had appeared as a surprise witness just before the noon recess, Earl was ready for him at the afternoon session when he took him over.

"Would you agree with a well known writer on medical subjects," Rogers asked in his pleasant manner, "when he says so and so?"—the "so and so" being contradictory to the witness's testimony.

"No, I certainly would not agree with such an 'authority'," replied the expert, for the attorney's quotation from the alleged medical writer was wholly favorable to the defense.

"Then I suppose you would also take issue with this same authority when he farther writes on the subject that——," and Rogers went on to quote his medical author from memory at considerable length.

"No reputable writer on that subject would express such an opinion," declared the physician with considerable asperity.

At this stage of the cross-examination the district attorney seemed to be getting fearful that Rogers might be digging a pitfall for the state's witnesses, so he interrupted the examination.

"Who, may I ask," interposed the prosecutor, "is this alleged authority being quoted so glibly by counsel for the defense? We have a right to know if such a medical writer really exists."

"Certainly you have the right to such information," murmured Earl as he lifted a book from the table and handed it to the district attorney. "I have been quoting from this excellent and authoritative work on the subject, which I had the good fortune to consult some years ago during my own medical studies. It was written by the learned gentleman now on the witness stand."

The state's case collapsed at this point as did the prosecutor and his star witness.

But the flawless memory of Rogers and his intense preparation for trials were but an integral part of a constantly growing mass of natural and acquired advantages in his profession. Ballistics, identification of bullets by the evidence left on them by guns' rifling, and like things hardly known then except to the scientific investigators of the Sûreté of Paris and police laboratories of Vienna and Berlin, were pretty well mastered by him even before they were studied by the police departments of this country and Scotland Yard.

Earl Rogers was no orator in the accepted sense of the term in those days. He abhorred the orotund declamation peculiar to forensic giants of his times. But he was more eloquent, more convincing than any of them, with his incisive and pleasant-toned appeal. He possessed the real artist's gift of restraint; always his auditors felt a sense of something in reserve behind his softly-modulated voice and persuasive logic.

Once he was trying a case with Frank Dominguez, who was for many years in his office. The latter was a stocky, bull-necked descendant of the California Dons. He was addicted to the florid style of address. Earl, who could never remain in a courtroom while an associate was arguing a case, was pacing discontentedly up and down the corridor, rolling and inhaling his eternal brown paper cigarettes. Another attorney came along the hallway.

"How's the case coming along, Earl?" he queried.

"Jesus Christ!" ejaculated Rogers as he gritted his teeth.

"Why, what's the matter?"

"Too goddamn' much noise!" was his taciturn reply as he nodded his head toward the room where Dominguez was bellowing.

But with Earl profanity was the exception. It took some such irritating incident as Dominguez' bombast to move him to curses. Nor was his cleanness of speech in an age of lusty expression the result of his religious training. He felt that resort to profanity would weaken his vocabulary, that one addicted to blasphemous speech would come to rely upon expletives instead of seeking the word which would express his thought correctly.

Of all Rogers' innovations in legal procedure none was more radical, nor in time more universally copied, than his change of court instructions to juries. It was only another instance of his tearing aside the old order of things and replacing them with inventions of his ingenious mind; but by members of the bench and bar it has been regarded as the most effective of judicial practices introduced by him.

Before his advent there had never been any deviation from the ancient manner of reading to the twelve men at a trial's close, an abstract treatise on law that usually went over their tired heads. But Earl injected a human note into those dry dissertations on the law's complexities so that they took on a personal tone.

One of the best exemplifications of this new method of jury instruction was furnished by the Melrose murder case—which took its place beside the Catalina Island affair as one of the great trials in the Rogers career.

CHAPTER XII

IF any accused slayer ever approached trial with definite assurance of winding up at the thirteen steps leading to the gallows, it was M. M. Melrose.

The killing climaxed a bitter neighborhood feud at Acton, a small ranching community north of Los Angeles, early in 1903. The victim was William H. Broome, a prosperous rancher, and the fatal encounter occurred in front of the Acton hotel. Melrose, who had come from the South with some reputation as a bully and gunfighter, had been made postmaster a short time previously. He also operated a small ranch on which he grew garden produce. Just before the killing he had delivered some garden truck in a wheelbarrow to the Acton hotel.

The evidence showed that after shooting down his victim Melrose emptied his pistol into Broome's back as the wounded man lay writhing on the ground. The slaying was apparently cold-blooded and without provocation.

In taking the case Earl Rogers realized that he was up against an almost hopeless task and that he would be compelled to resort to every adroit device he had ever created, plus possible new devices, to save his client from the hangman.

Realizing the preponderance of evidence against him, he urged his staff of investigators to work as they never had before in securing the intimate history of every man on the venire from which the jury was to be drawn. In impaneling that jury he exerted his sharp powers of analysis to the utmost in efforts to determine their mental attitudes; employed all his subtlety in attempts to create bias for the defendant in their minds as he questioned prospective jurymen.

Through his own devious ways Rogers seemed able to keep himself informed of every move that was even contemplated by the district attorney's force. He used his newspaper connections to the limit in creating public opinion favorable to the man he was defending. He resorted to his now thorough knowledge of surgery and anatomy with excellent results and impressed his three skilled medical friends into service.

Yet, notwithstanding his use of every device he had ever perfected, in spite of every subterfuge occurring to his nimble wits whenever the breaks came his way, this long-drawn-out battle proved the most desperate of his career. Probably at no time in his long criminal practice had he ever come closer to violating his rule of never accepting what looked like a sure loser.

In the final test, with virtually all the evidence against him, unable to clear his client through his favorite strategy of flashing attack and disconcerting surprise evidence, like a skilled boxer who is forced to cast aside his science and slug, Earl settled down to a courtroom siege whose main device was that of putting the district attorney on trial.

Acton townspeople flocked into Los Angeles for the trial, virtually deserting their community. In early days the country thereabouts had been developed by frugal and hard-working farmers of German stock. When newcomers arrived social and business barriers were set up. The late comers were as intolerant of the pioneers as the latter were of everyone and everything differing from them. The two factions were fanatically opposed to each other. Clashing at every contact, political or social, they accused each other of poisoning stock, of killing domestic animals, and even of desecrating graves. Broome was of the old-timers, Melrose the most militant of the more recent settlers.

So much feeling had been aroused in the vicinity of Acton by the killing that neither side had any opportunity of getting a man on the jury who was even acquainted in that section. Panel after panel was exhausted. When the trial proper began the state was regarded as having a case in which a verdict of guilty was a foregone conclusion.

The prosecution placed its chief reliance on a witness whose testimony came as a distinct shock to the defense—an eye-witness who was admittedly nearly a half-mile away from the scene of the killing. Such a situation would be discarded as implausible, if not actually ridiculous, in any mystery story or moving picture. The witness, a straight-laced, thin-lipped New England school teacher, declared on the stand that she had viewed every movement in the fatal encounter; that she had seen the men meet and apparently speak and that without any belligerent action on the part of Broome, Melrose drew his revolver and shot Broome in the back. And the woman declared emphatically that she had witnessed the slaying through a pair of field glasses which she was trying out as she sat on the porch of her home.

This testimony seemed so fantastic in its coincidental nature that Rogers took over the witness with eager confidence; but try as he might Earl could not shake the woman's story. Nor could he create any doubt as to her integrity. When counsel for the defense in desperation resorted to his favorite weapon of sarcasm, the little school teacher came right back at him, greatly to his discomfiture. Every attempt to make her lose her equanimity drew from the witness an acidulous rejoinder that fairly wilted the gardenia in Earl's buttonhole. It was an experience that he never forgot and by which he never ceased to profit. From that time on he carefully refrained from hurling verbal boomerangs at feminine witnesses.

The defense relied almost entirely on the testimony of the defendant himself, plus "the second gun," to support a theory of self-defense. It was perhaps the first instance of Rogers' finding the weapon of the dead man. The defense was that

Broome had been gunning for Melrose and that he had with him a shotgun which he had set against a tree just inside the gate of the Acton hotel as Melrose came along the road with his wheelbarrow.

Another important witness for the prosecution, a German rancher named Schulte, almost sealed the fate of Melrose. He declared that he had seen the meeting of the two men and had been horrified to see Melrose hold the weapon against the back of the man on the ground and fire a second shot.

When the prosecution turned over the German to Rogers, the latter dramatically summoned Luther Brown, who had been sitting beside him, and bade him lie on the floor. He had the witness adjust him in what Schulte had said was Broome's position when shot in the back.

After a number of preliminary questions, he aimed his trump query at the witness.

"Mr. Schulte," he asked as he placed the muzzle of a pistol against Brown's spine, "if you saw the defendant fire a second shot as he held his weapon this close to Broome's body, how is it that there were no powder burns discovered upon his person by the prosecution's postmortem examination?"

At this question Deputy District Attorney McComas, directly in charge of the case, was seen to grimace as if stricken suddenly by cramps. Later it was learned that the possibility of powder burns had been overlooked by the district attorney's office during the coroner's inquest.

"I guess he used schmokeless powder," hazarded the rattled witness in his rich Teutonic dialect.

Counsel for the defense smiled significantly. Of course he did not hide that smile from the men in the jury box.

Melrose was placed on the stand and declared that Broome had been the aggressor in the quarrel, that he had walked in front of the barrow to annoy Melrose and had vilely abused him. Not content with this personal vilification he had made allegations as to the chastity of the defendant's wife, going so far as to designate her as "no better than a railroad whore." Then, when the defendant had remonstrated, Broome had started for the gate, inside which was standing the shotgun. Fearing that Broome would kill him, he drew his revolver and shot him.

Again Rogers exercised his flair for the dramatic. He had the very tree against which the supposed shotgun of the dead man had been leaning brought into court. A shotgun was placed against it and the defendant illustrated his story by means of these exhibits.

But even the eloquent, forceful argument of Rogers failed to convince more than two jurors that his client was not guilty. The jury was discharged after being deadlocked at ten to two for twenty-four hours.

A strenuous effort was made to have the case dismissed but there were several important reasons for the state to oppose such disposition. The district attorney, John D. Fredericks, had not been in office very long. He felt that his professional reputation and future career were seriously jeopardized by his failure to obtain a conviction in what the public had called "an open and shut case." He demanded that it be reset for an early trial.

There was another reason for the state's refusal to dismiss the case. Melrose had been a supporter of Fredericks in the election and the latter did not want it charged that he was using his office to favor a political friend. The new trial was placed on the court calendar for about a month later.

The prosecution knew that it had to strengthen its case. The autopsy surgeon had testified for the state that Broome had been shot through the back of the head; also in the back. There was also the matter of powder burns, lack of which had been commented upon by the defense.

So District Attorney Fredericks ordered McComas, his chief trial deputy, and his chief medical expert witness,

Dr. E. O. Sawyer, to exhume Broome's body and verify the autopsy surgeon's testimony. They were also instructed to see if powder burns could be found on the back of the dead man.

The exhumation occurred dramatically at a Los Angeles cemetery where the remains of the slain man had been interred. The scene would have done credit to the weirdest fictional murder mystery.

In the dead of night the assistant prosecutor, two doctors and a detective had the body exhumed. As the coffin was lifted from the grave and placed on two supports, the witnesses were startled by a terrific flash. As their vision cleared, they discerned the figures of five men lined up at the other side of the tombstone. Beside them stood a newspaper photographer getting ready for another flashlight photograph. There was a low chuckling laugh which was instantly identified by McComas.

"Earl Rogers, what in the goddamn' hell are you doing here?" he demanded.

"Just dropped over to watch the show," replied the grinning Rogers.

"Who tipped you off?" snarled McComas, now deeply enraged.

"On the advice of counsel I refuse to testify," went on the unperturbed Rogers. "I believe there is no necessity for introducing my friends." He indicated his assistant, Luther Brown, and his three medical musketeers, Doctors Claire Murphy, Bob Day and Ed Pallette.

Convinced that there was no way of getting rid of Rogers and his aides, the other side went ahead with its examination of the corpse. Before anything was done, however, Rogers called attention to evidence that the body had previously been exhumed. Certain screws had been removed from the coffin lid and the head cloths had been displaced.

Rogers took up a position at the head of the casket.

"All of you gentlemen will notice," he observed sternly while the others shivered in the graveyard's midnight chill, "that this body has been exhumed before now."

"Well, who did it? You?" growled the exasperated McComas.

Rogers did not reply.

The examination proceeded. There were no bullet holes in the dead man's skull. The skin surrounding the hole in Broome's back was so discolored that the search for powder burns there was futile. The prosecutor turned from his regard of the deceased's spine to glower at the grinning Rogers.

"Damned funny he should have taken a notion to begin decomposing first just where we wanted to examine him," growled McComas, as if the late William H. Broome had betrayed the prosecution.

In statements to the press as well as at the second trial Earl stressed to the limit what he called the "midnight grave robbing." At last he had found a charge upon which to place the prosecution on trial.

"What," he demanded, "was the object of exhuming the body in secrecy at midnight? Who had already exhumed it? There would have been no object for the defense to do so. Do you suppose we would have been foolish enough to have tried filling any bullet holes in the skull with putty?

"But, on the other hand, if holes had been made in the skull with a punch and the body buried again, no doctor would have been able to say now, a month afterward, that they were not bullet holes."

The newspaper reporters rose to the occasion with a whoop. This was the hottest stuff Earl had ever furnished for the front pages.

And while Melrose's counsel chortled in glee, the prosecution forces were, in the idiom of the day, "fit to be tied."

At the second trial of Melrose, Rogers again introduced his tree and again "killed" Luther Brown while the latter ran for the shotgun that leaned against the prop. Secure now in the knowledge that none could belittle his dramatic demands on the prosecution witness for powder marks on the back of the deceased, he again blasted Mr. Schulte's testimony by citing the absence of any report of such marks by the state's autopsy surgeon.

Rogers virtually placed on trial the harassed prosecutors for robbing graves and manufacturing evidence to convict innocent people, and kept them so busy defending themselves that they were unable to make out a case with all the evidence in their favor. Before he got through with the trial he had convinced a majority of the jury that the district attorney had dug up Broome's body for no other reason than to punch or drill holes in the decedent's skull to prove that Melrose had shot Broome through the back of his head. There was another hung jury but this time the score was ten to two in favor of the defense.

Fredericks again resisted all attempts by Rogers to secure a dismissal of the case and it was set for a third trial. After having been held up to public scorn as a ghoul who dug up dead men to poke holes in their skulls for the purpose of getting convictions, the prosecutor was determined not to surrender.

At the third trial Rogers not only used all the evidence that had twice saved Melrose, but he wound up the judicial show with an epilogue that will never be forgotten by those who heard it. Before beginning his address to the jury he announced that he was going to repeat all the epithets Broome was alleged to have applied to Melrose and his wife, and asked the women to leave the courtroom; but not a feminine auditor budged out of her seat. Some of the language which they bore with apparent equanimity would have singed the hair off a dog's back.

But so much hostility and bitterness had been aroused by the two former trials, Rogers had so drawn on his mental resources during their course, that the third trial had become wholly a contest of endurance.

Earl had become an adept at waiting for openings and there was nothing for him to do throughout that weary session but wear down the other side by ceaseless pounding. Hostile witnesses were questioned until through sheer fatigue they had come to contradict themselves; even the prosecutors were so wearied that they could no longer forestall Earl when a break came his way.

So when the third trial had dragged through to another disagreement the harried prosecution, realizing the utter hopelessness of ever obtaining a conviction, recommended a dismissal, and the year-long legal battle was over.

As indicated, a certain technical aspect of the Melrose case was, in the opinion of legal experts, of far greater significance than the freeing of a presumably guilty man from the gallows. It was only in the succeedings years, however, that the bar fully realized the complete importance of the revolutionary innovation which Earl Rogers had introduced in the manner of submitting jury instructions to the court.

Just as he dramatized his every action in court, Rogers succeeded in dramatizing the hitherto perfunctory and prosaic final instructions which the court reads to the jurors before they retire.

It had been the age-old custom for courts to instruct juries on the law in the stilted, legal verbiage of the statutes. Jurors listened respectfully to the judge's droning of the law's application to the case, but seldom did it mean anything to them. Rogers introduced the personal element and the dreary instructions were transformed into a vivid personal story, an account of dramatic action which caused twelve tired men to prick up their ears and listen.

That part of the court's instructions submitted by the defense became in effect a dramatic continuation of the argument of the defendant's counsel. But coming from the judge himself, it was even more effective than if couched in the eloquent language of the pleader.

No better illustration of the old and the new way of charging the jury can be found than those accepted by Judge Smith from the defense in the Melrose case. The defense's instruction as to the law covering reasonable doubt in the old, impersonal manner, would be as follows:

"The jury are instructed that in a case of homicide, where the shooting is admitted, and the defense is that of justification, that before a defendant can be lawfully convicted it devolves upon the people to prove, beyond a reasonable doubt, that the killing was not justifiable, or excusable. And if the jury, from the evidence, or want of evidence, entertain a reasonable doubt after hearing all the evidence, as to whether a defendant, at the time the fatal shot was fired, was under the reasonable apprehension that the deceased intended to inflict upon him great bodily harm, then the jury should give the defendant the benefit of such doubt and acquit him."

And here are the Rogers written instructions on the law of self-defense as read to the jury by the court:

"If the jury believe, from the evidence, that the defendant, Melrose, was lawfully and peacefully engaged upon a public street in the town of Acton, and, without fault on his part, was pursued by Broome (while the defendant himself was endeavoring to avoid conflict) a distance of some 500 feet, and that the deceased, Broome, during the pursuit, applied to the defendant, Melrose, profane and opprobrious epithets and language, and threatened him with bodily violence and announced his determination to the defendant, Melrose, to enter into combat with the defendant.

"Under these circumstances, if the defendant, Melrose, being without fault at the time, and with the deceased, Broome, being the aggressor there before the deceased, Broome, could have placed himself rightly under the law, he, Broome, must not only have declined and endeavored to avoid further combat, but must have made known his declination to the defendant, Melrose, clearly and in such manner that the defendant as a reasonable man under all the circumstances could not have failed to realize that the deceased, Broome, was declining further combat.

"The question for your determination in this behalf is not whether Broome actually did decline further combat and endeavor to escape, but as to whether the defendant, Melrose, as a reasonable man, under the then existing circumstances, must have known that the deceased, Broome, was declining further combat.

"And so, even if you should believe beyond a reasonable doubt that Broome may have been endeavoring to escape through the gate of the hotel fence, referred to in the testimony, yet, if the circumstances of his gun being placed in the vicinity of the gate, and of his previous threats against the defendant, Melrose, and his previous conduct toward the defendant, and all the circumstances and surroundings at the time, were, in your judgment, such as to prevent the defendant, Melrose, from realizing that the deceased, Broome, was endeavoring to decline further combat, then the defendant, Melrose, had a right to stand his ground, and even to pursue the deceased for the purpose of winning his own safety.

"The question for you to determine is not alone what the intention of the deceased, Broome, was, but rather what the defendant, Melrose, as a reasonable man under the circumstances feared Broome's intentions to be. And if you entertain a reasonable doubt as to whether the defendant Melrose feared that Broome intended to inflict great bodily injury upon the defendant; and then and there acting under the fears then existing in his mind, Melrose slew the deceased, then you must acquit the defendant."

The psychological effect on a jury of hearing the law interpreted in terms of the specific case itself and in such a pertinent, intimate manner could not but be tremendously effective. It was not long before criminal lawyers everywhere were following the lead of Earl Rogers. Courts as a rule rejected such instructions, upon first presentation, as too revolutionary, but the system gradually became a matter of common usage in many courtrooms.

As for Melrose himself, he became thereafter Earl Rogers' devoted retainer. He went with Earl to San Francisco a few years later during the famous graft trials and acted as the lawyer's personal bodyguard.

CHAPTER XIII

WITH characteristic disregard for tradition as exemplified in his revolutionizing of the court's instructions, Earl Rogers likewise changed radically the age-old custom of jury selection. Before he got busy and turned things topsy-turvy in the criminal courts, there was only one accepted method of questioning men in the jury box. Qualifying a talesman had always followed an immemorial, cut-and-dried procedure, consisting of pointless and futile verbiage.

After giving his name, address and occupation, the prospective juror would be asked if he had read or been told anything about the case about to be tried; if he had formed an opinion of the defendant's guilt or innocence; if it were an unqualified opinion or if his conclusion were such that it might be changed by evidence—and so on through the long ritual of ancient, holy, and monotonous folderol.

Even to the layman it was obvious that any man under examination could by his replies bring about any result he desired. If, for instance, he happened to be a business man who wanted to evade jury service he usually had an opinion that was so fixed that no amount of evidence could change it. If, on the other hand, he were a professional juror, that genus of courtroom habitué to whom the few dollars per diem came in handy, he would glibly declare that he knew nothing about the case, and, if he did, that he had formed no opinion. Most of the professional jurors were known to both sides of the case and those known as convicting jurors, or otherwise friendly to the prosecution, were subjected to attack by the defense. And vice versa.

All of this meaningless routine was gradually ignored by

Rogers. He skimmed over the unavoidable preliminary questions as rapidly as possible. It will be recalled that he was already armed with the chief facts about the talesmen. Closely but unobtrusively sizing up the man during fifteen or twenty minutes of agreeable conversation, he would ascertain the venireman's nature and character, analyzing adroitly without disclosing his discoveries; then, sedulously careful to keep within the scope allowed by judicial regulations, he would sow in the future juror's consciousness the seed of bias for his client.

It was all done so insidiously that it was some time before the prosecutors realized that Earl was in reality trying out the validity of his defense before the trial proper was commenced. Not only that, but he was informing the jurors already accepted as to phases of his defense that might not even get into the record, while actually ascertaining whom to exclude from the jury or to accept.

For illustration, if the defense in a murder case should hinge upon threats or abuse by the man who had been killed, Rogers would ask the prospective juror, as in the Melrose case:

"If you, Mr. Smith, had been called a vile name by a man we shall call Jones, and if Jones then insulted your wife by calling her 'no better than a railroad whore' and had then threatened to shoot you, would you have run away or stood your ground?"

Opposing counsel would complain indignantly to the court against that line of questioning, but Earl, by the subtle manner in which he would get over his points, seldom left openings for objections that would be sustained by the judge. Either his court-room antagonists had to reconcile themselves to being outmaneuvered or adopt similar methods. In time members of the bar engaged in criminal practice were following the Rogers technique with varying success according to their abilities.

However, this was one Rogers innovation that passed with other elements in criminal procedure, the elimination of which has robbed the criminal courts of much of their drama. Crowded court calendars have done away with leisurely examination of jurymen. In California especially, where there is more litigation to the square mile than in any other commonwealth, more speed was necessary to keep the courts from becoming hopelessly clogged.

In 1927, the California legislature enacted a statute reading:

It shall be the duty of the trial court to examine the prospective jurors, to select a fair and impartial jury. He shall permit reasonable examination of prospective jurors by counsel for the people and for the defense.

If Rogers were alive today he, perforce, would have abandoned his effective device along with many of his other radical innovations that have been banned. But those who knew his fertile mind are certain that he would have replaced them with other methods equally ingenious.

If the more alert and discriminating members of the bar after a while came to appreciate and adopt Earl's finesse with veniremen, they were for years unaware of the clever methods he used to employ before ever they appeared in the courtroom.

In those days when a venire of about sixty men composed the entire list from which jurymen were drawn, Rogers would retain in his phenomenal memory the names of each of the threescore talesmen, and he also remembered much of every man's personal history as ferreted out by his investigators.

During the months court was in session he usually contrived to encounter each of the prospective jurors in a manner that seemed wholly casual, stop for a brief chat or drop into step with the other for a few moments, just long enough to accost him by his correct name and inquire about his wife's health since her recent illness or ask how daughter Minnie liked the new school she was now attending, or perhaps pass a word or two concerning the general tone of the business the juryman followed.

Naturally each man so met would be mildly flattered by the attorney's knowledge of his name and family affairs, not thinking that Earl's retentive memory held like information concerning fifty-nine other men who might appear before him as jurors. In these dexterous contacts he was never obvious or intrusive, passing on his way after just enough conversation to leave a pleasant impression.

And he needed all of his adroit devices to achieve his almost unbroken list of successful murder defenses, for it was far more difficult to secure acquittals in his time than is the case today. Although it is true that in some respects a criminal pleader was allowed more latitude twenty years ago, all those advantages have been more than offset by changed conditions.

Before beginning his closing argument to the jury Rogers invariably knew which of the twelve men were "tough." He would plan a campaign to win them over and this phase of the trial took on the aspect of a game to him. He would contrive some particular argument which his knowledge of the unfriendly juror would dictate, then concentrate on winning him over. The object of his attack never knew it as Earl never aimed his verbal guns in the direction of his target. Unwilling to disclose his purpose by even a glance at the subject of his specific argument, he would have an associate, sometimes his daughter Adela, watch the juror to get the latter's reaction without betraying his own design. Whenever there was doubt as to any number of the jurors, Earl would argue for the benefit of a juror who he could sense would be a dominant figure in the jury room. After a jury retired to deliberate he could nearly always tell who would be the most difficult to win over. Of course those were the days before women served on juries. Without any reflection on the other sex, it is not likely that the dashing, debonair Earl Rogers would have had any greater difficulty in winning favorable consideration from a jury of today.

No man equipped even with the remarkable memory of Earl Rogers could have much success in getting acquainted with jurors in these times. In California especially the old system of a small venire has been abolished. Under the present laws the list of citizens drawn for jury service numbers approximately five thousand names in a community like Los Angeles and no citizen is permitted to serve as a juror more than twenty days in two years. This has done away with the professional juror and the jury investigation system. It would take a fortune to look into the private affairs of five thousand jurors and, until a case is actually called for trial, neither the identity of the court nor of the prospective jurors summoned to that particular court is disclosed.

A knowledge of some of these Rogers methods will go a long way to explain why he spurned the clumsy and crude devices of the ordinary criminal lawyer.

The public has come to believe that all important criminal lawyers have to be unethical, if not actually corrupt; that suborning of perjury occurs in every criminal case and that disagreements of juries usually result because of the fixing of at least one man to cause a mistrial. In all of the Rogers cases in which hung juries prevented a verdict, there was never an 11-to-1 ballot for conviction, the customary vote where there has been jury tampering.

Although the layman is likely to consider as an indication of perjury the contradictory testimony of witnesses in a criminal trial, there are probably relatively few witnesses who consciously give perjured evidence. Even widely divergent stories told on the stand with every evidence of veracity may be honest versions, differing only because of imperfect perception, unconscious bias and the working of certain unconscious elements in the human make-up which modern psychology explains.

In a recently published volume, Dean John H. Wigmore, an acknowledged authority on evidence, declares that the most contradictory stories told on the stand are due to an unconscious mental bias and self-interest, to which are added the imperfections of the perceptive elements.

"No perception," says Dean Wigmore, "is ever complete or accurate. Always it is a mixture of perception, pre-perception, illusion and suggestion. To the inaccuracies and incompleteness of perception, those of memory are added. Memory involves not only knowledge, but also forgetting, illusion, suggestion, and wrong conclusions."

These unconscious phenomena, according to the learned Dean, more often color testimony than does willful perjury.

It is a generally accepted truism in legal circles that clients who do not tell the truth in court lie also to their attorneys. The popular belief is that a man charged with a crime tells the entire truth to his counsel, but according to Earl Rogers —and other noted criminal lawyers confirm him—the reverse is the rule. Rogers once told a law class before which he was lecturing that it was a frequent occurrence for persons charged with crimes to supply perjured testimony on their own initiative when learning that there was a flaw in the defense. And it is not unlikely that counsel for the defense were aware of it.

Earl Rogers was far ahead of the average modern psychologist in his knowledge of mental phenomena, and was a past master in sensing the ingrained prejudices of a witness. He knew the tendency of all untrained human minds to remember things imperfectly and could suggest to such witnesses with imperceptible craft what they immediately believed to be their own complete recollection of the incident. When such subtleties could not be employed, he had a way of putting questions which literally compelled a witness to give the answer desired.

In the cross-examination of witnesses, Rogers seldom did any fishing for an opening, or to discover a flaw in the story of the witness. He knew the human animal so intimately and had so perfected the art of cross-examination that he knew in advance what the answers would be. He would wait patiently for the opening he was playing for—then he usually followed one of two courses. It was the custom, almost the undeviating practice, when a cross-examiner had found such a weakness to attack in force immediately. The old time criminal lawyer would try to tear the witness's testimony to pieces, using, as the point of attack, the newly discovered discrepancy.

Not so Rogers. If it served his purpose best he would ignore the opening, would appear ignorant of the flaw in the testimony until he proceeded to bring it out with deadly effect in his argument to the jury, too late for the dismayed prosecutor to remedy the defect in his case.

The other alternative when he had extracted from the harassed witness the answer he wanted—the flaw in an otherwise sound story—was to smile and fold his arms, a characteristic Rogers pose. He would turn so that the jury could see his satisfied smile and allow the twelve good men and true to discover for themselves wherein he had gained an advantage.

Prosecutors opposing Rogers invariably showed extreme caution in cases of this sort. They always suspected traps and occasionally failed to make any effort to undo the damage for fear of getting into a worse situation.

Few of Rogers' successors, among them some of his most apt pupils, have ever been able to manipulate this ingenious device. Those who have tried have usually either failed to go far enough, or have gone too far.

About this period prosecutors were beginning to compre-

hend another distinctive Rogers artifice, the subterfuge employed by him of creating a disconcerting diversion whenever
things looked bad for his client. Perhaps it was a damaging
bit of evidence being given by a state witness on direct examination, or an unfavorable response during the cross-examination of a defense witness. At other times the diversion came
during an especially severe arraignment of his client by the
prosecutor in his argument to the jury.

The devices he employed to distract attention until the
immediate danger was over were as diversified as Earl's
prismatic wardrobe and, being of necessity spontaneous, they
were often more terrifying to his own associates than to the
opposition.

The most common act employed by him in such emer-
gencies, widely copied later on, was to accuse the opposition
of employing unethical tactics, thereby starting a heated
three-cornered fight between the court, the prosecutor and
himself. But as his methods along this line became partially
recognized he was constantly forced to invent new devices
in order to effect his purposes without getting fined or jailed
for contempt.

Perhaps the most striking illustration of Earl's ingenuity
when suddenly confronted by such a dangerous condition
occurred in the course of a homicide trial at Santa Ana
during the very heydey of his career. A man named Trent
had been charged with the slaying of a neighbor during a
family quarrel. Earl had made a very effective defense based
on the defendant's action, the deed that had resulted fatally.
The weapon was a garden rake. The prosecution held that
Trent had struck his victim with it. Rogers made two of the
state's witnesses say that the defendant pushed the victim
with the rake, his purpose being to prove that Trent was
merely protecting his wife by pushing the other man away,
and as that action was of a protective nature, there could
have been no murder committed.

Rogers was assisted by one of the younger members of his office staff, Milton M. Cohen. Both had concluded their arguments to the jury and Earl, as was his custom, left the courtroom while the district attorney made his final plea for the death verdict. As usual he paced up and down the corridor, rolling and smoking cigarettes, pausing at the door occasionally to hear what was going on.

The prosecutor was making a good job of it, pounding home a concluding argument that Earl suddenly feared would send the accused man to the gallows. Wild-eyed, obviously overcome by some fearful emotion, he burst into the courtroom. He rushed to the side of his youthful colleague, seized him roughly by the shoulder and began abusing him in violent language.

The whole courtroom was thrown into confusion by the turbulence of the attack. The young lawyer cringed, speechless. The district attorney stopped his argument in the midst of his peroration. The jurors turned their glances to the unusual scene being enacted at the counsel table. In his astonishment the judge allowed the wild tirade to continue for some time before he recovered his presence of mind and began rapping for order.

Then Rogers seemed suddenly aware of his disgraceful conduct. He instantly became the picture of abject contrition. He turned to the court and began to apologize profusely for his action. He said that he had left the courtroom with definite instructions to his associate, Mr. Cohen, to see that the record was protected, and that the latter had failed to follow his orders. The court insisted that there had been no reason for Mr. Cohen to interrupt the district attorney and that so far as the defense was concerned the record *had* been wholly protected.

Earl bowed in humble acknowledgment. Then he turned to the district attorney and made profuse apology for the interruption. Not content with this he addressed himself to the jury and apologized further. Those who knew Rogers well always had a high regard for the thoroughness of his apologies. No one could be more gracious, more sincere or more eloquent while asking forgiveness.

But when Earl had finished apologizing to the jury, the prosecutor moved forward with a wry smile and hands up-raised in a gesture of surrender. He turned to the court and declared: "I have been a public prosecutor for a long time and have taken part in criminal trials for thirty-five years, but this is the first time I ever heard of a trial in which the counsel for the defense made the final argument to the jury."

Of course the jurors had completely forgotten the climax which the district attorney had tried so hard to reach and it was hopeless to attempt any recovery of the lost advantage. The defendant was promptly acquitted. And, of course, Earl had a good laugh when his young assistant, feeling that he had failed in his duty, attempted that evening to resign his place in the Rogers law office.

Earl's faculty of invention was exhaustless. Every trick he invoked in a court was a fresh surprise to that particular judge and generally just as unexpected to his associates. He always held out something on his colleagues. But then, no one ever enjoyed Earl Rogers' complete confidence.

CHAPTER XIV

OF all the elements which contribute to the success of a lawyer engaged in criminal practice none can be more helpful than friendly coöperation of the police. Coming into contact with the man who has committed the crime, generally before anyone else after the illegal act, the police have a clearer conception than any others of the actual circumstances attending the violent deed. Usually the accused is panicky when apprehended by the officers and in his agitation makes admissions or otherwise imparts information that later will prove vitally important either to prosecution or defense attorneys.

For many years Earl was the recipient of whole-hearted aid from the Los Angeles police force. It was in the nature of a goodwill offering, without any expectation of reward; rather the repayment of an obligation, or an evidence of grateful appreciation.

Early in 1904 William Randolph Hearst started a new daily newspaper in Los Angeles, *The Examiner*. The militant publisher had been induced to measure swords with that grim old battler, General Harrison Gray Otis, by forces opposed to the policies of the latter's powerful morning *Times*. To cut into that soundly entrenched daily's circulation and advertising seemed a rather hopeless task. Hearst, of course, was strongly pro-labor union and pro-common people. Otis was supposed to stand for the ancient public-be-damned policy, to be against any form of labor organization and in favor of the form of capitalism pictured by the most zealous radicals.

The *Examiner* started with a terrific splash, but a public educated to the conservatism of the *Times* merely shuddered at the glaring headlines and refused to subscribe to what had come to be known as yellow journalism. Business houses refused to advertise because of the pressure brought by the closed-shop leaders. The Hearst executives realized that they must have an overpowering argument in the form of a great circulation before they could prevail on the merchants to use their space.

On the constant outlook for circulation-building issues, the *Examiner* found one about two months after the paper had made its sensational début. Two apparently innocent men were shot and killed by city detectives. It was a grand opportunity to use the biggest and blackest headline type in the cases of the *Examiner* composing room, to fill the streets with newsboys shrieking of the cold-blooded slaying of harmless citizens by the ruthless Los Angeles police. They went to it as only a Hearst editorial staff could go to it in those stirring days.

The story of the killing was something like this: Joseph Choisser, about sixty years old, and his eighteen-year-old son Louis had recently come to Los Angeles from Illinois. They rented a room at the Broxburn Hotel, corner of Hill and Fifth streets, opposite the California Club. Soon after their arrival in town, the police received a telegram from the sheriff of Hardin County, Illinois, asking that father and son be apprehended on a charge of swindling, the result of a business transaction.

Three city detectives, Hawley, Cowen, and Murphy, went to the Broxburn to apprehend the pair. According to the story told by the detectives, father and son resisted arrest and both were shot and killed by the officers. There was nothing unusual about the case on the face of it. Police endeavoring to arrest fugitives were offered resistance and in a general pistol battle the fugitives were slain. The coroner was notified, impaneled a jury, and the officers were exonerated.

Ordinarily that would have been the end of the story, but

an *Examiner* reporter, conducting his own private investigation among the inmates of the hotel, stumbled upon evidence that varied considerably from the story told by the trio of plainclothes men. The *Examiner,* scenting sensations and circulation, threw its entire local staff into the front line and the excitement began.

According to the story told at the inquest by the three policemen, the elder Choisser was sitting on his bed with a gun beside him when the officers entered his room. They declared that Choisser reached for his gun as Murphy seized him and the brief struggle ended by Cowen shoving his gun under Murphy's arm and shooting Choisser through the heart.

The testimony of the detective trio further had it that the younger Choisser, who had been hiding within the room, then began shooting at them; that they rushed out followed by the boy, who was still firing; that in returning his fire the young man was slain.

Examiner reporters discovered four residents of the Broxburn who told an entirely different story of the double slaying. The newspaper violently demanded that the affair be investigated further. The community was aroused to a high pitch. Charges of murder were made against Hawley, Cowen, and Murphy and they were brought before Justice Chambers for preliminary examination. The district attorney assigned an assistant, William P. James, now a federal judge, to prosecute the case. Earl Rogers was engaged by the police, who also retained Judd Rush and Le Compte Davis, two of the city's most eminent attorneys.

The legal battle that resulted in the justice court to determine if the officers should be held to the grand jury was more bitterly fought than most murder trials in the higher tribunal.

Arthur Clough was the most important of the state's witnesses. He testified that he and his wife were getting ready for bed in a room near that occupied by the Choissers when he heard the commotion; that he thereupon stood upon the foot of the bed and leaning his arms upon the transom sill saw what had happened in the hallway. One shot had been fired in the room, declared Clough, when Louis Choisser ran out of the room and into a nearby one occupied by J. S. Atkinson, seeking aid for his father. With Atkinson he re-entered his own room and in a moment emerged, unarmed, calling back to Atkinson to remain until he could bring a doctor.

As young Choisser ran down the hallway, according to Clough's testimony, Detective Cowen shot him through the heart and Detective Murphy sent a second bullet through his back. Atkinson and two others living in the hotel gave corroborative testimony and declared that there was no gun in the hallway where young Choisser fell.

These stories had already been printed in the *Examiner* and when they were repeated under oath on the witness stand, the case looked very black for the three defendants. Clough's testimony was corroborated further by his wife. It looked still blacker when the prosecution made a showing that two state witnesses had been approached with propositions to absent themselves from the city until after the hearing. Simultaneously a story broke in the *Examiner* to the accompaniment of screaming headlines, and photographs, giving the details of the alleged attempt of "a tall man with black hair and moustache" to corrupt the two witnesses.

The foregoing will give something of an idea as to what Earl Rogers was up against. He centered most of his attack on the eye-witnesses, without appreciably affecting their testimony. He made a showing that Clough was quite a frequenter of saloons but the witness declared that he was "stone sober" the night of the tragedy.

Rogers undertook to get an admission from Mrs. Clough when she was on the stand. He had learned a valuable lesson in the Melrose trial as to the cross-examination of women witnesses and his manner with Mrs. Clough was courtly and gallant, but he kept insisting that her spouse was under the influence of drink on the night in question.

"No, Mr. Rogers," she replied, "my husband was cold sober the night the Choissers were killed. Although I must admit that at other times he has drunk more than is good for him."

"Like others I might mention," she added as an after-thought, and favored Earl with a level gaze that caused him to join with a wry smile in the titter that ran through the courtroom.

LeRoy Smith, one of the two state witnesses who had been played up by the *Examiner* as victims of attempted in-timidation and bribery by the police, was given a severe grill-ing by Rogers when he was turned over for cross-examina-tion. Earl wanted to know how it happened that an *Examiner* reporter had a photograph of the witness and the story of the attempted bribery within a half hour of its occurrence. He intimated that the whole tale was nothing but a fabrica-tion of yellow journalism.

"You got that photograph of yourself for the reporter in a hurry, didn't you?" queried Earl in caustic tones.

"No, I didn't want to give it to him," hedged Smith, "but he—"

"What did he do to get it—chloroform you?"

"Do I look like I'd been chloroformed?" retorted the wrathful witness.

"Yes," was Rogers' contemptuous reply.

"You say I do?"

"Yes, you asked me; so I told you."

Here Prosecutor James, probably fearful that the cagey de-fense counsel was angering Smith for the purpose of leading him into one of the usual Rogers traps, objected to the line of questioning upon the ground that it was incompetent, im-material and irrelevant. "It is very interesting to listen to

Mr. Rogers' dissertation and the very lurid and sparkling adjectives that he is using," observed the prosecutor, "but that's all there is to it. It is leading nowhere, so we object upon the grounds just stated."

Judge Chambers agreed with James, so Earl reluctantly let the witness go after using him as a peg upon which to hang his opinion that the *Examiner* was trying to railroad the policemen to jail.

When the turn of the defense came, it was generally believed that unless something sensational were sprung, the detectives would be held on a murder charge. Rogers began his case with an air of assurance that presaged surprises. They were not long in coming.

The first witness was an assayer named J. B. Hawley, an expert on firearms and ammunition. No reference had been made by the prosecution to the finding of a bullet in the door casing inside the Choissers' room. The detectives had alleged that young Choisser had fired at them after the shooting of his father.

The witness testified that he had analyzed the bullet found on the inside door-casing of the room. This analysis was of the oily substance used in the grooves around bullets to make them take the rifling of pistol or rifle barrels when the bullets are discharged. The expert unequivocally declared that the bullet in the door frame inside the room was the same as those contained in the guns owned by the slain men; that it showed a substance different from that on the police cartridges. This evidence was history-making, as it was the first instance of the use of such expert testimony in a Western court. It tended to prove that young Choisser, inside the room, had fired at the policemen, as they had testified. The state had nothing with which to refute it and the accused men thereby had convincing corroboration of their story that young Choisser had opened the gun battle.

Rogers next introduced the testimony of Detective Paul

Flammer, later made chief of the city's detective bureau. Flammer swore that soon after the shooting he had examined the sill of the transom over the door leading to the room occupied by Clough. He had found, he said, that the dust thereon was virtually undisturbed, which obviously could not have been the case had Clough rested his arms on the sill, as stated by him, while witnessing the tragedy in the hall outside.

The Los Angeles chief of police, Elton, then took the stand and corroborated Flammer's testimony. The chief also swore that he had made his examination with a magnifying glass, but had found no marks other than a few faint finger-prints.

This testimony of the police chief and the detective wholly discredited Clough's damaging story, but the prosecution seemed unable to refute the officials' evidence. Perhaps the Broxburn Hotel chambermaid had been a listener at the hearing and, belatedly conscience-stricken, had hurried home to dust off the long-neglected transom.

With the bullet from the door casing identified by the expert as having been fired from Choisser's gun, and Clough's testimony destroyed, Judge Chambers could not very well hold the accused officers.

So Cowen, Murphy, and Hawley were set at liberty, and from then on Earl Rogers had the Los Angeles police force added to his already efficient staff. Earl always regarded the case as one of his outstanding achievements.

Perhaps he considered it to be one of his best criminal defenses because it afforded him his first opportunity to make vital use of his elaborate study of the indention of gun-barrel rifling on bullets and of the substances with which bullets were lubricated. His scientific bent had led him to follow closely the investigations of the institutions at Leipsic, Frankfort-on-Main, and at the University of Heidelberg. Probably the familiarity with the German language which Earl came to possess was acquired during these studies.

CHAPTER XV

"COLONEL" GRIFFITH J. GRIFFITH, one of the most colorful characters of the Los Angeles of a generation ago, did not seem a human reality. Rather he appeared a gnome or kobold out of a book of grotesque tales, a human caricature. He was a roly poly, pompous little fellow who held himself to be above the estimates of his acquaintances, or public opinion, or even the courts. He had an exaggerated strut like a turkey gobbler, disporting an oversize cane somewhat like that carried by Louis XVI as seen in pictures of the gardens of Versailles.

Griffith gave a great tract of land—river bed, vales, and mountainside—to the City of Los Angeles in 1898. It is today one of the showplaces of the West, Griffith Park, second largest municipal park in the nation. It contains an aviation field, three golf courses, tennis courts, bridle paths and mountain drives, and an open air Greek theater of classic beauty.

Mrs. Christina Griffith, wife of the "Colonel," was the daughter of one of Los Angeles' first families. She was wealthy in her own right, a popular factor in women's civic activities, and socially prominent. As a leading member of the Catholic church she was an active social welfare worker.

Mrs. Griffith had conveyed to her husband considerable real estate for his use as collateral in a deal he was handling, but when she requested its return upon consummation of his business transaction he became at first enraged, and then settled down to a smoldering hatred and distrust of his wife which he nevertheless concealed with all the cunning of his warped intellect.

Notwithstanding his delusions of grandeur the little turkey-cock Colonel was really a first-class business man who had amassed property worth millions, despite the circumstance of being at least half drunk during all the years of his successful business career. He had made most of his fortune in mining and real estate. The Griffith reports on western mines had been used by engineers for years. His constant alcoholic excesses, however, filled his mind with weird hallucinations. One of Griffith's obsessions was that his church-going wife was in league with the Pope and all his followers to destroy him. So he decided to thwart this dark plot by eliminating his unsuspecting spouse. No more fantastic scheme to destroy a fellow being was ever conceived in a demented brain.

One day in the beautiful old Arcadia Hotel on a breeze-swept bluff overlooking the rolling surf of the Pacific Ocean at Santa Monica, where they had been spending a month's vacation, the Colonel prepared, grandiosely, to end his wife's life. Bloodshot eyes blazing with alcoholic frenzy, he handed to her a prayer book and forced her to get down on her knees with the opened book before her.

Brandishing a cocked pistol, Griffith took from his pocket a slip of paper upon which he had written questions he was about to ask her. Then he told her to close her eyes. As she did so she realized he intended to kill her, and in horror-stricken accents implored him to spare her. As her terror increased she begged him to let her live for the sake of their twelve-year-old boy.

But now the frightened woman knew from his ominous silence she could not alter his purpose to murder her and pleaded for a few moments' respite to pray. He told her she could have long enough to commend her soul to her Maker. But as she began hysterically beseeching God for mercy on her soul her crazed husband started to question her. His first senseless query was, "Have you ever been unfaithful to me?"

"Oh, Papa," she wailed despairingly, "you know I have always been true to you!"

Ignoring her tremulous protestations of chastity, the Colonel solemnly asked if she knew who had poisoned Briswalter, a neighbor who had died from an infected leg some months previously. But by now the terrified woman had almost lost her power of speech. As she sobbed inarticulately in her attempt to reply, the physical effort forced her eyes open, barely in time to prevent a bullet from crashing through her brain, for as her vision took in the weapon that almost touched her forehead she saw his finger contract on the trigger. Involuntarily her head jerked to one side, and the bullet struck her in the left temple.

The bullet's shock and the roar of the gun galvanized her trembling limbs into action. Screaming in terror she flung herself through the window before he could shoot again, and fell upon the roof of a veranda two stories below. The fall broke one of her legs, but fear of death spurred her to the effort required to drag herself through a window into a room.

With a towel she stanched the flow of blood from a terrible wound which had destroyed one of her eyes, and summoned help. As the Arcadia's proprietor entered the door she saw her husband's face beside him and screamed: "Please, Mr. Wright, don't let him come in! He shot me. He's crazy!"

When the other man interrogated Griffith the latter declared his wife had accidentally wounded herself.

Mrs. Griffith's family, thoroughly outraged by Griffith's brutal assault on "Teeny," as Mrs. Griffith was known to her friends, decided to make an example of the Colonel. They retained three eminent lawyers to act as special prosecutors with District Attorney Fredericks. One was ex-Judge McKinley, a leader of the Western bar. Another was Isidore B. Dockweiler, also a well known lawyer. The third was Henry T. Gage, who had been Governor of California, and some years later became Minister to Portugal, where during the dethronement of King Manuel he played a rôle of international importance. For years Gage had been ranked as an attorney almost on a par with the peerless Stephen M. White.

For years no criminal trial had excited such intense and widespread interest as that which marked the opening of the Griffith case. Its personal and dramatic elements promised to make it the greatest forensic show since Earl had cleared William Alford of the charge of murdering Jay E. Hunter nearly five years before.

Not only were the principals and their relatives outstanding members of California's social and business spheres, but the impending clash between Henry Gage and the adroit Rogers, whose methods were still inscrutable even to most of his own profession, had bar and public alike thrilled with expectancy. In some quarters the lively partisanship existing among the two pleaders' followers overshadowed the direct issues of the case itself. A few lawyers close to Rogers knew that Gage was the only member of the local bar whom Rogers really feared.

Rogers asked the court for a continuance of two weeks, declaring that a case involving so many probable witnesses and such diverse testimony could not possibly be prepared within the brief space of three days. But the prosecution maintained that the eminent counsel, ex-Judges Works and Silent, who had been in charge of Griffith's interests until Rogers took them over, had had plenty of time to get their case in order. The court announced that it would be ready to listen to argument on postponement when the counsel for both sides appeared upon the day set for trial.

When Rogers and his associates and their client came into court on opening day, Gage had with him a group of witnesses who were prepared to testify on oath that the defense had had abundant opportunity to prepare its case. Earl merely glanced at the array of prosecutors and the many witnesses with whom they were to combat his attempt to gain more time, and smilingly announced that Griffith J. Griffith was ready for trial.

Despite his natural placidity Henry T. Gage's features displayed a flush of surprise that was close to consternation as his young adversary pulled this coup. Certain that Earl would wage a stubborn fight for continuance, District Attorney Fredericks and the special prosecutors had come prepared for several hours of interrogation of witnesses and argument against such delay. As a result of Rogers' unexpected move they were not ready to proceed to trial without some preliminary conferences, but Rogers was all set and his confused opponents had to go into action immediately at the impatient command of the court.

Earl grinned complacently at Gage. He had scored the first surprise of the legal battle.

As the warring hosts squared away for the battle the courtroom was packed almost to the point of suffocation. Leaders of the city's social life and of the bar occupied most of the seats, and the aisles were filled with standing spectators.

And if the prominence of the persons involved had not sufficed to draw a record attendance the splendor of the lawyers would alone have been enough to fill the hall of justice. Newspapers commented on the fact that ex-Governor Gage, his great mane of iron gray hair notable in any assemblage, was conscious that he was the only man in the courtroom who was wearing high boots. Like the present Governor Rolph of California, that touch of pioneer days was always part of his immaculate apparel, the boots being worn under the trousers. Isidore Dockweiler with his poetic haircut and classic countenance was a glass of fashion. Judge McKinley, always garbed like Daniel Webster, resembled a steel engraving of the days of forensic immortals. District Attorney Fredericks, whose features were similar to those of Abraham Lincoln, heightened his resemblance to the martyr president by his flowing black locks.

Of the defense counsel, Luther Brown was garbed as if for a trip to the race track and Major Jones was impeccably furnished. Earl Rogers wore a beautifully tailored slate-colored frock coat, sparklingly new patent leather shoes, and what the *Examiner* reporter described as "Williams and Walker stockings with as many colors as Joseph's coat."

The defendant was arrayed in clothes of fashionable cut. His curly jet-black hair and little mustache that seemed a charcoal mark upon his ruddy face contrasted sharply with his snowy linen. For the first time in the recollection of the oldest inhabitants he was as sober as Judge Smith himself. Rogers had insisted upon that detail, saying he would do all the drinking for the defense until the trial was over.

"All of counsel for both sides," continued the *Examiner* reporter, "were smooth-shaven with the exception of Major Jones, who had enough whiskers to go around."

As a result of his alcoholic line of defense, Earl had the courtroom cluttered up with alienists, brew-masters, plain and fancy drunkards, and everybody he felt could qualify as experts on the art of drinking and its effects on the human mind. He even went to such lengths—probably because of the importance he attached to keeping a jury laughing—as to elicit from one of the first prospective jurymen he questioned on the effects of hard liquor the fact that in Ireland, where the venireman was born, Catholics and Orangemen did not drink at the same bar.

As the two opposing leaders, Gage and Rogers, went about the impaneling of jurors, it was evident that the matter of religion was to play an important part in the case. Not a venireman who was suspected of being a Catholic was allowed in the box. Nor was any man even slightly acquainted with Rogers allowed by Gage to qualify. Venireman Harris, a dignified person who wore elaborate mustaches, was excused by the prosecution because of his acquaintance with the defense counsel; he admitted that he met Earl every two years. By the time nine jurors had been selected the venire was exhausted and court adjourned until the judge's call for a second panel could be complied with.

"From the questioning of veniremen it was evident," wrote the *Times* reporter covering the case, "that Rogers was going to attempt to prove that Mrs. Griffith had too much religion and the Colonel too much champagne."

The jury box was filled early on the second day and Mrs. Griffith took the stand and testified to the nature of her husband's murderous assault upon her in the Arcadia Hotel. At the bidding of her attorney she stepped close to the jurors and lifting her heavy veil showed them how her eye had been shot out.

When Gage turned her over to Rogers for cross-examination the exquisitely tailored defense counsel questioned the lady with a soft-toned deference that almost led her into a trap. Taking a slip of paper from his pocket he said it was the list of questions her husband had held as she knelt with the prayer book in her hands. As Rogers read the queries he asked her if those were the interrogations the defendant had read to her in the Arcadia. She replied to each question that it was substantially the same, as nearly as she could recall it. But when he read the last on the slip she declared he had asked her no such question. It read:

"Will you swear on your sacred honor and by all the Gods you have been taught to worship that you will be true to me and will find no farther fault with the Hollywood monument?"

It was evident that the defense would try to identify that question as having been asked by Griffith. As showing an illogical, inconsistent, and rambling way of formulating ideas on paper, it would be of weight as indicating insanity. But the witness declared she could not identify the piece of paper as the one her husband had held as he shot her.

Later in the trial Earl let it be known that the defendant

[125]

had been afflicted for fifteen years with chronic alcoholic insanity, in proof of which he would prove that:

Griffith had accused his wife of having improper relations with a porter at the Nadeau Hotel;

He had told friends that soon after his marriage his wife and a sister of charity had attempted to poison him in the United States Hotel;

He had stated that Bishop Conaty wanted him slain so that his property would go to the Catholic church;

He believed that the late Senator Stephen M. White had been poisoned by Catholics because White had told the Colonel—probably when both of them were well under the influence—that he believed the friars should be expelled from the Philippines, and that soon thereafter White had died;

That he slept in a bath house to escape from his wife and the Pope's followers.

At play of wit Rogers proved himself the master of both Gage and McKinley, beat them to it every time they had an acrimonious encounter. Once when Gage sternly demanded of a witness for the defense that he answer "yes or no," Earl suavely informed the bench—something that many attorneys and judges do not yet seem to understand—that "there is no law requiring a witness to answer yes or no, and never has been."

But at his own forte of dissecting hostile witnesses Rogers met his equal in the ex-Governor. With the exception of Stephen M. White, who had died three years before the Griffith case began, there had been no Western attorney the equal of Gage at cross-examination until Earl had developed into a past master at that insidious art.

Rogers, unprepared at the trial's opening, nevertheless had gathered some valuable witnesses early in the case by spurring his staff of investigators to feverish activity. One such witness, Louis B. Garrett, upon whose facts Earl had built up a body of testimony which seemed to admit of no doubt, testified to his belief that at the time of Griffith's crime the latter was mentally unsound, citing one convincing incident that seemed certain to stump the prosecution.

This incident was Griffith's irrational talk when the witness's father had died. He testified that at the time of his bereavement he went to Griffith, an old friend of the deceased, and asked him to serve as pall bearer at the funeral. But Griffith, according to the testimony, refused to attend the obsequies because he feared that if he exposed himself publicly he might be assassinated by Catholics. Then Gage took the witness for cross-examination.

After condoling with him on the death of his parent, whom the former governor took occasion to say he had known very well and had respected as a fine gentleman, the cross-examiner asked if Griffith's refusal to serve as pallbearer were the only incident upon which the witness had based his belief that the defendant was of unsound mind.

"No," replied the man on the stand, unaware of a warning scowl from Rogers, "there were many others."

"Before or after the one you have just related?"

"Before."

"About how long before?" asked Gage.

"Oh, just a few weeks—maybe not over a week," and he went on to relate in considerable detail the nature of several conversations with Griffith which seemed conclusive proof of mental derangement.

"And these circumstances which occurred about a week before your father's death had convinced you that Griffith was really insane?" continued Gage in his suavely disarming manner.

Rogers' nimble and clairvoyant mind was following Gage's mental processes as clearly as if they were an open book, anticipating every question and realizing far in advance what the cross-examiner was leading up to.

But his attempt to create a diversion at the crucial moment

and pull the witness away from his line of testimony was futile this time. He was up against a mind as alert and resourceful as his own. When Earl interposed a string of objections in his effort to start an argument, Gage merely smiled away the attack and proceeded to lead the witness toward disaster.

"You were absolutely convinced by defendant's delusions concerning religious persecution, his illusions of grandeur, and his other abnormal mental symptoms, that he was not sane at the time of your father's death—were you?" Gage calmly persisted, despite Rogers' renewed objections that failed to warn the man being questioned, although the latter was also a lawyer.

"Absolutely!" declared the unwary witness. "Any reasonable man would have realized that he was crazy."

"And yet, knowing this, you nevertheless tried to get an insane man to act as pall bearer at your dear old father's funeral?" asked Gage with sad reproach.

So completely had Gage thus discredited the witness's testimony that the baffled and disgusted Rogers made no attempt to repair the damage by redirect examination.

But despite his great handicap of going into the case with only thirty-six hours research against the careful preparation of ex-Governor Gage and Judge McKinley, the young attorney contested every move of his able opponents with a skill and constant change of strategy that kept them tensely watchful. His rapier keenness or agreeable plausibility at cross-examination fully matched the subtle questioning of his shrewd antagonist.

But it was in the handling of hostile medical expert witnesses that Earl displayed pronounced superiority over his learned opponents. Rogers, as usual, boned up on his subject every night after court sessions, and the manner in which he cross-examined prosecution doctors and alienists on "chronic alcoholic insanity" and "alcoholic paranoia" made some of them dizzy. Spitza, Gower, Peterson and Haines, Clouston, all the other authorities on delirium tremens, appeared to have been medical classmates of Earl's as he bombarded the prosecution's witnesses ceaselessly.

When Gage, bewildered, tried to interpose objections, Earl badgered him and drew some biting sarcasm from that leonine-headed old Nestor of the bar. "I have observed you for years," growled Gage after one passage, "and must say that you are always growing—downward, like a cow's tail."

Rogers had evolved one hypothetical question with which he unfailingly hamstrung every medical expert who went up against him. When he had wrapped it in loops and coils and diamond-hitches around the quivering consciousness of experts who didn't suit him they were left dazed and helpless, and neither Gage nor any of his associates nor the judge himself had the remotest idea as to how to undo the terrible entanglement of technical barbed wire. But if nobody except Rogers and the medical victim knew what it was all about, it nevertheless effected its purpose of making of the witness a total loss to the prosecutors.

After Rogers had twice sprung that lengthy verbal horror on the experts, its effect on everyone was immediate. As soon as he glared at an alienist and began rolling that hypothetical question under his tongue the courtroom began to empty, and by the time he had propounded it over a space of twenty minutes he was without hearers except the judge, the witness who was being third-degreed, the jurors who couldn't escape, and whichever woe-begone prosecution attorney had been picked on by his colleagues to ride out the gale.

But Henry Gage decided that he, too, must take a dive into the hypothetical maelstrom if he wished to preserve his standing as a criminal pleader, and on the fifth day of the trial he let loose at Dr. George W. Campbell, testifying for the prosecution. For five years Campbell had not looked upon the wine when it was red, but admitted that before he had gone dry he had often hoisted the flowing bowl with the defendant. As all the state's experts prior to Dr. Campbell had been sunk without trace by Rogers' hypothetical torpedo, it was felt that desperate measures must be employed to save their last expert alcohol witness.

But when Gage had wound up his twenty-minute query Earl was all over him with a barrage of objections that precluded any answer from Campbell. Gage made a few futile attempts to repel Earl's attack, but he had exhausted his knowledge of the subject when he had unloaded his elongated query. He felt he looked foolish as he gazed helplessly from the doctor to the judge. But, always resourceful, he finally had a happy idea. He withdrew the question.

Then Rogers went after the witness and in a minute the court was sunk again in a morass of technicalities and all the spectators and spare attorneys were flowing into the corridor. At last even patient Judge Smith blew up.

"Mr. Rogers," he pleaded, "if you will agree that an insane delusion is an insane delusion there will be more celerity to the cross-examination."

But Mr. Rogers wouldn't agree to any such thing, with the result that Dr. Campbell never got a chance to say that he considered Griffith sane.

Having disposed of all the prosecution's expert doctors the crafty defense counsel put on a real expert, and asked him never a hypothetical thing. That was Dr. E. M. Butler, head of the Keeley Cure of Los Angeles. He said he considered Griffith's a case of chronic alcoholic insanity, and the best Gage could do to the affable salvager of drunks brought a satisfied smile to Earl's ascetic features.

On the next to the last day of evidence, Rogers sprung one of his usual sensations. Pausing suddenly during cross-examination of a witness, he declared to the court that he had been hissed by two women spectators.

"Ever since I came into this courtroom to defend Griffith,"

he continued, "this baiting of myself has been going on. One of these women is the sister of the late William H. Broome, a man who was killed in a fight with M. M. Melrose, for whom I acted as attorney. The other woman is her companion. For six months they have followed me into courtrooms and hissed and jeered me. It has become unbearable, and if it goes on I shall have to ask that the courtroom be cleared of spectators." Rogers had called the women by name.

Judge Smith said that if any hissing occurred again he would visit a severe penalty upon the offenders. At this the two women covered their faces with their handkerchiefs, and rose to leave the room.

Having smothered all the prosecution's medical savants with his murderous hypothetical gas attack, Earl wound up the defense in a blaze of expert glory. Of the final day for taking testimony, the *Los Angeles Examiner* said:

Saturday was about as fine a field day for experts as has appeared on the calendar for some time. There were experts on mixed drinks and other forms of insanity; experts on law and experts on foolishness; and experts on experts.

Rogers called to the stand in a swiftly moving procession, bartenders, barbers and bellboys, following a series of bankers and barristers. There was also an undertaker and more doctors. If any practicing physician in Los Angeles had been overlooked by either side in this trial, he was indeed an obscure member of his profession.

A bellboy at the Arcadia Hotel, where the shooting occurred, and who had been called by the prosecution after the defense had scratched his name off its list, testified that the defendant was "crazy like a fox"; that the only signs of abnormality displayed by Griffith were in the meagerness of his tips and in his manner of ordering only a pint of champagne at a time. He would take a drink, testified the bellboy, then have the bottle recorked and placed on ice until he wanted another drink.

Two barbers testified that Griffith exhibited what they termed "nuttiness" in telling "bum stories" and jokes that were mostly "old chestnuts." One of the tonsorial experts said that in his opinion Griffith's intellect "was nothing to brag about" but that he wouldn't risk an opinion as to his sanity. Other witnesses testified concerning Griffith's insistence upon telling stories with "long white whiskers."

Bill Salter, owner of a saloon and described by the *Examiner* reporter as being attired in "a nobby race track suit of lemonade tint," solemnly declared that "after about the tenth drink the Colonel didn't know right from wrong." As an illustration, the witness declared that once Griffith had informed him that he, the Colonel, looked just like President McKinley and that he "was the same to Los Angeles that McKinley was to Washington, D. C."

Attorney Oscar Lawler was another witness for the defense. He testified that Griffith had once entered his study and delivered a lecture on "The Philosophy of Mirthfulness." Asked his opinion of this lecture, Mr. Lawler declared that it was "pure drivel." Griffith had told the witness at another time that he had been asked by the Republicans to run for mayor of Los Angeles, being assured that the Democrats would not oppose him with a candidate.

"And how did you advise him on this occasion?" asked Rogers.

"I told him that he ought to run for the United States Senate instead," was the reply.

Despite Earl's strategy that prevented any worth-while expert medical testimony from getting into the record, he must have realized the great weight of evidence against him, for in his address to the jury he seemed to be trying wholly for psychological reactions, ignoring most of the testimony that either side had introduced.

But Gage, artful with the craft gained through long years in courtrooms, had been counting upon a psychological finish himself. He had decided to beat the defense at its own game. Earl's involved hypothetical questions and other technical assaults upon the prosecution's witnesses he referred to as nothing but "brazen attempts to confuse the real issues."

"The incontrovertible, eloquent facts," Gage told them, "are that Griffith J. Griffith, in his brutal attempt to murder the faithful and affectionate companion who had clung fondly to him during all the years of drunken persecution he had inflicted upon her, has terribly and irreparably injured her.

"His vicious assault upon the loving wife who had borne him a son has done far more than destroy forever one of her eyes, with all the physical suffering, all the mental anguish such disfigurement means to a beautiful and sensitive woman; it has left forever an awful scar upon her soul, that of her outraged love, the destruction of the beautiful romance a good woman weaves about her husband and motherhood.

"But what does that matter?" he asked them accusingly. "No rich man has ever been punished for such a crime in this part of the United States."

With that challenge ringing in their ears, the jurors were not long in returning a verdict that sent Griffith to San Quentin for two years.

Although the public generally, and members of the bar in particular, considered the lightness of the sentence a virtual victory for Rogers, he was so despondent over the verdict of guilty, according to his close friends, that he was on the verge of committing suicide. He had begun to look upon himself as unbeatable and his pride was shattered.

An aftermath of the case illustrates the aversion Rogers had to anything but cash, especially to real estate, in the nature of fees. Griffith, being short of ready money at the time, wished to convey to his attorney a large tract of land along Los Feliz Boulevard in lieu of a few thousand dollars; but Earl would have none of it; said he wouldn't even pay taxes on it.

Today that property is one of the most desirable residential sections of that part of Los Angeles known as Hollywood. Rupert Hughes and other famous writers, Harry Chandler, millionaire owner of the *Los Angeles Times,* and scores of others rich and prominent have beautiful homes upon the ground Earl turned down. It is worth millions.

During Griffith's two years in the penitentiary, and until his death a few years later, the erratic millionaire interested himself in prison reform, many of the better features of modern penology being due to his activities. But his delusions of grandeur persisted to the end. He left an endowment to build the beautiful Greek theater that is a notable feature of Griffith Park, and he willed money to construct the fine conservatory there. He died several years later to go down in local history as the funniest and most tragic rich man Los Angeles ever knew—an unusual distinction.

CHAPTER XVI

For a decade and a half after the Griffith trial Earl Rogers had a hand in virtually every criminal case of importance in Southern California. In his profession his reputation grew steadily and his exploits were almost as well known among members of the bar east of the Mississippi as on the Pacific Coast.

The Harry Thaw trial, most celebrated murder case of that period, almost drew Rogers to the East. There are various versions as to overtures on the part of the Thaw defense and Rogers' reasons for not participating in the trial of Stanford White's slayer.

The generally accepted story among intimate friends of the Los Angeles attorney was that he would not go East because he did not want to "play second fiddle" to Delphin M. Delmas, the San Francisco attorney who had already been engaged by the Thaw defense.

Delmas undoubtedly wanted Rogers for his deftness at cross-examination, but Earl confided to friends that he would go East in only one capacity—that of chief counsel for the defense. During the trial Earl was lecturing on medico-legal jurisprudence at the University of Southern California and he frequently commented upon the progress of the case. More than once he expressed the opinion to his class that Thaw could have been liberated but for the fantastic "dementia Americana" defense of Delmas; that he had a perfectly sound defense of unwritten law without the necessity of a ponderous, highly technical insanity plea.

The two most interesting Western court dramas of the period following the Griffith case were the Canfield murder trial and the Federal action against Tom Hayes. In the former Earl made his début as a prosecutor, the first of but two appearances on the side of the law during his entire career.

The tragedy which first brought Earl into court as a prosecutor was the murder of Mrs. Charles A. Canfield, wife of the millionaire partner of Edward L. Doheny; herself a leader in the city's social and charitable activities. A kindly, gracious woman, her generosity was indirectly the cause of her tragic death.

Morrison Buck, formerly a coachman for the Canfield family, was the slayer. He knew from personal contact the charitable nature of his former employer and had himself been a beneficiary of her generosity. One day soon after he left her employ he called at her home and asked her for money to aid him in going into business. He wanted to start a bakery.

Only the murderer knew just what conversation took place and his story was a rambling, incoherent tale. This much was known, however, that Buck, when refused a loan, pulled a revolver and deliberately shot Mrs. Canfield as she stood in the doorway of her home on Alvarado Street in the heart of what was then—in 1906—the most select residence district of the city.

The sound of the shot attracted the attention of Mrs. Canfield's daughter, Daisy, later the wife of the screen star, Antonio Moreno.* The girl was at the front window. She saw at a glance what had occurred.

"He's killing mamma!" she screamed.

At that Buck fired a second shot into the woman's breast. As she fell dead Buck calmly seated himself in a chair, gazing indifferently at his victim as she lay at his feet on the veranda floor. There he remained, callously unconcerned, until an officer who had been attracted by the shots came hurry-

---

* Mrs. Moreno met a tragic death in an automobile accident on a mountain road near Hollywood in February, 1933.

tained by District Attorney Fredericks, but Earl Rogers displayed such profound knowledge of that branch of pathology relating to mental diseases that it is doubtful if the doctors were at all needed by the prosecution.

In cross-examination Rogers shocked Buck into desired mental reflexes. He explained that all forms of insanity depend upon delusions, hallucinations, and illusions, and after giving his analysis of the defendant's responses to his surprise questions declared that Buck displayed no such signs of aberration.

Attorney Warner, alarmed by the visible effect upon the jury of this damaging procedure, heatedly importuned the court to instruct the jurors that Rogers was not qualified to pass upon such special pathological subjects. But Earl informed the judge that if it were necessary he would produce in court his certificate as a regular member of the faculty of the College of Physicians and Surgeons. Such confirmation of his standing as a lecturer on medico-legal jurisprudence and like subjects was, however, rendered unnecessary by the testimony of Dr. I. E. Cohn, superintendent of the Napa State Asylum for the Insane, who unqualifiedly corroborated the prosecution attorney's observations.

Despite his statement that important witnesses for the defense were absent, defense counsel produced an impressive array of men who testified to Buck's mental defectiveness. His brother, William Buck, had come from Arizona to aid his accused relative. He told how Morrison Buck had been severely cut at the base of the skull by a cleaver in the hands of a drunken Mexican in the Pinal mountain mining camp of Globe.

On cross-examination Rogers, whose investigators had delved into the witness's career, drew from William Buck admission that he himself had killed a butcher in Globe with a cleaver and had been sentenced to life imprisonment in Yuma. The witness added that he had been pardoned when he killed a fellow convict during a mutiny in the Arizona penitentiary and thereby saved the warden's life.

A nephew of the defendant told how the latter had been kicked on the head by a horse. Several others testified as to head injuries which Buck had received at different times during his life. Following a long series of such asseverations, Attorney Warner dragged Buck over to the jury box, seized him by the hair and jerked his head down so that the jurors could view the numerous scars on the cranium of the accused.

But the alert Rogers got hold of Buck's head before Warner could return him to the witness stand and delivered an interesting illustrated lecture upon the effects of every variety of head injury known to medical science. The gist of this erudite symposium was that head wounds which affect the brain always leave scars that are attached to the skull, and he induced the jurors, severally and collectively, to feel Buck's head so that they might be convinced of the truth of Rogers' assertion that the defendant's scalp was perfectly mobile where the wounds had left their evidence.

Again counsel for the defense appealed to the court that Attorney Rogers was not qualified for such expert examination, and again Earl, holding onto Buck's locks the while, proved his expertness by the prosecution's own medical experts.

When this last attempt of the defense to establish proof of insanity had failed Buck fell in a faint. Immediately Earl recalled Dr. Cohn to the witness stand and the latter testified that although in his career he had observed and examined thousands of insane patients, he had never known one to swoon.

When the corps of defense experts were called, Rogers, with a knowledge of pathology obviously greater than theirs, picked their testimony to shreds and discredited them. Morrison Buck was found guilty and hanged.

After the trial Gage hazarded the opinion that had Earl Rogers been defending Buck, the killer would have gone to an insane asylum instead of the gallows.

There was no one to save from the gallows in the Hayes case, but it really meant more to Rogers than any of the murder cases he had defended up to that time. Being asked to aid in the defense of Hayes was the first recognition Earl had been accorded by the more distinguished section of the Los Angeles bar. And finding himself in an entirely different setting, he quickly adjusted himself to the more austere dignity of the Federal court and the company of the state's leading civil lawyers. The effect on his raiment was as marked as that on his court manners. He was an entirely different Earl Rogers and his changed demeanor and appearance attracted more attention than his accustomed flamboyant methods.

Quiet, sombre suits took the place of the loud checks; the fawn colored waistcoats were placed in moth balls, as were the spats and gaily-hued cravats. Earl's manner underwent a similar transition. He took on the repressed air and quiet dignity of the learned chief counsel, John H. Chapman. He became a new, strange Earl Rogers.

The bitter fight to prevent an independent competitive railway line from entering Los Angeles and acquiring an outlet to the Pacific was the direct cause of the Hayes tragedy. For it was a tragedy more lasting in its effects than most murder trials. And, before it was finally disposed of, the financial, social and political structures of Southern California were shaken to their very foundations.

Tom Hayes, christened Howard Thomas, was one of the best-liked men of Southern California. He was a power in politics throughout his region, and in beautiful and prosperous Riverside County he was an absolute czar. When President Theodore Roosevelt visited the Coast during his first term he was not only guest, but boon companion, of Tom

Hayes. Not only was Hayes a power among southwestern California Republicans, he was the social arbiter of his section of the state as well.

At that time the multi-millionaire Montana miner, Senator W. A. Clark, and his brother, J. Ross Clark, were building the Salt Lake Railroad to the Pacific Coast from Salt Lake City. They were being secretly and steadily hampered in their venture by the powerful railway interests whose terminals were already established on the Pacific Ocean. State and county governments and those behind them had to be cajoled, bluffed, or bribed to secure rights-of-way for the new line.

The Salt Lake's agents learned that Tom Hayes was Riverside's political boss and went to him to secure rights-of-way across that county. Tom told them who would have to be reached among the bankers, politicians, and public officials if they wished to overcome the power of the Southern Pacific. To facilitate building of the line, with its certain and incalculable aid to Riverside County's industries, Hayes acted as go-between.

In the fall of the year a story was circulated to the effect that Tom Hayes had, in the interests of the Clark road, engineered vast land frauds, so-called, and he resigned as cashier of the Orange Growers' Bank.

Several months later Clyde Daniels, son of the bank president, who had been sent to Congress by Hayes in the rôle of political boss, reported that he had discovered false entries in the bank's books amounting to $90,000. A complaint was issued charging Tom Hayes with embezzlement.

The next day a run on the bank occurred which caused it to close. Through extraordinary influence, Justice of the Peace Stephenson of Riverside was prevailed upon to issue warrants for Hayes' arrest at midnight, when it would be impossible for him to furnish bail. It looked very ominous for the erstwhile banker-politician.

Hayes heard of the coup and concealed himself in the Riverside Country Club, where he was kept hidden for three days by the Chinese cook, Lo San, until he had retained attorneys and bondsmen.

It was generally believed that Hayes was being made a scapegoat for men higher up, who pocketed many thousands through his activities. He had, according to friends, received only a comparatively small portion of the railroad slush fund, and the money embezzled from the bank was probably used in behalf of others. Chapman, who was regarded as one of the state's finest civil lawyers, was engaged to defend Hayes. He immediately recruited Rogers.

Realizing that the wealthy men who had profited by Hayes' work were prepared to aid the prosecution and thus clear their own reputations, Earl went to United States Senator William A. Clark and to lesser men connected with the gigantic land deal and told them in unmistakable words that unless the pressure against Tom Hayes were relaxed during his trial, he, Earl Rogers, would have them all in court immediately. At once there was noticed less fervent desire in some quarters to send Hayes to the penitentiary.

There were two outstanding features of the trial: one, Earl Rogers' remarkable ability to become adept on short notice in almost any human art; the other, that of an old Chinese servant's sheer loyalty.

After the case Federal Bank Examiner John Wilson declared himself to have been absolutely astonished by Rogers' complete grasp of all the ramifications of bank bookkeeping.

At one point in the taking of testimony Rogers tossed onto the table one of the bank's books being used in evidence, and solemnly declared, "If a single column of figures in that book has been added up correctly Mr. Hayes will plead guilty." Either it was a magnificent bluff that worked, or Earl knew what he was talking about, for after a conference with the bank officials the prosecuting attorney let Rogers' challenge pass.

Lo San, the Country Club cook, swore on the witness stand that Hayes had made no effort to conceal himself in the club house, and even after being indicted for perjury he loyally continued to swear with a succession of "No, Ma'ams" to prosecuting attorney and judge that Hayes never had tried to hide.

Not particularly noted for his eloquence before a jury, Rogers astonished court and spectators by his argument and he was commended openly by Federal Judge Olin Wellborn at the conclusion of his plea to the jury.

But when the jury returned a verdict of not guilty, the court expressed doubt that justice had been done. There were rumors that one of the twelve had held out for acquittal until the other eleven joined him and Judge Wellborn did not hesitate to state his opinion that the verdict was not legitimately arrived at.

A couple of years after he was freed of the charges Tom Hayes died of a broken heart. At his bedside were his wife, his daughter Wanda, and Earl Rogers. Of the men who abandoned Hayes in his hour of great stress none ever prospered thereafter. A judge and several others who had profited heavily by the land deal died broke. One official in high place who had shared in the graft, and then left Hayes to sink, committed suicide.

But the trial had done a great deal for Earl Rogers in the way of investing him with an added dignity and the acquisition of a new courtroom personality.

CHAPTER XVII

THE first decade of Earl Rogers' career as a criminal lawyer had its climax in his participation in the sensational San Francisco graft prosecutions. It was by far his most notable assignment, as it projected him into a desperate legal battle that was attracting the attention of the nation.

These graft trials marked this country's high spot in municipal corruption. And in the quarter century which has elapsed since, no city of the United States has equalled them in their flagrant ramifications, their sensationalism, or the bitterness of that struggle.

San Francisco was stricken by fire and earthquake in 1906, and before the smoking ruins of the picturesque metropolis were cool, its body politic was torn asunder by an exposé of wholesale bribery and official venality that created almost as much consternation as nature's upheaval.

While men who had betrayed the public trust were dragged down to disgrace and ruin in a campaign of reprisal against their perfidy which inflamed press, pulpit and citizenry, others were elevated to lofty pedestals by hysterical popular praise and hero worship. Among the latter were Francis J. Heney, Hiram Johnson, and the late William J. Burns.

Heney became a national figure as a fighting prosecutor, Johnson was catapulted into the governorship of California, the United States Senate and almost into the Presidency. It will be recalled that in 1920 he was offered the Vice-Presidential nomination and spurned it, having already been a candidate for the Presidency. Coolidge accepted the nomination and became the nation's chief executive upon the death of

President Harding. Burns gained fame, fortune and high official honor as chief of the United States Secret Service.

Beginning soon after the holocaust of 1906, the graft trials continued for three years—a municipal war that stands alone in American history.

Earl Rogers was not in the case when it began. It was not until the higher-ups were drawn into the seething maelstrom and several had been convicted that the Los Angeles lawyer was requisitioned.

Before that Abe Ruef, the political boss of the city, had been found guilty of extortion, and Eugene Schmitz, the violin-playing mayor who was Ruef's willing tool, had been convicted on a like charge. It was disclosed by a series of confessions that every member of the Board of Supervisors had taken money in exchange for his vote to grant the United Railroads an overhead trolley franchise—the major incident of the graft scandal.

The saturnalia of official corruption had originated in the desire of the street railway corporation to override the desire of some of the leading citizens of the Golden Gate city to have the unsightly trolley poles replaced by underground conduits.

When Rogers projected his colorful personality into the picture the entire city was divided into hostile camps, money was being poured out on both sides, the press of the country was editorializing on the unique situation almost daily, and even the President of the United States, Theodore Roosevelt, did not hesitate to comment publicly on the proceedings.

It was the attempt of the fiery Francis J. Heney to reach the highest of the higher-ups, Patrick Calhoun, that brought the case to its most acute stage. Millions of dollars were available to prevent Calhoun's conviction.

Patrick Calhoun was the head of the San Francisco street railway system known as the United Railroads, but was not a resident of the city. He was a Southern aristocrat, descendant of John C. Calhoun, the great American statesman and former Vice-President. He had been an attorney of distinction before he became an industrial leader. He was reputed to have participated in the last pistol duel fought in the South.

The dynamic Heney had been attorney-general of Arizona Territory in its quick-trigger days. He had quit this position in wrath because President Grover Cleveland had refused his demand that Arizona's governor be removed on charges preferred by Heney, although Cleveland did remove Governor Hughes a few months after Heney resigned. Heney had shot and killed in self-defense a powerful political boss of the Territory, after the latter had threatened publicly to kill him on sight.

At the behest of ex-Mayor James D. Phelan of San Francisco, Rudolph Spreckels, and other prominent men who were preparing to fight the plunderers of San Francisco, Heney returned to that city, fresh from his victory as Federal prosecutor of the Oregon timberland grafters, a case in which high Federal officials were involved.

Eugene E. Schmitz had been a musician in a San Francisco theater before Ruef's machine elevated him to the position of mayor. As a member of the Musician's Union he had been groomed for the Union Labor Party nomination by the scheming Ruef and was swept into office in an election dominated by union interests.

Abe Ruef, San Francisco's political czar, was born in the Bay City and knew every racial, religious, industrial and political angle and complication of his day and age. An attorney, he was one of the shrewdest political manipulators in the West, and his worst enemies were forced to admit that if he had been able to make the mayor, the supervisors, and his other henchmen obey his instructions explicitly none of them ever would have been brought to justice.

The charge against Calhoun and his chief counsel, Tirey L. Ford, was the bribery of the board of supervisors through

Ruef. They were alleged to have had the sum of $200,000 consigned to the United States mint in San Francisco, which amount upon Calhoun's order was turned over to Ford for payment to Ruef. The latter had already confessed to bribing the city officials. (Some years after the trial Ruef admitted that $85,000 of the $200,000 had been used to buy the supervisors and that he and Mayor Schmitz had divided most of the remainder.)

It was the conviction of Louis P. Glass, head of the Pacific States Telephone & Telegraph Company, that brought the anti-prosecution forces to a realization that Heney was too much for them, with all their high-powered attorneys and their millions of dollars. Glass was found guilty of bribery, but did not go to the penitentiary as the verdict was set aside on appeal months later. But the defense forces were in a state of panic. Ford and Calhoun were next on Heney's schedule.

Strenuous efforts had been made by the Calhoun forces to offset the financial and moral support being given the prosecution by such civic leaders as Spreckels and Phelan. Desperate attempts to silence the *San Francisco Bulletin* and its militant editor, Fremont Older, had failed. Older, with his newspaper, led the attack on the corruptionists.

The defense determined that Earl Rogers was the only one who could stop the fire-eating Heney. Garret McEnerny, chief counsel for the defense, made a trip to Los Angeles to put through the deal.

The way for the employment of Rogers had been paved some time previously by the action of the defense in acquiring the services of Luther Brown. Luther, who had been known for some years as Earl's chief jury investigator, had been brought to San Francisco at more money than he had ever seen before and placed in charge of the so-called investigation of prospective jurors.

Brown's work was highly effective, according to those on the other side. He was alleged to have corrupted a group of trusted operatives working for Detective Burns and in this manner was getting the state's reports on the veniremen before Heney himself received them. In many instances, according to Heney, the state's reports on the jurymen were actually written in Luther's office. On their face these reports showed that the men investigated were favorable to the prosecution; but actually these prospective jurors were planted by the defense.

It is more than likely that Luther Brown himself had suggested the advantage of employing Earl Rogers. Luther was firmly entrenched as a necessary adjunct to the defense and he realized that Rogers was about the only available criminal lawyer who could cope with Frank Heney. It has been said that Brown sold the idea of hiring Rogers chiefly on the argument that Earl would be invaluable in harassing Heney. Luther also realized that the resourcefulness of Rogers was a necessity at this stage of the prosecutions and that the defense was in sore need of his ability as a cross-examiner. Whether or not he was employed as a prosecutor-baiter or in any other subordinate capacity, Earl Rogers did not hesitate to arrogate to himself the functions of a generalissimo immediately upon entering the case. That was the Rogers way. He was the star of the show and the array of celebrated counsel merely members of the supporting cast.

Earl took with him to San Francisco the two youngest members of his staff, Jerry Giesler but recently admitted to the bar and Ernest Noon, whose status at the time was that of office boy. Despite their youth they took an important part in the Rogers campaign.

Although the physical San Francisco had been razed by earthquake shock and flames, in spirit it was still the colorful and alluring metropolis of old. It was rebuilding rapidly and everyone was busy, either working or grafting, freehanded and reckless despite the calamity which had so recently visited them. It seemed that nothing could dull the buoyant nature transmitted by the vigorous Forty Niners and the fearless Comstock gamblers of the days of Flood, Fair, Mackay, and O'Brien. Lucky Baldwin and his dare-devil contemporaries still linked the present with the golden past.

San Francisco women were the same eye-filling show, with their smart dresses and the beautiful complexions about which Robert Louis Stevenson and Rudyard Kipling had raved in their books. Theaters that had not been destroyed were open again in greater proportion to population than anywhere else in the land. Everyone seemed able to patronize the gay French restaurants. Holiday excursion boats were always crowded in their trips up and down the beautiful bay. Bizarre Chinatown was continually thronged with sightseers.

From those of exalted caste on Nob Hill down to the hilarious crowds who made merry along the far-famed Barbary Coast there was an animation and a gay camaraderie that had never ceased since the first bearded Argonauts began to rear their proud city upon the easy-going Spaniards' pueblo of Yerba Buena. Aptly it was called the Paris of America.

Into this cosmopolitan picture Earl Rogers with his fifty suits of clothes, his swanky walking-sticks, and his flair for the theatrical fitted perfectly. At once his air of culture and elevated mannerisms were an open sesame to the upper circles of society for himself and his beautiful wife. With their two children, Adela and Bogart, they moved into the St. Francis Hotel, and later to a house in the city's most reserved residential district. They had chauffeurs and bodyguards. The effect of that sparkling environment was apparent in recent years when Earl's daughter, Adela, used it as the background of her widely read novel, "A Free Soul."

It was not long until Earl was recognized as a leading spirit among the boulevardiers of Van Ness Avenue; he was soon as well known along the Barbary Coast as he had been on Spring and Broadway in the City of the Angels.

Until the advent of Rogers the graft trials had been marked

by an air of humdrum routine, despite the undercurrent of human passion and partisanship which swayed the city's population. But from the day when Rogers stepped into the courtroom with his aura of drama, his ofttimes flamboyant attire and esthetic pose, the legal arena became a theater. When he appeared the first day with his cutaway morning coat, faced with broad black braid, his shirt and necktie a symphony of hues that blended more or less harmoniously with his checked waistcoat; striped trousers the last word of fashion's mode; his glossy patent leather shoes offset by spats, he created a sensation. The cynical newspaper reporters declared that no such sartorial splendor had graced a San Francisco courtroom since the days of the gorgeous Forties.

And when Rogers, acting for the defense in impaneling the jurors for Tirey L. Ford's trial, fastidiously flicked a handkerchief from his coat sleeve to mop his brow, the grinning Francis J. Heney was so amazed by this final touch of elegance that he almost turned a back-somersault.

All of San Francisco's civic buildings had been reduced to piles of brick and mortar by the earthquake and fire, so the graft trials were held in a Jewish place of worship, Sherith Israel Temple. Strangely enough, also, Ruef, the city's leading Jew, had been one of the first to be convicted in the Synagogue.

The opening skirmish between the courtroom gladiators came on September 7, 1907, in the Ford case, when Earl started the forensic fireworks. Ugly intimations of jury tampering and crooked detective tactics were loosed from the beginning of the day's session. Rogers charged men in the employ of Detective Burns with pursuing "indecent eavesdropping tactics" in the courtroom.

Extreme tension was created when Rogers arose and with sinister suavity addressed Judge Lawlor on what he said was a question of personal and professional privilege.

"I think it is extremely indecent," said Rogers, "that as the

defendant and counsel for defense are consulting in this courtroom we should have sitting next to us, and listening with all
their ears, employees of Detective Burns."

Prosecutor Heney rose to reply. "I believe," grinned Heney,
"the counsel for the defense should be more specific. That is,
he should specify the number of auricular organs each employee of Burns is listening with. 'All their ears' is very in-
definite. Maybe one of them is deaf in one ear." Rogers
merely glared at him. Heney had won the first round in
what one newspaper reporter described as the "goat-getting
contest."

"Insofar as men sitting there are concerned," continued
Heney, "I have seen about a half-dozen of the most desperate
characters in California, including Dave Nagle and three
men who have the reputation of killing prisoners at Folsom,
sitting in this courtroom, and they are supposed to be in the
employ of the United Railroads. Honors are about even if
it comes down to that sort of thing."

Heney's intimation that honors were about even was a
tacit admission that the prosecution had begun to fight fire
with fire. By that time any killer could get employment from
one side or the other, although the enormous fund at the
disposal of the defense made of their corps of gun men and
other shady characters a virtual army.

In referring to the men and women employed by the graft
defense, the *San Francisco Call*, in an editorial article in its
issue of September 26, 1907, said:

The retinue of the trolley magnates as exhibited in the Ford
case, makes a remarkable picture. Behind the expert lawyers of
last resort troops a motley train of gun fighters, professional
plug-uglies, decoys, disreputable "detectives," thugs, women of
the half world and the wolfish pack of gutter journalism. It must
be, indeed, a hard case that needs such bolstering.

How will Mr. Calhoun square with his protestations of high-
mindedness the presence and the efforts in his behalf of such

creatures of the slums and stews as "Bogie" O'Donnell and "The Banjo-Eyed Kid"? Are these and the others of their kidney laboring in the same behalf as friends and sympathizers of Mr. Calhoun or merely as his hired men?

Bickering about the character and activities of the sleuths of both sides continued between Rogers and Heney until Judge Lawlor put a stop to it and ordered Burns' men to sit as far away as possible from Rogers and his client.

In austere contrast to this rout of wrangling lawyers, men of violence and the hard-faced women abetting their devious schemes, was the daily presence of a solemn-visaged Rabbi. Aloft and still as an eagle in the gallery, where Jewish women of his congregation sat when he read the ancient liturgy of his people's religious service, he was an impressive figure. Up there in the shadows his falcon's nose and flowing beard lent to him the illusion of a reincarnation of Michaelangelo's immortal sculpture of Moses as, glooming and inscrutable, he beheld this daily profanation of Jehovah's Temple. The fantasy of his resemblance to the great lawgiver of his race was heightened by his immobile pose as thoughts none but himself might divine came and went behind his boding eyes.

Although Heney laughed derisively at Rogers' fastidious twice-a-day change of raiment and his ofttimes supercilious manner, the Los Angeles lawyer was for many days the center of all interest among court attendants and visitors. The news reporters were delighted by his affectation of the Anglicized "A" and other high-brow accents. In the beginning he threw the observant and cagey Heney almost completely off his guard by his affectations.

To make light of the constant reference of the district attorney and his assistant to the tentacles of graft in the city, he phrased the popular American idiom as "grawft" and asked prospective jurors if they were acquainted with "William J. Burns, said to be a detective."

CHAPTER XVIII

THOMAS F. LONERGAN, one of the boodling supervisors, was the key witness in the trolley franchise scandal. He had confessed and implicated the other members of the board. Over him was waged a bitter struggle as Rogers endeavored by his rapidly-shifting attack to discredit his evidence.

Lonergan's signed confession and his adherence to that story under Rogers' slashing cross-examination seemed to be attack-proof until Earl suddenly flashed before the witness a written statement by Lonergan in which the latter set forth that when he voted for the trolley permit he had not been promised, nor did he understand, there would be any monetary consideration allowed him for voting in favor of the measure. When Rogers drew from the witness the admission that the signature was his the prosecution's forces were thrown into confusion.

Later it was learned that the statement had been obtained by one Dorland under the pretense that he was a magazine writer who was preparing an article on the San Francisco graft prosecution, and Lonergan, never supposing it would become known to any of the graft counsel until after the prosecution was over, had signed the statement without even reading it. Lonergan, the driver of a bakery wagon, harassed and confused by Earl's rapid-fire questioning, stammered out what appeared an improbable explanation of how he had been induced to sign the paper in Rogers' hands.

Heney himself did not know of the ruse by which the Lonergan statement had been obtained, but he went into action at once with a trump card he had been holding in reserve. On re-direct examination he asked Lonergan if he had been followed by a man during the noon recess. The witness testified that he had.

"Was that Mr. Melrose, a detective of the Southern Pacific?" asked Heney.

"I don't know Mr. Melrose," replied Lonergan.

"Is the man who followed you the one sitting directly back of Mr. Ford?"

"That is the gentleman; that is him."

"He was following you around during the noon hour?"

"Yes, sir."

Then Heney proceeded to get before the court the fact that Melrose, who had been freed of the charge of murdering Broome in a year-long fight by Earl Rogers, was really Earl's bodyguard, although on the railroad's payroll. This fact had no direct bearing on the case, but it put Rogers on the defensive and gave the puzzled Heney a chance to mark time until he could get at the true aspect of Lonergan's act.

Before the trial was many days old the verbal duel between Rogers and Heney had become as deeply interesting to press and public as all the rest of the legal war put together. Once Heney jeered that Rogers was trying to "sit in the lap" of a witness whom Earl was coaching in his elusive manner that left no opening for legitimate objection.

But the same day the fiery prosecutor was moved to complain to the court that he objected to the manner in which Rogers was laughing at him while he was conducting the examination of a witness.

"I am not laughing at Mr. Heney," declared Earl.

"Well, let's call it smiling insultingly, then," amended the prosecutor. "Anyhow, I object to the attorney's facial expression during the prosecution's efforts."

"Well," conceded Rogers, "if the eminent and learned counsel will indicate what sort of facial expression he wishes me to assume I shall be pleased to try to accommodate him."

Heney knew that Rogers was employing his well-known

badgering tactics and kept himself well in hand. Once when Heney inadvertently stepped behind Rogers the latter whirled about as if greatly agitated and exclaimed in a loud whisper to those near him, "Never let that fellow get behind you! He's an Arizona gun-man. Shot a man to death in Tucson, from the rear."

Heney only grinned.

Rogers' persistent baiting finally did irk the prosecutor considerably. Once, as Heney addressed the jury, he made gestures with a rolled newspaper, which happened to be then opposed to the defense. Pausing in his talk, he laid it down on a table, fully ten feet away from the jury, but immediately Earl was on his feet protesting that the prosecutor was showing the jurors an article concerning the graft prosecution in the newspaper.

At that moment a court clerk was handing a paper to Judge Lawlor and the latter failed to hear Rogers' objection. Angered beyond control, for the only time during the case, Heney stepped close to Earl and whispered belligerently: "You dirty skunk, if you ever pull anything like that on me again I'll knock your goddamn' block off!" Rogers merely grinned amiably. He had finally forced Heney to show the effect of the constant badgering.

But a few days later it came Rogers' turn to lose his poise. Frank Leach, superintendent of the mint in San Francisco, was on the stand and had testified as to Ford drawing the $200,000 from the mint. Rogers tried desperately to shake his story on cross-examination. Leach could not be tricked into changing his story in any respect.

Earl had been out the night before and had not been to bed. His nerves were badly frayed. Baffled by the witness, he became incensed and a note of abuse crept into his queries. The other defense attorneys grew uneasy. Leach was a man of impeccable reputation. They feared, and rightly so, that Rogers was jeopardizing their client. They stood it as long as they could, then took action against him. There was a hurriedly whispered conference of the whole battery of defense counsel and Earl was finally induced to withdraw for the time being and take a rest. He agreed only when he was convinced by his associates that his nerves were badly frayed from the severe strain of "overwork."

Leach was dismissed from the witness stand and Rogers, picking up his hat and cane, withdrew in great dignity for the badly needed "rest."

At the entrance of the Synagogue, Earl met Jack London, then the reigning fiction writer of the country. They had foregathered on numerous occasions and now by mutual consent they started out for the Water Front. Habitués of the Embarcadero and the Barbary Coast still talk about that great wet duet. It continued for three days and during that time they visited practically every resort on the Coast. On either the second or third day they ran into Tom Sharkey, who was still the idol of the Water Front despite his two defeats at the hands of Jim Jeffries.

Tom was well filled with steam beer and needed no persuasion to join the roistering couple. Old timers recalling those days seldom fail to mention the climax of that meeting. It occurred in one of the more important Water Front saloons, the White Elephant. After a few drinks and some fight talk, Sharkey, tightening his belt significantly, took his position at the end of the bar. Pounding on the mahogany with his huge fist until he had gained the attention of the long rows of drinkers, he demanded belligerently: "Is there any man in this house has got anything to say again' Dundalk?"

It was Tom's favorite challenge. Dundalk was Tom's birthplace in Ireland. As there were among his hearers several true born Irishmen who were not from Dundalk, disparaging remarks in abundance about that famed seaport of County Louth were immediately forthcoming.

Details of the ensuing battle are not available. Those who participated in it were scarcely qualified to give them and those who didn't take part also gave rather vague versions. However, Jack London emerged minus his coat and one leg of his trousers and Earl Rogers had a cut lip and a well-blackened optic. It required several patrol loads of husky San Francisco policemen to quell the war. Earl and Jack were hustled by friendly officers to a Turkish bath and put to bed.

The prosecution was severely handicapped by its inability to connect Tirey Ford directly with the bribing of the supervisors. When Heney decided to try Ford first instead of Calhoun he was certain that he had Ford on the verge of a collapse and a willingness to tell his entire part in the wholesale corruption of the supervisors. But Ford refused to break. Only one man could give direct evidence of the alleged graft activities of Ford and Calhoun. This was Ruef. Heney had been assured that Ruef would turn state's evidence if proper inducements were extended, such as an immunity bath. But Abe failed to supply the testimony.

Nevertheless Heney had a powerful case against Calhoun's chief aide and the defense was desperately trying every possible means of averting an almost certain conviction.

Some of their methods were more than questionable. An attempt was made to kidnap Editor Fremont Older of the *Bulletin,* the mainspring of the prosecution, and railroad him to prison on a charge of criminally libeling Luther Brown. He was actually kidnaped and taken on a train bound for Los Angeles, where a judge friendly to the Calhoun side was said to be awaiting his arrival. He was rescued by officers with a court order at Santa Barbara before the train arrived in Los Angeles. As Brown was an associate of Rogers, the latter was generally credited with authorship of the idea.

Attempts had been made also to kidnap Lonergan and frighten him into silence by compromising him with the help of a woman. It was openly charged that Rogers had brought the woman from Los Angeles for that purpose. This abortive effort to defeat the prosecution was made on the eve of Lonergan's appearance on the stand.

The case finally went to the jury without the introduction of any evidence by the defense. It ended in a mistrial, the jury standing eight to four for acquittal. Ford was immediately brought to trial for bribery of another supervisor. This was even a stronger case than the first one. The jury brought in a verdict of "not guilty." Trial on a third indictment ensued with similar result.

Quite remarkably, in not one of the Ford trials did the defense present a word of testimony. Calhoun and Ruef were both called to the stand in the last trial but both refused to answer questions. The result of the three trials brought only one inference, and no serious denial was ever made that there was wholesale jury-purchasing.

Before Calhoun could be brought to trial, the appellate court set aside the convictions of Ruef, Schmitz and Glass. They were released from prison and Ruef remained free until late in 1908, when Heney again prosecuted him, this time for the trolley bribery. The trial was begun while the third Ford trial was in progress, Heney leaving the former case to Prosecutor John O'Gara.

If public feeling had been violent during the preceding trials, it would be difficult to describe conditions in San Francisco during the new hearing of Ruef. Attempts were made to murder Supervisor James L. Gallagher, who had been won over by the prosecution. Gallagher had been the "pay-off man" for Ruef, it will be recalled. A residence occupied by Gallagher and his family was almost entirely destroyed by dynamite. The occupants miraculously escaped. Other buildings owned by Gallagher were dynamited. A man named Claudianes confessed that he had been hired to assassinate Gallagher and was sent to prison for life. In the first trial the jury disagreed and in the interim before the next trial several persons were tried for jury bribery and one man, named Blake, was convicted.

In the midst of the second Ruef trial an attempt was made to assassinate Heney. Gallagher, the state's star witness, had just left the stand and was talking to Heney when a man approached the prosecutor and, holding a gun six inches from his head, fired point blank. Heney fell, apparently mortally wounded, with a jagged hole under his right ear. The assailant was Morris Haas, an ex-convict who had been a prospective juror in the first Ruef trial and had been exposed by Heney. He was taken to jail. During the civic furor over the attempted assassination, Haas was found slain in his cell. A revolver was found beside him and the police said it was suicide. They couldn't explain whence the revolver came and friends of Heney declared that he had been murdered to seal his lips.

That Heney was not mortally wounded was due to the fact that he was laughing when shot. His mouth being open, the bullet had barely room to pass between the upper and lower jawbones, was thus retarded and lodged in his throat,

When Heney was wounded Hiram Johnson volunteered his services, with several other prominent lawyers. The trial proceeded, Gallagher told his story, and Ruef was found guilty and sentenced to four years at San Quentin.

Rogers, who had returned to Los Angeles at the conclusion of the third Ford trial, went back to San Francisco to defend Calhoun. Fully three months were required to select a jury out of 2,370 veniremen who had been called into court. The defense was reinforced by several other noted attorneys. More than half of the people in the court room were detectives or undercover men employed by the state or the defense. Heney, still weak from his wound, was determined to link Calhoun, the man at the top, with the bribery of the supervisors. Gallagher again on the stand testified that he had been given $85,000 by Ruef, of which he had retained $15,000 and paid the supervisors $4,000 each, but no evidence could be adduced that Tirey L. Ford, Calhoun's agent, had passed the money to Ruef.

When Gallagher was finally turned over to Rogers for cross-examination, he was subjected to such a terrific bombardment that the newspaper accounts of those few days contained little else than Earl's questions and the witness's replies.

Nothing was overlooked in the efforts of the defense to protect Calhoun. The newspapers gave almost as much space to the by-plays as to the trial itself.

When the defense charged that the prosecution had burglarized Calhoun's safe and purloined documents relating to the case, the city was flooded with small colored cards on which were printed the picture of a safe surrounded by a question mark and the query: "Has YOUR safe been cracked yet?" When an apparently upright citizen allied with Calhoun was arrested by the prosecution on a jury-tampering charge, thousands of cards were circulated reading, "Have YOU been arrested yet?" Rogers was credited with authorship of this unique scheme.

Every prominent man on both sides of the legal struggle was shadowed constantly. Even the shadows were in turn shadowed. A San Francisco resident who wasn't being dogged by detectives in those parlous days certainly didn't amount to much. Taking advantage of this state of affairs, Rogers staged one of his flamboyant, bombastic spectacles. It was intended to impress upon the public that the defense attorneys were being pursued by human bloodhounds.

Announcing, especially to reporters of the newspapers friendly to his side, that he could not secure in San Francisco sufficient privacy to prepare his case from day to day, Earl leased a ferry-boat.

The old side-wheel barge cruised around the bay all night while Rogers ostensibly was delving through documents having to do with the next day's court session. Heney, hearing of the deep-sea law office, gave an interview to the only newspaper on his side. He expressed the opinion that Earl had gone off on another spree caused by his certain knowledge that Calhoun was headed for San Quentin. This time, said Heney, Earl wasn't going to risk having to terminate his celebration prematurely.

Earl gave the newspapers another opportunity to play him up on the front page during the following week-end recess when he was haled before the justice court at South San Francisco, charged with resisting an officer. Fast automobiles were a passion with him and he loved to get everything he could out of a car. Buron Fitts, present district attorney of Los Angeles, who started his career as an office boy for Rogers, tells of how he once escaped the wrath of Rogers when he wrecked the latter's car, by telling Earl that he was going seventy miles an hour when the accident happened. Earl forgot the smashed automobile in his joy at its achievement. But this was many years later.

When a constable boarded the running board of the Rogers car which contained members of his family at the San Francisco suburb and demanded that Rogers stop while he made out a ticket for speeding, Earl promptly knocked the constable off the car. The officer tried to enforce his command by drawing a gun, whereupon Earl, who was wholly unarmed, sprang from his seat and started chasing the constable across the fields. He was arrested the next day on an assortment of charges. The trial was given much space as it had many humorous features, including the action of the justice in hiring a hall because of the importance of the trial. Earl who had sent for Attorney Will Anderson of Los Angeles to defend him, raised the point that the arresting officer had not had his appointment confirmed when the incident occurred so he was not in reality an officer.

However, Judge McSweeney held Rogers to the superior

court and fined him for contempt of court as well, but that was as far as the case ever went.

The San Francisco press and public had enjoyed at least a brief respite from the grim deadliness of the Calhoun trial.

Again the defense placed no witnesses on the stand and the case went to the jury on the evidence of the state and the arguments based on the plea that Calhoun had not been connected with the bribery. The result was another hung jury. It had voted first eight to four for acquittal and the last ballot was ten to two. Calhoun was again brought into court on another indictment, but Heney had just been defeated for district attorney and this meant the breaking down of the graft prosecution. Millions had been spent by the big corporations and the taxpayers were bitterly complaining of the burdens resting on their shoulders. Calhoun went back East, a badly broken man. Earl journeyed to his own habitat in Southern California.

CHAPTER XIX

Before Rogers, with his family and his wardrobe, returned to Los Angeles, Patrick Calhoun had made Earl an offer of a retainer of $25,000 a year to represent his interests, his legal requirements for the traction magnate not to interfere with the attorney's regular practice. As a condition, however, Earl would have had to foreswear strong drink.

Earl was indignant at such a proposal. "Hell!" he declared to the traction magnate, "do you think I'd sacrifice my independence for money?"

But his real reason for not remaining was his desire to get back into the less stormy atmosphere of his home town. He had collected nearly $100,000 in fees and almost as much for living expenses, all of which came from the coffers of the United Railroads. Yet he returned to Los Angeles with little to show in the way of actual cash—perhaps not more than a few thousand dollars. The Barbary Coast, the bars and the cafés of San Francisco's downtown tenderloin had got most of it.

Rogers also had the fear of making a fresh start away from the haunts which knew him best. In Los Angeles he was sure of himself and certain of what he could accomplish professionally. It was for the same reason that he turned down an offer to go to New York, made a short time previously. He had visited the metropolis on several occasions. Once he went there on a rather mysterious mission to recover some valuable jewels that had been stolen from the wife of a wealthy race track man who had powerful political connections in New York. Through some involved method he recovered the gems.

Earl had also attracted the attention of the New York bar by his remarkable success on the Coast and once he had been sent for by the late Delancy Nicoll, the noted corporation lawyer. Nicoll induced Rogers to come on to New York from the Coast for the sole purpose of cross-examining a particularly difficult witness.

Before accepting that task Earl wrote Nicoll that he would essay breaking down the witness only if no one was to know that he was going to New York and that he should have a chance to observe the man for at least a week before putting him on the stand.

When Earl reached New York he stayed at the hotel where the witness was quartered. He did not have the man shadowed or investigated, nor did he ask him any questions concerning the case; but daily he ate at the same table with him, smoked with him in the hotel lobby as he covertly studied him, and when the day for questioning the witness came the California lawyer had so thoroughly studied the other's mentality that he tore his story to shreds during twenty minutes of cross-examination and won the case for Nicoll.

One version of the assignment, probably started by Earl himself, was that he had dashed to New York, put the witness on the grill with all the results desired, and boarded a train for the return trip to the Coast without even unpacking his bag, after collecting his fee of $5,000. That story was at least a bit exaggerated. It is inconceivable that Rogers, with $5,000 in his pocket, would have quit New York without one little incursion into its then widely-heralded tenderloin. But Earl had a very normal weakness for exaggeration, especially when drinking.

As a result of this visit Rogers received an offer through an important politician to leave the Coast for New York. It was reported that he had received an offer of legal business which would guarantee him a minimum of $100,000 annually. He gave this offer serious consideration and finally rejected it. He had no desire to start all over again as he felt this meant. Besides he loathed the East and especially New York which he always maintained lacked personality. He felt also that despite the assured income his place was where he had won his spurs; where his name was a household word, his face and figure as familiar as the incline railway on Angels' Flight in the heart of Los Angeles. Furthermore, his self-esteem would not permit him to assume the rôle of a little toad in a big puddle even were he well paid for it.

On the Pacific Slope Earl Rogers could walk into any hotel lobby and be accorded a reception such as only the highest dignitary would receive. In any barroom from San Diego to Seattle he would be hailed as a pal and good fellow. The leading sporting houses knew him as a liberal spender and any time he deigned to visit an exclusive house, they would "close the door" for him if he gave the word. That meant no one save Rogers' party could make merry in that particular resort until Earl departed. It is perhaps beside the point to add that frequently when Earl had "passed out," some solicitous friend would phone his home or office and the "rescue squad" would take him to his favorite Turkish baths.

Earl's incursions into the bawdy houses, however, were often inspired by the urge for oratorical outlet of his warm self-appraisal as much as the desire to indulge in debauches. His habitual care to conceal from social and professional acquaintances the overweening self-esteem that was his predominant characteristic drove him to the social frontier to vent his repressed vanity. Often he would indulge his sardonic humor by bewildering his audience with academic discourse on metaphysics or owlish dissertation on St. Paul's definition of faith. There in the cloistered gloom of the bagnio, free from restraint of the outside world's less sympathetic appraisal of his conceit, he would fairly hypnotize his hearers with brazen eulogy of his own superior mentality, illustrated by stories of his superhuman intellectual feats.

"In such baffling cases," he was wont to orate, "they at first used to imagine others might solve those mysteries. They would appeal to the police, to the detectives, even to the bright newspapermen.

"Then," he would conclude grandiloquently, "everything else having failed, they would come to *me*," as in the awed silence he would lay his forefinger dramatically upon his own chest.

Yes, Earl Rogers felt that he was of the West, and to be more specific, of Los Angeles. Here he could get front row seats at any theater when the mayor of the city failed, or a ringside seat at any championship bout. He usually sat with one of his cronies, Nat Goodwin or Charlie Van Loan. He never missed a stake race at Lucky Baldwin's Santa Anita track on the outskirts of Los Angeles. In a crowded cabaret, a special table would be placed on the dance floor for an Earl Rogers party; and Earl would pridefully mix his own salad dressing under the admiring observation of guests and waiters. He never visited a café without going into the kitchen, selecting his own steak and instructing the chef how he wanted it cooked. Here they all knew him, the rooters at the ball games and the fights, the millionaire horse owners, the bookies and the touts at the tracks, the performers on the stage, the speed demons at the famous road races, the song and dance artists of the cabarets. He was seldom known to miss a first night or an important fistic bout. On Sundays he rode with the Vaqueros, for he was a splendid horseman; and he always got a thrill out of beating the chess champion in his favorite club. He loved to manipulate the chessmen but he hated card games because he believed that luck was a greater requirement than skill at cards. After racing was outlawed in California, Earl made frequent trips to the track at Tia Juana and once his presence was noted by the running of the "Earl Rogers Handicap." No wonder he rejected offers to live elsewhere.

There was no dearth of business for Rogers upon his return to Los Angeles from San Francisco. There was a rapid succession of murders and Rogers officiated at five of them, one after another, with only enough time between to get over the usual spree which marked the end of a trial. In each case there was an acquittal. One of them, the McComas case, went down in the annals of Los Angeles as one of its most colorful and dramatic courtroom plays. Like the Alford, Boyd, and Melrose cases, it became another high spot in the career of Earl Rogers. This trial occurred before Rogers returned to San Francisco for the Calhoun case. The defense was entirely different from any that Earl had ever presented and surpassed in boldness any stroke he had previously wielded to free a client.

The crime was the killing of Charlotte Noyes, his sweetheart, by debonair Billy McComas, as colorful a character as ever came inside from the frontier. He was a handsome big six-footer, athletic and graceful. His vocation was that of mining engineer; by avocation he was an adventurer and lover. He had many women during his eventful life. He never married any of his loves, however; just loved them and left them strung along his life trail. He was not related, so far as known, to the assistant district attorney of that name.

The early life of McComas as disclosed during the trial was as rich in adventure and drama as an entire series of dime novels. Back in the Eighties his lawyer-pioneer father, with his wife and one of their boys, were driving out of Silver City, New Mexico, when they were waylaid by Chatto's band of Apache assassins ranging northward out of the Sierra Madres of Old Mexico on one of their many bloody forays. Billy had been left at home.

The redskins killed Judge McComas after torturing him, outraged his wife before brutally murdering her, and carried the child away with them. For years after the McComas murders, expeditions of vengeful men from Arizona, New Mexico and Northern Sonora scoured the Southwest in quest of the captive boy. Every rumor brought into mining camp or cow town by scout or prospector of a white child seen with Apaches sent a grim bunch of frontiersmen hot-footing it into far cañons on a chance of rescuing Billy McComas' younger brother.

But after a lapse of five or six years an Apache squaw at San Carlos reservation in Arizona told of the McComas boy's real fate. She had taken charge of him after the massacre of his parents and tried to mother him, for she had recently lost her own child of about the white boy's age. But, horrified by the sight of his parents' tragic fate, the child sobbed continually; and finally, angered by his crying, an Apache buck crushed in his head with a rock.

This tragedy of his family won young Billy McComas the sympathy of everyone throughout the Southwest, and before he had grown to full manhood the pity felt for him by girls and women had made of the rascal a conscienceless philanderer. His first adventure of note with the fair sex was when at the age of twenty he became school teacher in what was then the little mining camp of Bisbee, up in the towering Mule Mountains of Arizona.

Before he had filled the job more than three months, his attentions to the older girls of his classes moved the school trustees to advise the young Don Juan that he had better go back to the mines and make way for the prim school ma'am they had picked to relieve him.

After mining for a while he tried his deft hands at dealing faro; but being a fellow of ambition, education, and intelligence well above the other gambling men, he studied mining engineering and was graduated with honors. He was working at that profession in a desultory way, between more profitable affairs of the heart with impressionable ladies of means, when the killing of his current sweetheart in Los Angeles occurred.

It was wholly consistent that Earl should defend McComas, for there was considerable in common between the men. They differed fundamentally in that Earl often spent his money lavishly upon women instead of extracting it from them by the well known McComas dry-cleaning process. But they were both handsome fellows, fastidious dressers, precise in their use of English.

The general opinion of those acquainted with the McComas technique was that, having run through all of Charlotte Noyes' money and being refused further funds, McComas in a fit of rage had shot her. But of course that wasn't the Rogers version of the tragedy.

Brought to trial, the slayer's story of the killing was that his mistress, in a passion of jealousy, had hurled a cup of sulphuric acid in his face; that in his agony and blindness, and not knowing the identity of his assailant, he had drawn his gun and fired wildly. The defense presented by Rogers was daring and fantastic. He pleaded that the act of McComas was the automatic reflex of a man accustomed to fire-arms; argued that the natural response of a gunfighter to an act such as acid-hurling or any sort of assault would be to draw his gun and fire without thought of the consequences—merely as an impulse of self-preservation.

But the story that has found wide credence ever since the trial was that Rogers himself had been the author of the acid attack and that McComas, at the suggestion of his attorney, had thrown the acid in his own face after the slaying, fantastic as that seems. The prosecution went so far as actually to charge that the defense was faked.

When McComas appeared for trial he was represented by Rogers and his then associate, Paul Schenck. His face was still bandaged. It might not be amiss at this point to state that, according to Schenck, McComas had phoned that lawyer immediately after the killing and that he had told of the acid-throwing at that time. This would absolve Rogers from any manufacturing of the defense, as Paul Schenck insisted that Rogers did not get in touch with McComas until Schenck had himself notified Earl of the tragedy. Among those who went on McComas' bail was the chief executive of Los Angeles, Mayor Harper, some indication of his standing in the community.

District Attorney Fredericks had assigned his deputies, Fleming and Horton, to conduct the prosecution and Judge James was on the bench. Hundreds were unable to enter the courtroom, which was jammed at each session.

The state's contention was that McComas had slain the woman without provocation. Witnesses testified that they heard three revolver shots and a woman screaming as the firing began. Only two empty shells were found in the slayer's revolver and the state's claim was that he had replaced an exploded shell with a new cartridge. Rogers retaliated by declaring that a gun found in the woman's bed had been tampered with by the state.

Critics of Rogers who sarcastically referred to his unfailing ability to find the second gun in many of his cases where he relied on a plea of self-defense, were given food for thought in this incident. The second gun was found this time by the prosecuting attorneys, when they examined the premises the second time. It was discovered at the foot of Charlotte Noyes' bed, under the bed clothing, where no one could have reached it in a hurry.

Rogers and Schenck were present at the beginning of this second search of the room, but they had stepped out into the hallway. When, in less than a minute, they unexpectedly returned, the district attorney's men had just found the weapon. It has been intimated that it may have been a trap arranged by Earl. He had claimed that the woman had fired a shot at McComas. But the second gun, found by the prosecution forces during his brief absence from the room, contained no empty cartridges.

In the course of the trial Rogers maintained that it was obvious the prosecutors had found the gun while he and Schenck were absent from the room for less than a minute, had hurriedly replaced the discharged cartridge in Charlotte Noyes' gun with an unexploded one, but, flustered by his unexpected reëntrance, had hurriedly shoved the pistol down beneath the bedding. How else, he very logically demanded, would it have been where the woman never would have placed it, where she never could have reached it in a moment of emergency?

He called attention to the fact that the only evidence concerning shots in the Noyes apartment was that three reports had been heard. Where had the third shot come from, with only two empty cartridges in McComas' gun, he asked, unless it had come from Charlotte Noyes' pistol, and had then been replaced by a full cartridge by some interested persons?

Of course the prosecutors were driven to intimation that Rogers had planted the second pistol. But if he had he must have done so with the legerdemain of a stage magician while he and Paul Schenck and the district attorney's men all were in the room together.

Even the most discerning of his contemporaries have never been able to reach any definite conclusion about that second gun which was proved to have been the property of Charlotte Noyes. Anyhow, he turned the discovery of the gun to better advantage than did the state, half-convincing the jury that the prosecution had done the planting.

But Rogers' feat of purloining the state's chief witness was his crowning achievement in the McComas case. The witness was Dr. George W. Campbell whose evidence regarding the woman's wound was the most damaging given against the defendant. The doctor had also given expert testimony at the preliminary examination and one phrase which he had used was employed as the lever by which Rogers converted him into one of the most effective witnesses for the defense. When Rogers took the doctor over for cross-examination, he completely ignored the testimony which the physician had just given under the direct examination of Prosecutor Fleming. Instead he began questioning him about any acid burns he might have seen on the person of the slain woman. The doctor admitted that he had noted such marks on her face and right hand. The cross-examination continued:

Rogers: Doctor, what do you mean by "return spray"?

Prosecutor: We object to that question. There was nothing in the direct examination about any "return spray."

Rogers: Do you understand the phrase, "return spray"?

Prosecutor: Same objection.

Court: He may answer that.

Doctor: Yes, sir.

Rogers: What is meant by that expression?

Doctor: Well, as an example of a return spray—you might see an illustration at the beach as the wave would strike and be thrown back in drops. The farther back, the greater the surface over which you would get the spray. That is what we mean when we use that term.

Rogers: That's what you meant in using the term? Then you did use the term?

Doctor: I did.

Rogers: When?

Doctor: I forget, but it must have been at the coroner's inquest or during the preliminary hearing.

Prosecutor: Same objection. He didn't use it here during the direct examination.

Rogers: If at any time heretofore he has used it in connection with this case, he may use it now.

Court: If at any time you have used that term as descriptive of what you saw, you may explain as to the conditions to which you applied it.

Doctor: I applied it to the form and line the acid drops took on the face.

Rogers: Face of the woman?

Doctor: Face of the woman, Mrs. Noyes, at the time I studied the case.

Rogers: Describe the conditions it left on her face.

Doctor: I found that from above downward, on the right side of the face, was a line of acid drops—or the marks they had left. The lighter ones being above, gradually becoming heavier as they passed downward. Showing me that the line of fluid, acid, had formed itself by gravity and struck the face in that manner, in that perpendicular manner, along the right side of the face.

Rogers: You mean she was standing up, don't you?

Doctor: I believe she must have been. The burns became deeper from above downward, and the lower one on the face contained considerable eschar.

Rogers: Which means dead tissue?

Doctor: Which means dead tissue. It was deeper in the lower one than in those above it.

Rogers: Now, Doctor, what is your reason for saying that she was standing up?

Doctor: The acid burns had been caused by a return spray, and the heavy drops took the lower course. The heavier ones were below, gradually became lighter above, showing that the force of gravity had lined it. She must have been in an erect position to receive it that way.

Rogers: Speaking of a return spray, Doctor, will you please tell us very explicitly what you mean by the term?

Doctor: Well, I mean a come-back, from the acid striking anything.

Rogers: You mean by that, then, what we might call a splash-back.

Doctor: Yes, sir; as the ocean would strike the beach and spray back.

ROGERS: In your judgment, is that the way those burns
were inflicted on this woman?

DOCTOR: Yes, sir.

ROGERS: Did you so testify at the autopsy or the preliminary
hearing?

DOCTOR: I must have.

ROGERS: Did you further say at that time that she had
thrown acid upon some wall or some body, and there splashed
back upon her some of the acid?

PROSECUTOR: I object to that.

ROGERS: Pardon me, but I have not finished my question.—
And when you said that at the preliminary hearing, Mr.
Fleming objected and the court sustained him, as usual?

PROSECUTOR: I move that that be stricken out.

COURT: "As usual" may be stricken out.

ROGERS: I mean that Mr. Fleming is always right in his
objections.

COURT: *Is* that what you mean, Mr. Rogers?

ROGERS: Entirely so. I mean Mr. Fleming is a good lawyer
and therefore his objections usually are sustained.

Rogers repeated the last question and the Doctor answered
in the affirmative.

ROGERS (*Arising after being seated*): I just realized—I
didn't until I had sat down—what your Honor means by
inquiring about my remark a moment ago. Your Honor
certainly understands that I meant nothing except in the
way of persiflage with Mr. Fleming. I did not catch your
Honor's meaning at first. I certainly intended no discourtesy.

Both the court and Rogers smiled benignly. Mr. Fleming
also smiled, but his smile gave the spectators the impression
that someone in his near vicinity was smoking a wet cigar.

The chief witness for the defense was a sister of McComas
who had come from Arizona to testify in his behalf. She
told a dramatic incident in the life of her brother. Questioned
by Rogers, she said that some sixteen years before, while

engaged in a mining venture, her brother was blasting out a prospect hole twenty feet below the surface. He had lighted the fuses of a round of six holes loaded with dynamite and then had made his way quickly up the ladder to safety. As he reached the surface his horrified eyes came on a level with the deadly triangular head of a huge rattlesnake which was coiled and ready to strike.

As McComas hesitated between a choice of being blown up by dynamite or being struck by the deadly reptile, the first hole exploded, quickly followed by the five other blasts, tossing rocks upward in half-ton spurts. When her brother regained consciousness he was lying on the ground. A rock hurled upward by the blast had destroyed the sight of his left eye.

That concluded the story and the prosecution saw no reason for cross-examination. The woman was followed by another witness who testified as to the loss of McComas' eyesight. There was a parade of character witnesses, including Mayor Harper and other prominent citizens, and then the defendant was called to the stand. He made a good impression and the state was unable to shake his story to the effect that he had shot in the dark without knowing who had thrown the searing acid in his face as he entered the room. He declared that he had then run down to the Pepper Hotel, a short distance away on Seventh Street, where he asked the clerk to telephone the police and then returned to the scene of the tragedy.

In his argument to the jury Rogers launched a vicious attack on the prosecution. He accused the state lawyers of having planted the gun at the foot of the bed because they knew the head of it had been searched previously. As he excoriated the prosecutors, Assistant District Attorney Fleming got up and left the courtroom. Rogers, paying no attention to the act, continued addressing the empty chair as though the chief prosecutor were still there.

Counsel for the defense then referred to the alleged slayer's return to the scene of the crime. "I have defended fifty-two men accused of murder," he declared impressively, "and this is the first time I ever knew of a man visiting the scene of the tragedy if he could find any excuse for staying away. And this, then, is your cold-blooded, scheming murderer!"

Next he dramatically had McComas step forward to a position in front of the fascinated jurors. He ordered him to strip the bandages from his face, disclosing that the acid had burned the skin away all about his right eye.

"If the defendant had deliberately thrown acid in his face to prepare a fake defense, as the prosecution contends," asked Rogers, "would he not in your judgment have thrown it on the left side of his face where he had already been blinded, as his sister has testified?"

He declared that the sight of McComas' good eye was saved only because of the fact that he was wearing glasses.

Then counsel for the defense went into a discussion of the instinct and speed with which a man familiar with a six-shooter's use always draws and shoots when suddenly confronted by great danger or overpowering shock. Naturally, the defense counsel maintained, a man of such training and almost inherited instinct, would shoot like a lightning stroke subconsciously if attacked; especially so when the maddening pain of acid hurled in his face rendered him temporarily insane with agony.

While Rogers addressed the jury on this phenomenon of human reaction he held a vial of sulphuric acid in his hand, occasionally shaking it to keep the jurors' attention upon the deadly chemical. As always, he paced pantherlike, back and forth while addressing the jurors. As ever, he did his pacing behind the chairs in which the attorneys for the prosecution were sitting, because that never failed to annoy them.

"Unless you have been burned by this colorless hell's-fire, known better by laymen as oil of vitriol, you'll never be able to realize the searing agony it produces upon contact with our flesh," intoned Earl.

He was approaching his associate, Paul Schenck, and as he passed his seated partner he dropped half a teaspoonful of the acid on the latter's leg. It instantly gave off a whiff of blue smoke as it burned a hole in Paul's pants, ruining an expensive fawn-colored suit, and in the same flicker of an eyelash seared a hole in his hide.

Earl's horrified associate sprang four feet into the air with a howl of agony that brought all in the courtroom to their feet.

"What the hell are you doing?" he yelled.

"You see," Earl calmly observed to the startled jurors, "what just a few drops will do to a man's leg. Think of a cup of that hurled in his face!"

Then as Schenck squirmed with pain and ruefully regarded the ruin of his new $80 suit, purchased for the occasion in order to share in the vestured splendor of the senior counsel, Earl, without even a glance in his direction, passed to another phase of the defense's case.

The prosecution's close was confined almost entirely to a defense of itself, which Rogers had planned by his charges of unethical conduct in its effort to hang "an innocent man." The state, however, had only asked for a verdict of manslaughter, which Rogers had turned against the prosecution by declaring to the jury that "they are begging for any kind of a conviction."

The case went to the jury, which was out all night, and upon the foreman's statement that no agreement was possible the jurors were discharged. They had stood ten to two for acquittal.

At his second trial McComas was liberated on a verdict of not guilty.

The sequence of dramatic episodes following McComas' acquittal were as striking as every other incident of that colorful Don Juan's life. The beautiful Charlotte Noyes had owned a devoted admirer in the person of a noted cartoonist whose unusual skill at portraiture still ranks him at the head of his fellow artists. But when dashing Billy McComas came along, the illustrator's love for her became hopeless in her infatuation for the handsome big cavalier from Arizona.

One evening after his acquittal, McComas with a gay party of friends from Los Angeles was dining at the famous Ship Café that was built against the ocean pier at Venice. The cartoonist, unobserved by the merrymaking quartet, sat gloomily at a distant table, covertly observing them. When they went onto the floor to dance, the artist slipped over to their table and with his gifted pencil rapidly sketched the face of Charlotte Noyes upon the table-cloth, reversed McComas' plate over it, and returned to his corner to observe the other man's reaction.

When McComas and his companions returned to their seats McComas noted the changed plate before him and in idle curiosity lifted it. But as he stared at the features limned on the cloth before him he turned white, rose unsteadily to his feet as his overturned chair clattered to the floor behind him, and with his friends left without dining.

Some years later he became involved in the death of another of his many sweethearts. A woman with whom he had been intimate was found slain in her apartment in San Francisco. McComas himself reported to the police that he believed the woman had committed suicide. He was held temporarily but was given his liberty on a showing that the body was so placed against the inside of the apartment door that he could not have made an exit without disturbing it. The police reported it as a suicide.

CHAPTER XX

THE law permits an inconsistent defense and, as even the veriest tyro knows, the law is elastic. It is doubtful, however, if any more severe test was ever placed on the law's elasticity than that made by Earl Rogers in his efforts to save young Hal Hardy from the gallows.

Perhaps not since the ancient Greek Sophists from whom the Los Angeles lawyer may have got the idea, had anything quite so inconsistent been advanced in a court of law.

Hal Hardy was the scion of a well known Kentucky family, who had wrecked his life through overindulgence in the product of a distillery of which he had been manager back in the Blue Grass State.

While drunk Hardy went to a tamale stand at the corner of Sixth and Main streets and ordered a tamale from the proprietor, Billy Moore. An argument ensued and Hardy left. He returned a short time later and without warning shot and killed Moore. There was not a single extenuating circumstance attending the murder.

Realizing that the evidence was all against the accused man, Earl went to the prosecutors, Assistant District Attorneys W. Joseph Ford and Percy Hammon, and offered to have his client plead guilty to a charge of manslaughter. Hammon, having a profound respect for Earl's legal knowledge and adroit mind, urged his associate to accept Rogers' proposition, but the pugnacious Ford rejected it, declaring that with the evidence they had to hand, the state would have no trouble hanging Hardy.

When the case came to trial Rogers astounded the court and staggered the prosecution by pleading a triple defense.

[180]

First was an alibi; the defendant could not have slain the dead man because he was elsewhere at the time of the killing. Second was self-defense; if Hardy shot Billy Moore it was in defense of his own life. Third, insanity; if the defendant was really present and did take the life of the decedent without provocation, Hardy must have been insane.

The Sophists of antiquity could not have beaten that one. It may be recalled that the suppositious case cited by the Hellenic quibbler had to do with a copper kettle. Recompense had been demanded by the owner for damage done the vessel by a borrower. The Greek of the second part denied the validity of the claim on three grounds: first, that he never borrowed the kettle; second, that if he had, it was damaged when he got it and third, that the kettle was in good shape when he returned it.

There would seem to be a definite relation between the two cases, so widely separated by the centuries and it is more than likely that Earl Rogers was familiar with the kettle story.

If the district attorney's office and the rest of the legal brotherhood were surprised when Rogers announced the nature of his bizarre plea, they gasped when the learned court, despite an evident astonishment, made no comment on the unusual proceedings. Earl, however, had at hand a wealth of authorities, most of them of the days of Rufus Choate and Daniel Webster, as sound and unassailable as they were ancient and forgotten of Rogers' contemporaries. With that array of authorities he squelched the warlike Ford before the latter could even start the bombardment of objections he had at first contemplated.

Realizing that the testimony which the prosecution's forces could produce would be overwhelmingly to the effect that Hardy had slain Moore without provocation, Rogers' constant and strenuous cross-examination of state witnesses was employed by him mostly in the nature of a smoke screen. Its object was to divert the prosecutors' attention as greatly as possible from his primary motivation, that of implanting in the jurors' minds the impression that the defendant was not mentally responsible at the time of the killing.

Always Earl's examination of witnesses had a definite object in view from the asking of his first question. If he were not driving carefully toward some preconceived conclusion, he was engaged in angering those on the stand to the end that they would become confused in their damaging testimony against his side of the case at bar.

Few lawyers knew more about the law of evidence than Rogers. Added to this was his deep insight into the psychology of witnesses and prosecutors so that in an especially difficult case he was more than ordinarily dangerous to the prosecution. In the Hardy case Rogers was particularly offensive to the prosecution, in his attitude towards both the state's witnesses and attorneys. More than once he angered prosecutors by his contemptuous attitude towards important witnesses and he capped the climax in his baiting tactics by telling both of the prosecutors, Ford and Hammon, that when he took over the witness then on the stand for cross-examination he would make him say just exactly what he wanted him to. In response to this taunt Ford retorted:

"Well, Earl, what are you going to make him say?"

"He's going to testify that the defendant was insane," was the smiling boast.

The man on the stand was Tom Davin, a peppery Irishman who told a very damaging story of the shooting. Hammon was questioning him and as he finished and indicated that counsel for the defense could interrogate him, Ford whispered to Rogers:

"Come on, Earl, with your miracle."

Rogers approached the witness.

"Mr. Davin," he began suavely, "didn't you turn to one of

the persons present directly after the shooting and say, 'Beat it, fellows, he's hog wild'?"

Ford was on his feet with an objection which was promptly overruled.

Rogers smilingly turned to the witness, after a side grin at Ford.

"You did say something like that, didn't you, Mr. Davin?"

The remainder of Davin's testimony as supplied by the transcript follows:

DAVIN: Yes, I guess I did say something like that.

ROGERS: Well then, what did you mean by "beat it"?

DAVIN: Well, what I meant by "beat it" was to back up.

ROGERS: Pack?

DAVIN: No, not pack—*back, back up!*

ROGERS: "Beat it" means to back up?

DAVIN: Sure. Back up. American slang phrase.

ROGERS: What did you mean by "hog wild"?

DAVIN: It's an American slang phrase.

ROGERS: Well, what does it mean in English?

DAVIN: What does it mean in English, you say?

ROGERS: Yes, "hog wild." What did you mean by it, in English?

DAVIN: It's just slang.

ROGERS: You have been in this country how long, Mr. Davin?

DAVIN: Thirty-three years.

ROGERS: You have been talking English all this time?

DAVIN: What do you think I've been talking? (*The witness was clearly nettled.*)

Rogers figured that his quarry was ready for the kill. He advanced upon him until their persons almost touched. The face of the witness was a deep red. His "Irish was up." Rogers shoved his index finger almost into the flaming visage of the witness. His voice resembled the staccato bark of a machine gun.

"Tom Davin," he demanded, "by 'hog wild', you meant that the defendant was crazy, didn't you, crazy as a hog?"

The voice of the witness almost matched that of his tormentor as he yelled back wrathfully, "Yes, that's what I meant; crazy as a hog!"

"That will be all, Mr. Davin; thank you." Earl smiled as he backed to his chair although he was almost bowled over by Prosecutor Ford rushing up to repair the damage. But the still wrathful witness, with true Celtic perverseness, could not be led into any statement that would nullify or minimize his admission that he thought the defendant was crazy.

Rogers with this entering wedge produced a mass of depositions from Hardy's former home in Kentucky to the effect that the defendant had been a victim of dipsomania since youth, some of the sworn statements recounting that when under the influence of liquor he displayed all the symptoms of epilepsy. This evidence Earl proceeded to crystallize through his medically erudite cross-examination of Doctor Robert V. Day.

"Doctor," was Rogers' opening question, "will you describe the symptoms of the disease of dipsomania, as distinguished from inebriety or drunkenness?"

DR. DAY: Dipsomania is a disease that is essentially in the first place that of a degenerate.

ROGERS: Does it resemble epilepsy?

DR. DAY: It is similar in many ways and is generally considered, according to the best modern thought, analogous to epilepsy.

ROGERS: How, as to intervals, does it occur?

DR. DAY: It comes on periodically at intervals of varying length, frequently is known as a quarterly drunkenness. The periods may extend over weeks or months, depending on the case, or attacks, of that particular individual. Usually commences as premonitory symptoms in the way of depressions, uneasiness; the individual wants to do something, he knows not what.

ROGERS: Are those periods ushered in by uncontrollable desire to drink?

DR. DAY: Frequently he has an intense desire to drink right at the start; at other times the beginning of his alcoholic excesses is days coming on; but finally he has an uncontrollable desire to drink. He does not wish to, but cannot help himself, and as soon as he begins drinking he has the full toxic effect of alcohol, no matter in what form it is taken, although for the first two or three hours he may take very large quantities and still not show any visible effects of his indulgence.

ROGERS: Yet chronic inebriety and dipsomania are essentially different, are they not, Doctor?

DR. DAY: Yes. Chronic inebriety usually has exterior causes for the drinking. That is, something may go against him, and the disappointment drive him to drink. Or he may go to a banquet where he inadvertently takes the first drink, or go out with a roistering party of men—he may get started in many ways, but he doesn't experience the terrible obsession characteristic of dipsomania.

ROGERS: Is dipsomania regarded as a disease?

DR. DAY: It is.

ROGERS: And does the medical profession attempt to treat it by medicine?

DR. DAY: It does.

Counsel for the defense concluded his examination of the medical witness with a long hypothetical question including a summary of the depositions concerning Hardy's alleged dipsomania, the events preceding the killing of Moore, and ending with the query, "In your judgment, Doctor, at the time of this alleged killing would that man know the difference between right and wrong with respect to that killing?"

DR. DAY: He would not.

[185]

The fiery Ford went after Dr. Day mercilessly in his cross-examination, but was unable to develop a flaw in the expert's testimony. On the contrary, the doctor tied up the prosecutor in technical knots that he couldn't undo, and when Ford's violent questioning was completed Day's evidence actually had been strengthened for the defense. Dr. Day was one of the medical trio who had taught Earl surgery and medicine, and the lawyer in turn had instructed them well in the finesse of making prosecution attorneys look foolish.

As his last witness Rogers called to the stand a cousin of the defendant, who testified that for days preceding the alcoholic debauch which had culminated in Moore's death, Hardy had been behaving irrationally, alternating between intensive study of the Bible and spells of profane denunciation of the world and all the inhabitants thereof.

Rogers' strategy in offering his strangely inconsistent defense was made clear during his argument to the jury. It was made evident that had he depended entirely upon a plea of insanity he would have found his evidence insufficient to convince the jury beyond a reasonable doubt that Hardy was wholly incompetent, or that the killing was anything less than a brutal murder. Although he avoided any outright claim of constitutional or congenital insanity, he paraded before the jury his convincing array of testimony concerning the defendant's periodic spells of irresponsibility by which he succeeded in implanting in the consciousness of the jurors apprehension lest they wrongfully punish a man who had been unaware of the nature of his act.

When the jury brought in a verdict of manslaughter, Rogers turned to the chagrined prosecutor.

"You should have listened to me in the first place, Joe," he declared smilingly. "You could have put in the last ten days to good advantage at law school."

To which Ford replied in words that could hardly be reproduced in these pages.

CHAPTER XXI

ABOUT a quarter of a century ago, the City of Los Angeles, which had been rapidly nearing metropolitan proportions, began to suffer from moral growing pains.

Retired farmers from the Middle West and well-to-do business men from the same region who had amassed a competence, through some phase of mob psychology, began flocking to Southern California. Those who wished to continue active purchased orange groves or went into the real estate business. Those who felt they had worked long enough bought income property and devoted most of their time to pitching horse-shoes and reading the home-town papers.

These straight-laced folk who came in a constantly increasing flow from the cities, villages and farms of the nation's middle reaches were wholly out of sympathy with the affable old-timers of the West. Soon the mellow tones of the mission bells began to sound but dimly through the pious exhortations of earnest pastors horrified by what they conceived to be the carnalities and crimes of flaming youth; people long accustomed to look askance upon home-town neighbors who condoned even the fragrance of hops could not find it in their crusading souls to tolerate the easy-going and ungodly spirit born of the glamor and magic of California's fruitful vines.

For three hundred years, from the brave days of the first *conquistadores* to the no less happy Spanish-American régime of the Nineties, California's spirit had remained as sunny as its boasted climate.

But now the Midwest Puritans were invading the pleasant land of the Padres and the Dons, and before Los Angeles realized it the community had become a Middle West city. The incoming folk from the corn belt now outnumbered the native sons and daughters. A new spirit of sanctification was slowly but surely permeating the normally liberal-minded town. Before she knew it Los Angeles had a conscience.

Of course it was a tremendous surprise for the old-timers to learn that horse racing was a creation of old man Satan. From the far days when the *hacendados* of Monterey came annually to the City of the Angels to run their magnificent silver-maned dun horses against the superb steeds of the southern Dons, and to wager anything from money to fat herds on their animals' flashing speed, the institution of horse racing had been regarded there as mankind's noblest pastime. And the first wave of Anglo-Saxon pioneers had aimed to perpetuate the sport of kings by bringing their own Blue Grass thoroughbreds to contend with the older Spanish stock of the Far West. The warm Southwestern sun never shone on more stirring scenes than those first meetings of animals of both racial strains.

The Dons had gradually, if reluctantly, given up their bull-fighting; even the gay annual Fiesta when, with no sense of impropriety, merrymakers of both sexes for one evening in the twelvemonth happily quaffed their wine and beer together at the city's bars, was gradually fading before the stern glare of the invaders; and now, sadly, the native born were coming to realize that they were to see an end also of the fleet horses' inspiring speed.

Of course it was equally astounding to the bewildered pioneers that municipally controlled and medically regulated prostitution was even worse than horse racing, and that gambling in any form from betting on the ponies to a game of monte or poker was a certain road to ruin.

So, while the thoughtlessly placid natives shook their heads in wonderment, the city's long-haired stepsons and short-haired stepdaughters determined to clean up the community and make it more worthy of the title City of the Angels.

Leadership of the crusaders fell to, or was assumed by, Edwin T. Earl, one of Southern California's wealthiest men, who had amassed a fortune in organizing the orange shipping industry. Millionaire Earl owned a newspaper, the *Evening Express,* and he had ambitions to rule California politically. So he started the vice war to rid Los Angeles of all those things offensive to eyes, ears, and souls of the expatriates from the land of the tall corn and the prize hogs.

Naturally the first object of attack was the city administration, and Mayor Harper, its chief executive, was singled out for the initial assault. Harper had declined to close the redlight district, at the behest of the reformers, on the theory that segregated vice was preferable to the unregulated sort. He, like all the old-timers, could not be horrified by the presence near the historic Plaza of a street or two devoted to the happy-go-lucky dalliance that had gone virtually unnoted since not long after Governor Felipe de Neve had founded El Pueblo de Nuestra Señora Reina de Los Angeles back in 1781.

As segregated districts ran, that of Los Angeles was well regulated and gave the police little trouble. It was a colorful and vivacious spot, a place where male visitors and the proverbial tired business men went as often for dancing, gay badinage and cheerful companionship as for any other purpose.

And it was not lacking in variety. There were the more aristocratic parlor houses, with ornate ball-rooms and vigorous pianists, for the discriminating; rows of cribs for the less fortunate—or less fastidious—patrons, where along the sidewalks cheery strumpets of many races exchanged robust gibes and Rabelaisian quips with ogling males, though the watchful police never permitted them to wax too boisterous. It was the invariable rule that all of the girls had to be back in the district from visits to the downtown cafés and theaters by midnight. The term "restricted district" was no misnomer.

But all this was anathema to the folk from the sections where beer had been banned and cigarettes outlawed.

Desultory efforts had been made by the forces of reform to abate these conditions, but they had met with little success. Then Millionaire Earl hit upon a happy idea. He would employ Earl Rogers to make a thorough investigation of vice conditions, especially as related to the city administration. If anyone knew vice conditions, he figured it would be the spectacular criminal lawyer. And Rogers' knowledge was not founded upon any hearsay.

Of course it was necessary to link vice with public officials in order to eliminate the evils under attack and the lawyer was known to be sufficiently resourceful to accomplish that end. The move was a smart one also for another reason: there was always the possibility that those opposing the reformers might themselves engage Rogers.

The wealthy publisher gave the attorney carte blanche, and Earl put a crew of private detectives to work. The official investigator himself did a lot of personal investigating. High city officials were connected with the payment of protection money by the vice bosses. Mayor Harper, under fire officially and personally, resigned rather than be subjected to a recall election.

The forces of evil, the cohorts of the devil, the servants of Satan, were routed. Parlor houses and cribs were padlocked for the first time in the history of the city. The girls were scattered throughout the rooming houses of Los Angeles. Poker games were silent. A haze of holiness heavy as a Pittsburgh pall settled upon the disgruntled pioneers.

Los Angeles was at last "chemically pure," the phrase coined a while later by the city's favorite literary son and severest critic, Willard Huntington Wright, who has since undergone transition to S. S. Van Dine, weaver of mystery tales.

Simultaneously with the regeneration of the Angel City there was in progress an industrial conflict that was rapidly approaching a peak. For years leaders of organized labor had been repulsed in their efforts to unionize Los Angeles. The organized and well-financed mercantile and manufacturing elements of the city were determined to keep Los Angeles from following in the wake of San Francisco. Just overnight from Los Angeles, the city at the Golden Gate was perhaps the most thoroughly union dominated municipality in the nation.

It might not be out of order to review briefly the long drawn out struggle prior to the tragic Los Angeles denouement.

For more than half a generation prior to 1910 America's war of the classes had been increasing in magnitude, each recurring clash between capital and labor rendering the opposing hosts more determined, more implacable. Beginning with the American Railway Union's strike of 1894 which for a time completely tied up industry throughout the United States, resulted in the destruction of the railroad employees' organization and sent their leader, Eugene V. Debs, to prison, the succeeding years were marked by constantly expanding disturbance and mounting violence. By 1905 the Department of Labor reported more than 2,000 strikes for that year alone.

Strengthening their respective commands after each battle, the leaders of big industry and of the toilers became more ruthless with the passing of every month, until at times the wide-flung conflict assumed almost the proportions of national revolution.

When generals of big industry invoked the power of the Federal government by injunction against picketing and even at times against the calling of strikes, labor unions, believing such actions to be unlawful invasions of their rights as American citizens, retaliated by organized attacks upon their enemies, manhandling strike breakers and dispersing the private detectives and other mercenaries hired to protect plants affected by the striking workers. When troops were sent against them they retaliated with dynamite.

In the West the struggle between Capital and Labor was, during the middle years of that decade, most desperate in the mining districts. Plants in the Coeur d'Alene section of Idaho were destroyed by nitroglycerine, regular army troops patrolled the mine and mill towns; members of the Western Federation of Miners were deported.

Governor Steunenberg of Idaho was assassinated by a bomb which exploded as he opened the gate at his home. Soon Clarence Darrow for the miners and William E. Borah for the prosecution were waging a bitter court battle over the fate of Moyer, Pettibone and Hayward, union leaders accused of the chief executive's murder. The state alleged that the trio were involved in widespread conspiracies of which Steunenberg's death was but a relatively small item. Darrow won in a historic court fight and became labor's mouthpiece.

The Western hard-rock miners, like their militant contemporaries, the Structural Iron Workers, were mostly of American stock, forceful and unafraid; wholly different from the Middle West and Eastern coal miners, who, mostly of recently imported European stock, were cowed by what was to them the mysterious power of courts and police. The industrial battle of the Coeur d'Alenes grew into a general strike of the Western Federation of Miners that covered practically all of the Western states. A railway station at Victor, Colorado, was destroyed by dynamite and more than thirty killed. Investigation by that state's legislative body resulted in a report that anarchy existed with equal violence in the ranks of the mine owners and those of the workers.

By 1910 the wave of industrial turbulence had involved

the country's entire building industry. Steel skeletons of skyscrapers in the largest cities were being destroyed by explosions, bridges in course of construction everywhere were suffering a like fate, cars filled with building material were being burned in the yards. Each side blamed the destruction upon the other. United States troops, state militia, swarms of strikebreaking private detectives, who by that time were frankly professional gunmen, were being thrown against the ranks of union labor. In railway strikes mail cars were being hooked onto practically every train in motion that Federal injunctions might be secured by the heads of the railway companies. Constantly the conspiracy laws were being magnified to help break the strength of the workingmen. In the important court struggles Clarence Darrow invariably appeared in behalf of the workers.

As a result of the increasing domination of organized labor's strength in San Francisco, the owners of industrial plants there had begun moving their businesses to Los Angeles. In the Southern California community the anti-union forces, led by belligerent Civil War veteran General Harrison Gray Otis, had withstood every effort to make a breach in their impregnable open-shop stronghold. The energetic and forceful soldier-publisher had inspired the formation of the Merchants & Manufacturers Association, a powerful organization whose chief function was that of combatting the entrance of crafts unions into their city.

With his puissant newspaper, the *Los Angeles Times,* and backed by the thoroughly systematized and well-financed body behind him, Otis was not only the commandant of anti-unionism's highest citadel, but the moral force which his city and he were lending to all others warring against organized labor had become of greater strength than any other influence on that side of the class war.

So Los Angeles became the battleground of the most decisive engagement in the world's greatest industrial war, at least its most dramatic encounter. Organized workers everywhere contributed to the support of those who moved to the attack against the open shop as symbolized by Los Angeles; the Erectors Association, suffering heavily from the direct action blows of the Structural Iron Workers, opened their treasury to the forces led by General Otis, as did the heads of most other large industries. Before that fateful struggle in Los Angeles had ended the uneasy attention of the whole civilized world was focussed upon what proved to be America's Waterloo in the titanic struggle between Labor and Capital.

The conflict reached its climax in the fall of 1910 in the destruction of the *Los Angeles Times* building by a dynamite bomb which caused the loss of twenty-one lives. Infernal machines that had failed to explode were found at the homes of General Otis and F. J. Zeehandelaar, active head of the Merchants & Manufacturers Association.

CHAPTER XXII

THE destruction of the *Los Angeles Times* building occurred shortly after midnight October 1, 1910, and those whose lives were lost in the flames which rapidly consumed the building were all engaged in getting out the paper—editors, printers, and other newspaper workers.

The fiery General Otis immediately accused the labor unions of responsibility for the holocaust. There was nothing equivocal about his charges. There never was about whatever the General said for or against anything in the editorial and news columns of his paper.

Much indignation was expressed by the papers throughout the country which were in sympathy with organized labor. Few big city publications agreed with the stand of the *Times*. Labor leaders and other champions of unionism throughout the country denounced the explosion either as a frame-up by the anti-union forces or insisted that the explosion was accidental; caused by defective gas connections. The building was old and something of a firetrap as was evidenced by its rapid destruction after the explosion.

Prominent labor leaders journeyed to California with experts to prove their contention that the *Times* disaster was the result of an accident. More violent partisans charged that Otis had planned the explosion himself as a means of discrediting the unions and that the fire was an unforeseen sequel.

The Merchants & Manufacturers Association took charge of the situation. Captain John D. Fredericks, the district attorney of Los Angeles County, was in nominal charge of the case, but when the organization of business men raised a special fund of $100,000 before nightfall on the day after the disaster, its leaders sought aid in other quarters. A lengthy conference resulted in the hiring of Earl Rogers. Big business of Los Angeles had had little use for Earl, whom it regarded as something of a charlatan whose chief vocation in life was cheating the gallows of its legitimate prey. But big business realized that a crisis had been reached in the long-drawn-out battle with the unions to keep Los Angeles the open-shop capital of the United States. So, believing that Rogers working on the side of law and order could show the same resourcefulness that he had for years demonstrated on the other side, big business engaged him to aid in running down the criminals who were responsible for the destruction of the *Times* and its employees.

The entire $100,000 was placed at the disposal of Rogers, who was made a special deputy district attorney. He was given a couple of sticks of dynamite and carte blanche. The dynamite was the only clue, obtained from the infernal machine planted at the Otis home and which had failed to explode.

It was an unusual rôle for him, but Rogers assumed it with enthusiasm. His chief aides were Harry Dehm, an attorney on his staff, and Sam Browne, a detective in the district attorney's office.

The dynamite was traced by Rogers and his assistants to an explosive factory near San Francisco. The trail eventually led to the McNamara brothers, and although little publicity for that service was ever given the attorney, those responsible for his employment credited him with bringing in the first evidence directly linking labor leaders with the *Times* explosion.

In this secret investigation Rogers found himself working side by side with his erstwhile bitter enemy of the San Francisco graft cases, William J. Burns, who with District Attorney Fredericks reaped most of the credit for the solution of the dynamiting mystery. But it was Rogers, representing the prosecution, who presented the case to the grand jury, which resulted in the sensational indictments against J. B. Mc-Namara and his accomplices, chief of whom was his brother J. J. McNamara, leader of the Iron Workers Union, which had its headquarters in Indianapolis.

There is a heretofore unwritten chapter of the sensational denouement to the historic capital-labor war that may be set down here for the first time.

The key figure in the state's case—the man who played Nemesis to organized labor—was Ortie McManigal, self-confessed dynamiter in the employ of the Iron Workers. Malcolm MacLaren, a former Burns detective in the employ of the state, had brought him in and obtained from him an amazing confession. In fact it was so fantastic that he was at first regarded as a highly accomplished liar.

Without referring to any notes, the prisoner gave the prosecution an astounding memory demonstration, reciting scores of dynamite outrages he had committed in behalf of the union. He told of his movements chronologically, giving dates and places and incidents in connection with the destruction of steel work in process of erection. Upon investigation the story checked up in every detail as to time and place of the explosions. But McManigal's confession had little or no support. Although the McNamaras were indicted chiefly on his statement, J. B. for the actual dynamiting and J. J. as the instigator, the prosecution feared there was insufficient corroborative evidence to bring about convictions.

The whole country was aroused by the arrests and most of the union men of the nation believed that the prisoners were innocent and were being railroaded to the gallows by manufactured evidence. A defense fund had been contributed by hundreds of thousands of workers and by the American Federation of Labor, whose officials were taking an active interest in the trial. McManigal was widely denounced in labor circles as a tool of Capital. Labor leaders practically defied the prosecution to obtain any support for the dynamiter's sensational confession.

The trial was about to begin, with Clarence Darrow as chief counsel for the defense. The prosecution knew that practically all of the corroborative evidence needed reposed in the vaults of the Iron Workers Union in Indianapolis, where J. J. McNamara had been apprehended. McManigal had told them that there were copies of letters in the files of the union leader giving specific instruction to the actual dynamiters, as well as documentary evidence to substantiate the charges of illegal interstate transportation of explosives—as alleged in the various charges against J. J. McNamara. The informer also declared that explosives were stored in these same office vaults and allotted to the dynamiters.

Efforts were made by Captain Fredericks as leader of the prosecution to obtain the coöperation of the Indiana state authorities as well as of the Federal officials at the Indiana capital. These efforts were unavailing because of the political influence of the labor leaders. The prosecution was up against it. The anti-union powers were in a panic. They felt that their evidence against the indicted men was true, but feared it would prove insufficient in court. They realized that if no convictions were obtained they would have to bow to the steel workers' reign of terrorism. Millions were at stake, as well as the future of the entire structural steel industry. It was at this crucial stage that it was determined to appeal to the nation's highest official, the President.

President Taft was on a tour of the West preliminary to the campaign of 1912 which proved so disastrous to him. He was due shortly in Los Angeles for a two-day visit to discuss with the Republican leaders of Southern California plans for his renomination. General Otis was one of those leaders—a power in the party.

There was no time to lose, as the task of getting a jury

to try James B. McNamara, charged with murder as the actual dynamiter of the *Times*, was already in progress in Judge Bordwell's court.

It was most obviously an extremely delicate matter to ask the President of the United States to intervene in a capital-labor issue on the eve of a presidential election at which he hoped to succeed himself. The McNamara case had already become a political issue in a bitter municipal election in Los Angeles with Job Harriman, one of the defense attorneys, an active candidate for mayor of the city on the Socialist ticket.

Throughout the country, particularly in important centers of population, the capital-labor strife had reached a crisis as a result of the Los Angeles arrests. Those who were about to appeal to the nation's Chief Executive realized that millions of votes would be affected by any publicity given to presidential intervention and that even a less astute politician than William Howard Taft would sense the danger to his own political future. But it seemed to be the only recourse left for those who were behind the prosecution.

The arrival of President Taft was an important event in the city of Los Angeles and it was celebrated with a huge street parade and social activities that took up most of the Chief Executive's time. The night before he came in from San Francisco, there was an important conference at the home of General Otis at which it was determined to make the appeal to the President directly following a reception on the night before his departure.

President Taft made his Los Angeles headquarters at the home of his brother-in-law, Dr. Edwards, where the chief social function in his honor was given on the night of October 17, 1911. He was to leave the following morning for Salt Lake City on what the political writers called his "swing around the circle."

The Chief Executive had readily agreed to listen to a statement of the Los Angeles industrial situation in which he had evinced much interest and it was agreed to have the meeting occur in an upstairs room of the Edwards home after the last guests had departed.

Only three were present, the President, General Otis and Oscar Lawler. Lawler was attorney for the Merchants & Manufacturers Association and the person responsible for drafting Earl Rogers in the dynamite investigation. He had been United States District Attorney for Southern California and was prominent in the councils of the Republican party. Mr. Lawler, the only survivor of the historic conference, was selected to act as spokesman and he quickly laid before the President the facts regarding the dynamiting. General Otis supported his argument that justice could be obtained only through Federal aid. Justice, in this case, meant the conviction of the labor leaders.

The President hesitated. Then the General appealed to the Chief Executive on the broad general ground that if justice were done in this instance there would be an immediate clarification of all labor and capital issues throughout the country. The General said he knew that it was a delicate matter, and that he had considered the possibility of serious political damage to the President's campaign for re-election.

President Taft was impressed. He asked what, specifically, was wanted of him. Mr. Lawler told him that the United States Attorney General had the power to seize the vaults of the general offices of the Iron Workers Union in Indianapolis and that conclusive evidence would be found therein that there had been wholesale violations of the Federal law against transporting dynamite.

President Taft pondered the matter briefly. Then he arose and came to the side of Lawler, who had been standing throughout the interview. He placed his hand on the attorney's shoulder.

"You have been examining the facts in this matter for a long time, Oscar," he began impressively. "Have I your assurance, as one lawyer to another, that there has been a violation of the Federal laws and that by the means which you suggest the facts can be made available and the guilty parties brought to justice?"

"I replied in the affirmative," declared Mr. Lawler in telling of the meeting. Then the President walked over to General Otis, who had risen with him. "General," he said, "it is my duty as President to see that the laws are faithfully executed. Whatever effect the performance of that duty may have on popular opinion or on votes is of no consequence. Justice must take its course. If you do not hear from Attorney General Wickersham tomorrow, telegraph me at Salt Lake City."

A day or two later Federal authorities seized the contents of the vaults in the Indianapolis offices of the Iron Workers Union and the Los Angeles prosecution had the evidence which validated the confession of Ortie McManigal.

A little more than a month after that, the country was astounded by news that while the jury was still being selected to try James B. McNamara, both of the brothers had changed their plea to guilty. James B., pleading guilty to murder, was sentenced to San Quentin for life and J. J. was sentenced to spend fifteen years in the same prison.

Recently published books have made much of this startling debacle in one of the nation's most celebrated cases. In several of them it has been credited to the altruistic activities of Lincoln Steffens. In that publicist's autobiography, and in that of Clarence Darrow, Steffens is given credit for the sensational termination of one of the greatest gambles in modern industrial history, for it was generally regarded as the last stand of those militant leaders who had invoked the use of sabotage in its most extreme form, dynamite.

Yet Steffens had little to do with the actual denouement, according to those who participated in the final negotiations. The fate of the McNamaras was really sealed when President

Taft made it possible for the prosecution to complete its chain of evidence against the labor leaders. But their defense actually crumbled to dust when it was alleged that Darrow, their chief counsel, was implicated in the act of tampering with the jury.

It is generally conceded that Steffens did work indefatigably and zealously to bring about peace between Labor and Capital through a compromise in the dynamiting cases. But a score of years later those most closely identified with the prosecution, newspapermen covering the trial, and intimates of grizzled old, fire-eating, union-hating General Otis, laugh uproariously at the Steffens story that the *Times* publisher had agreed to any sort of compromise.

The good faith or honesty of Mr. Steffens has never been questioned, but those most familiar with that situation insist that if Steffens thought he had conferred with General Otis, he must have been a victim of mistaken identity. For it is related by Harry Chandler, son-in-law of the General and present publisher of the *Times,* that General Otis learned of the deal for the first time on the day of the court climax when it fell to the lot of Mr. Chandler and District Attorney Fredericks to break the news to the old gentleman. It was with fear and trembling that they broached the matter to him in the Otis home, according to Mr. Chandler. It is related that the General was instantly convulsed with rage when told that the state had agreed to accept pleas of guilty from the dynamiting brothers and that they were to be given sentences in the penitentiary.

General Otis, as expected, became furious at the prosecution's plan. He stormed about, declaring: "I want those sons-of-bitches to hang!" It was some time before he could be placated by the argument that it would be much better for his own cause if the trial were ended this way. It was pointed out to him that in pleading guilty the defendants would be denied the certain martyrdom that would be accorded them if convicted by trial, no matter how conclusive the case against them.

It has even been intimated that Steffens was the unconscious means by which panic was thrown into the ranks of the defense by carrying to Darrow information purposely dropped by the prosecution as to the impregnability of the state's case.

The press of Los Angeles did not at all accept the Steffens version of the manner in which the Golden Rule was brought into play to end the noted conflict. Local newspapermen knew Otis too well, and they knew what was happening to Darrow. The Associated Press man, David Lawrence, then a young reporter sent out from the East to cover the trial, was the only one who gave any credit to Steffens in his story, which declared that the climax was "brought about by methods unheard of in the prosecution of criminals."

According to the chief prosecutor, Captain Fredericks, the defense had been ready to sacrifice J. B. McNamara ever since the Indianapolis evidence had been obtained, but the question of a guilty plea by his brother never entered into the situation until Darrow's arrest on a charge of jury bribery. Evidence had been brought to the district attorney some time previously that Darrow had drawn large sums from a bank in San Francisco and another in Washington, D. C., mostly in $1,000 bills. This was the money allegedly used in the asserted bribing.

The prospective juror involved was George Lockwood, a Civil War veteran, who notified the district attorney that Bert Franklin, jury investigator for the defense, had offered him $5,000 if he qualified as a juror and voted for acquittal. When Lockwood told his story to Fredericks, an old friend, the latter advised him to go through with the deal in the interests of justice. Lockwood informed the prosecutor that Darrow's side had also told him that Robert Bain, a juror already accepted by both sides, would be "company" for him.

The Lockwood deal was said to have been consummated on a street corner in downtown Los Angeles and, according to the evidence brought out at the trial, Darrow was in the immediate vicinity and presumably a witness to the passage of the money. Franklin was arrested and jailed, and the following day LeCompte Davis, an associate of Darrow in the McNamara defense, called at the district attorney's office to arrange for Franklin's bail. He asked Fredericks what he was going to do about Franklin, according to the prosecutor's version of the incident.

"Depends upon what you're going to do about the McNamaras," replied the district attorney. He said that "things might be arranged by the two McNamaras pleading guilty."

"But J. J. isn't on trial," protested Davis.

On the following day Darrow appeared at the prosecutor's office, accompanied by Davis. Fredericks delivered an ultimatum that the bribery prosecutions would go on unless J. J. McNamara also entered a plea of guilty. His brother had already agreed to accept life sentence. He had even declared a willingness to go to the gallows if his brother were allowed freedom.

Darrow argued that J. J. McNamara symbolized Union Labor and that a plea of guilty on his part would crush the labor movement. He would never agree to such a plea.

"He'd better do it now," Fredericks replied, "because Mrs. Bain is sitting out there in the next room and is about ready to come through."

"Bain?" queried Darrow.

"You know Bain, who is on the jury," retorted Fredericks; "*You* know all about him!"

Silently Darrow motioned to Davis and they departed. A short time later Fredericks received a telephone message from Darrow that J. J. McNamara had been induced to plead guilty.

[204]

That is the former prosecutor's version of the incidents leading up to the collapse of the McNamara defense. The press agreed generally that there was a definite relation between it and Darrow's predicament.

CHAPTER XXIII

WHEN Clarence Darrow came to the Coast to defend the McNamaras one of his first moves was to make overtures to Earl Rogers to assist him. But Rogers could not do so. He had taken a prominent part in bringing the dynamiting brothers to the bar of justice and, even had he wanted to aid Darrow, he would have been disqualified.

However, when Darrow learned that there was no disposition on the part of the state to let down on him now that his clients were in San Quentin, his first thought was that Rogers was the man to defend him on the indictments charging him with jury bribery. There was no ethical reason why Rogers shouldn't, but Darrow, fearful and uncertain, delayed engaging him.

Finally, when the decision could be put off no longer, Darrow learned that Rogers was pleading a case in the Central California town of Hanford, so he decided to go there and carefully observe Rogers in action before determining whether he would use him in the desperate battle which must be waged if Darrow himself were to be saved from joining the McNamaras behind the gray walls of San Quentin.

Darrow, accompanied by his wife, went to Hanford where they saw Rogers in action in what, even though not a murder trial, was one of his greatest courtroom achievements. The litigation centered upon an apparently hopeless attempt to break the will of the late Patrick Talent, a wealthy land owner who had made a fortune in Montana mines before coming to California.

Some time before his death Talent had brought from Ireland two nephews, James and Richard McHale, brothers. He had promised to provide a living for them and see that they were generously remembered in his will. When Talent died, however, his only will, made on his deathbed, bequeathed all of his estate to his widow and made her the executrix. The nephews had no evidence that Talent was not in full possession of his senses when he signed the will cutting them off without a penny. But the contest was based upon that allegation.

Rogers had been engaged by the contestants when other attorneys had told them that the case seemed practically hopeless.

Beyond the unsupported word of the nephews their side had nothing whatever upon which to base their case, not an iota of evidence as to the conditions under which the will was drawn, so Rogers had to depend wholly upon what he could get in the way of testimony from those who had been subpoenaed for the defendant.

The chief witnesses for the widow were the attorney who had drawn the will, and a wealthy grain grower and long time friend of the dead man, named Phillip Ray. Under direct examination Ray had told a perfectly sound story of witnessing the signing of the will. Then the Los Angeles lawyer took him in hand.

Rogers began an interminable line of examination that after an hour had completely tired the judge, jury, and the witness. The court more than once regarded Rogers impatiently, seemed on the verge of warning him that the case could not be dragged along in that baseless manner indefinitely. But Rogers continued doggedly. Apparently fishing blindly for some possible opening, in reality he had his case thoroughly mapped out from the beginning. No matter how aimless his questioning at any phase of a case might seem, his cross-examinations always were directed toward some definite goal.

After questioning Ray about all the incidents the latter

could recall of his many years' close friendship with Talent, he finally got down to the day of the will's signing, and then launched upon a line of examination that seemed more useless and tiring than the hours of questioning which had preceded. He asked Ray at what time he arose that morning.

"What did you do then, Mr. Ray?" queried Rogers in his pleasant voice.

"I read the morning paper."

"And then?"

"I ate my breakfast."

"What did you do after breakfast?"

"I went to my office."

Earl droned on, asking humdrum questions, apparently without point, lulling court, jury, spectators, and witnesses alike into sleepiness as the warm Hanford afternoon made all living things drowsy. But always as he questioned he kept recurring to the life-long friendship of the two men.

"Was there any change in your friendship before Talent died?"

"None."

"At any time in the past had there been any misunderstanding between you?"

"Never," averred Ray; "we were always warm friends."

"And when you signed the will as a witness of your old friend's signature, what then did you do, Mr. Ray?" droned Earl.

"I left."

"Did you bid Patrick Talent good-by before you took your departure?"

"No, I left as soon as I had witnessed his signature."

"*What!*"

The drowsing court and jury were now wide awake, tingling with the dramatic cry of the attorney as he sprang at Ray, and shoved a quivering forefinger almost against the astonished witness's face.

"You mean to tell this court and jury," demanded Rogers in harsh, incredulous tones, "that you, the dear friend, the lifelong friend of Patrick Talent, knowing he was dying, *did not bid him a last good-by?*"

"I don't think I did," faltered the dismayed man on the witness stand.

"You don't *think!* If you bade farewell to your lifelong friend on his deathbed you would not be uncertain about it. You would *know!*

"*Did—you—bid—him—good-by?*"

"No," whispered Ray tremulously.

"If you did not say good-by to your dying friend," Earl solemnly intoned as his blazing eyes held Ray in a state of misery, "there could be only one reason—and that was that you knew he was mentally incapacitated, *that he did not know you!*"

Rogers stood menacingly before the witness, his somber eyes boring into the very consciousness of the other. "Is that not so?" he asked after several uneasy moments.

Ray sat helplessly for many seconds, his worried gaze shifting before the penetrating eyes of his tormentor. He did not reply audibly. But, eventually, he raised both hands midway to his shoulders and shrugged as if to say, "What is the use?"

That shrug of the witness's shoulders was the basis and the text of Rogers' dramatic two-hour plea to the jury to which a crowded courtroom listened in rapt attention. And no listeners were more interested or fascinated than Clarence Darrow and his wife.

But even more drama was crowded into the peroration of his plea to the jury when he called upon his acting ability for as weird a demonstration of theatricalism as has ever been displayed in a courtroom. Having wrung every possible bit of effectiveness out of that fatal shoulder shrug, Earl suddenly turned to the jury.

"Suppose Patrick Talent were to enter this courtroom now," he demanded.

There was a brief pause as Rogers assumed the character of the dead man. He had never seen Patrick Talent, yet those in the courtroom were amazed at his impersonation. He leaned over the rail of the jury box as Talent might have done, startling those members who had known the wealthy Talent.

"Suppose Patrick Talent came within this rail," he declared. "He would ask what this was all about and he would be told that it was about his will. He would be astonished. He would say: 'Why, I never made a will!'"

Rogers, still simulating the Talent mannerisms and even his voice, turned threateningly to the lawyer defending the case:

"Dixon Phillips, you know I never made a will. You know *you* made that will. *I* never did!"

Again Rogers turned to the jury, shaking off his impersonation as quickly as it was assumed. "And, gentlemen of the jury, Dixon Phillips would then jump out of that window!"

The jury returned a verdict for the contestants. The will had been broken.

Darrow was brought to trial for having attempted to corrupt Juror George N. Lockwood, five months after the dramatic end of the McNamaras. The great attorney who had saved so many men from the gallows, who had lifted his voice so often in behalf of the oppressed, who had so courageously fought for human rights against property rights, had undergone a marked change since the day the McNamaras appeared in court for the last time.

In his autobiography Lincoln Steffens says of Darrow: "When people ask me what sort of man Darrow is, I ask them an apparently irrelevant question: When? And my answer is that at three o'clock he is a hero for courage, nerve and calm judgment, but at 3:15 he may be a coward for fear, collapse and panicky mentality."

And now it was 3:15 for Darrow. The hands of the clock moved very little for him during the record-breaking thirteen weeks of the trial. He was in an almost continuous state of panic.

"He cannot conceal much," continues the Steffens analysis; "his face is too expressive."

Time after time during the trial, Rogers railed at Darrow under his breath because of the drooping chin, the fear-stricken eyes that so clearly told his trepidation. At times Darrow was absolutely without hope and only the rough prodding of the Los Angeles lawyer could make him realize that he was providing for the jury "a portrait of guilt," as Earl once put it, within hearing of the row of newspapermen. Only on occasion, when engaged in battling some hostile witness, was Darrow his old self; but he rose to hitherto unoccupied heights when called upon to address the jury in his own behalf.

Strangely enough little is said in Darrow's own life story of Earl Rogers' part in saving him from prison. In fact the inference gained from all of the various books dealing with the trial is that Darrow conducted his own defense.

Yet from the day the trial opened before Judge Hutton, it was Rogers who dominated every movement of the defense. It was Earl's great opportunity, a chance he would not have missed for worlds. It was the first well-timed stage entrance which Fate had offered him to bask in the white light of national publicity since the San Francisco trials, and now he occupied a much more important position. He confided to friends that he felt he had been slipping somewhat and that he needed Darrow almost as much as Darrow needed him. His ego told him that his selection to defend the nation's acknowledged premier criminal lawyer would naturally place him in Darrow's class. Before the trial was over even Darrow was ready to admit Earl's supremacy, especially in the realms of cross-examination and resourcefulness.

Darrow's position was a precarious one. The forces behind the open shop principle were determined to place him behind prison bars. The great structural steel concerns which had suffered most from the dynamiting depredations were said to be heavy contributors to the prosecution.

And, although he was universally regarded as the mouth-piece of union labor and its leading champion, the labor organizations were apparently indifferent to his fate. True, some of the funds for his defense came from the coffers of the American Federation of Labor, but the rank and file of the workers, crushed by the McNamara debacle, showed no interest.

Clarence Darrow, the great unselfish crusader in the cause of the down-trodden toiler, was suspected of having betrayed the McNamaras in their darkest hour to save his own hide. It was a tough spot for the famous pleader. Only a person with histrionic artistry in dissembling such as Rogers possessed could have succeeded in wholly masking his fear.

The Darrow defense staff consisted of Rogers, Harry Dehm, Horace Appel and Jerry Giesler. All have passed except Giesler, then a youngster in Rogers' office, now regarded as the leading criminal lawyer of his city.

The prosecution consisted of the district attorney, Captain John D. Fredericks, his assistant, W. Joseph Ford, who had so many times opposed Rogers, and Arthur Keetch, later elevated to the bench.

It appeared to be a sure case for the prosecution. Bert Franklin, Darrow's jury investigator, had without doubt made a proposition to the veteran George Lockwood. As already stated, the latter, not yet called for examination as a juror, had reported to Fredericks the attempt to corrupt him and the prosecutor had advised him to go through with it. Franklin, Lockwood had told the district attorney, had informed him that Darrow was allowing him to spend $5,000 on each juror purchased; that Franklin was to keep $1,000 of this and give any complaisant juror who agreed to vote for acquittal the remaining $4,000.

A meeting place was arranged at which Lockwood was to receive $500. The remainder of the sum was to be placed in the hands of a stakeholder, a veteran officer named White, to be delivered to Lockwood when the trial was over. Lockwood was told that this procedure had already been followed in the bribery of Juror Bain, then sitting in the jury box.

The place selected for the transfer of the money was a busy intersection in the heart of Los Angeles' wholesale district. As Lockwood accepted the $500, detectives from the district attorney's office swooped down and gathered in the entire group. As there was evidence introduced in the trial that Darrow was in the immediate vicinity at the time, the theory was advanced by the prosecution that his presence in the vicinity was due to his desire to be sure that Franklin didn't double-cross him.

With Bert Franklin turning state's evidence, the case of the prosecution was a veritable mountain of adverse evidence. Darrow's immediate connection with the bribery was sought to be proved by further evidence that he had withdrawn large sums of money from San Francisco and Washington, D. C., banks provided by the McNamara defense. The currency was alleged to have corresponded with that used in the bribery of the jurors, at least the $4,000 seized as Franklin was showing it to Lockwood.

Franklin testified that after his arrest Darrow had arranged for him to plead guilty to one count in the information charging him with attempting to bribe Lockwood, and that "I would be fined the sum of $5,000, which they would pay, and that he would give to me for the protection of my family until I could build myself up in the community, the sum of

$3,000." The following is an excerpt from Rogers' cross-examination as officially reported:

FRANKLIN: Darrow said, "Well, if arrangements can be made for you to plead guilty and get a fine, I will see that you get $3,000."

ROGERS: Isn't it a fact that the district attorney told you these things?

FRANKLIN: No, he did not.

ROGERS: Namely—

FRANKLIN: And you know he didn't!

ROGERS: Back up a moment until I get through with my question.

FORD: I object to the witness being told to back up. It is not a proper way to talk to a witness in court.

ROGERS (*to Ford*): Possibly so. (*Turning to Franklin*): You needn't back up.

Darrow's chief counsel was rarely at fault in matters of law and evidence, often proving the court in error along with the attorneys for the prosecution. Once Franklin refused to testify concerning his conversations with Davis about the former's proposed plan to plead guilty, claiming—and being backed up by the state's attorneys—that such discussions were privileged communications. The court, siding with the prosecution's contention, quoted the Civil Code of Procedure to the effect that such a conversation would come under the head of privileged communications.

Then Rogers quoted a decision by the Supreme Court of California, to the effect that a man who turned state's evidence and attempted to convict others by proof also convicting himself, "must be deemed thereby to have waived the privileges which permit him to withhold anything."

The court hurried to explain that he had not at first understood the question of law before him. Earl grinned.

COURT (*to Franklin*): Under the circumstances the Civil

Code of Procedure does not enable you to avoid the duty of answering the question.

So Earl, as usual, forced the reluctant witness to answer his interrogation.

Throughout the long trial Rogers, himself impervious to baiting, never overlooked an opportunity to keep his opponents on edge by his constant raillery. Fiery Joe Ford, particularly, he kept at boiling point all through the case by constant nagging, thereby handicapping that attorney's unquestioned ability.

"We wish to guard against any manufacturing of witnesses, too," said Ford to Earl during Franklin's cross-examination.

ROGERS: "Manufacturing, too," is a very good locution.

FORD: We want to guard against it.

ROGERS: "Manufacturing, too," means "manufacturing also." I don't object to that.

FORD: We also wish to guard against manufacturing testimony.

ROGERS: Is that an admission?

FORD: Oh, don't get childish!

Franklin and Lockwood were, naturally, the prosecutor's chief witnesses. After having confused Franklin's testimony in the eyes of the jury as much as possible, Rogers made a vicious assault upon the former detective, endeavoring to show that Franklin had actually been in the employ of the district attorney while acting for Darrow. He did not trifle much with Lockwood, who had a good reputation and looked the substantial citizen that he was.

A clash between counsel in the cross-examination by Rogers of John R. Harrington, formerly associated with Darrow in Chicago but now testifying for the prosecution, affords an example of the tense manner in which the opposing attorneys fought over introduction of every bit of testimony submitted, and serves as an interesting illustration of the thin line of demarcation between admissible and non-admissible evidence.

Harrington had testified that Darrow had showed him a roll containing $10,000, which the witness testified Darrow had told him he had drawn from "Tveitmoe's bank"—the bank in which Tveitmoe, a militant leader among labor unionists of San Francisco, kept his money.

ROGERS: How did you come to put that word "Tveitmoe's" in there? Wasn't it because Lawler, U. S. District Attorney, wanted to get Tveitmoe?

FORD: We object to that on the ground that it is not proper cross-examination, to ask how he came to say it.

COURT: Objection sustained.

ROGERS: In cross-examination I may assume—

FREDERICKS (*interrupting Rogers*): The objection has been sustained. There is nothing before the court.

ROGERS: I shall ask it again, then. Didn't you put in that word "Tveitmoe's" to please Mr. Lawler?

FREDERICKS: The same objection, for the same reason.

COURT: Overruled.

HARRINGTON: No, sir.

CHAPTER XXIV

WILLIAM J. BURNS, the detective, was the acknowledged star witness of the prosecution, chiefly because of his prominence and his reputation for honesty and veracity. The strategy to be used with respect to Burns was the subject of numerous arguments between Darrow and Rogers.

Rogers felt that it would be almost impossible to minimize the effect of the detective's testimony. Darrow clung doggedly to the determination to cross-examine Burns himself. Darrow won out, but his handling of the witness had not progressed far when the defendant-lawyer found himself seated at counsel's table and the quizzing of the detective being conducted by Rogers.

It is doubtful if any witness of the prominence of Burns ever underwent the manhandling that Rogers subjected him to. Sparks flew almost continuously and both men were frequently on the verge of physical encounter. Perhaps Burns suffered his worst moments when Rogers in the course of his questions found occasion to comment on the vocation of private detective. He sought to have Burns admit that nothing could be lower in the vocational scale than a private detective. His play of facial expression, the scorn, loathing and taunting triumph with which he regarded the noted sleuth brought from the latter appeals to the court to protect him against further irrelevant questioning. Failing in this, Burns virtually challenged Rogers to meet him in personal combat outside the courtroom.

Darrow had begun his questioning of Burns concerning the detective's testimony on direct examination as to the part one of his men, Guy Biddinger, played in the McNamara case. Burns had said, and Biddinger had corroborated him, that Darrow had sought to corrupt Biddinger, that he had given him an initial payment of $500 to keep Darrow informed of whatever moves were made by the McNamara prosecution. Burns had testified that Biddinger had given him the money and that he had turned it over to the district attorney.

Burns was having little difficulty in offsetting Darrow's queries and the latter became obviously nettled. Throwing up his hands in an expressive gesture, Darrow asked of no one in particular: "What are we trying to prove here at this time by this wonderful man?"

Instantly the ruddy-faced Burns turned a shade more florid as he snapped at Darrow, "I object to your referring to me in that way!"

"The witness's objection is sustained," interjected the court.

"I withdraw it then," hastily declared Darrow, realizing he had placed himself at a disadvantage.

Rogers immediately came to the rescue by intruding himself, demanding, "To what action does the witness refer?"

Rogers had been sitting where he could catch Burns' eye. With his usual craft, though, he had his back toward the bench so that Judge Hutton could not catch the by-play.

"Now, if your Honor please," blurted Burns, angered beyond his usual caution by Rogers' action, "I would like at this time to call your attention to Mr. Rogers' remarks that I carried a sword cane."

"That is not true!" said Rogers heatedly.

"This man also made a statement in the presence of the jury," continued Burns furiously, "that I was a suborner of perjury."

At this Rogers sprang to his feet, shouldering Darrow aside, and advancing towards the witness with pointing finger announced, "I make it again, sir; and do not take it back!"

The detective now was white with anger and Rogers also was quivering with rage. "Your Honor," cried Burns, "I ought to be protected, and be permitted, if you will allow me, to tell here what I know to be true."

Again the court entered the heated discussion, endeavoring to pacify the wrathful disputants. "Mr. Rogers," he warned the attorney, "you have no right to make such comment when the person discussed is on the witness stand."

"Well, he asked for it," retorted Earl. "I was sitting here listening to the cross-examination, annoying neither the witness nor anyone else, when Mr. Burns saw fit to pick a quarrel with me."

Judge Hutton rapped for order. "I shall fine each of you gentlemen twenty-five dollars," he announced.

"It's worth it," declared Rogers, as he borrowed the money from Jerry Giesler and handed it to the clerk.

The cross-examination of Burns lasted for days and was marked by altercations between lawyer and witness that nearly resulted in physical encounters. Once after he had goaded Burns into a fury which left him purple-faced and on the verge of springing from the witness stand, Rogers calmly turned to the court and asked for protection against the witness, who he had heard not only carried a sword cane in the courtroom but a gun as well.

Of the clash between attorney and detective, Joe Timmons wrote in the *Examiner:* "Rogers with his lorgnette took over Burns for cross-examination. Rogers can ask a man his name in a tone that calls him a liar, perjurer and crawling reptile all at once."

On another occasion Rogers sought to offset the effect of a damaging bit of testimony by his old method of staging a scene of violence. He was unable to shake the witness's story, so he went into a maniacal rage and wound up with a verbal barrage that reached its climax when he denounced the witness as a conscienceless perjurer. Judge Hutton interrupted,

excused the jury and fined Rogers $50 for contempt of court
with the alternative of going to jail "from now until nine
o'clock tomorrow morning."

Rogers declared in open court that he would not pay the
fine, nor would he go to jail. He immediately gained his re-
lease on a writ of habeas corpus. When he was called to account the next day, he declared to the court that the sentence
could not be invoked because "from now" had passed as had
"tomorrow at nine o'clock." As he had refused to pay the
fine and the alternative sentence could not be enforced, he
held that there was nothing before the court affecting Earl
Rogers. Judge Hutton took a recess to look up certain matters of law and when court was resumed no reference was
made to the case of contempt. Meanwhile the jury had forgotten just how damaging was the evidence of the witness.

On still another occasion Assistant District Attorney Ford
declared that Rogers was trying to hypnotize a witness. John
R. Harrington was the man on the stand, and Darrow, who
was cross-examining his former employee, was attempting to
show that Harrington had been a secret employee of the
prosecution at the same time.

Harrington's testimony was extremely damaging and Darrow's questioning was doing little good. Suddenly Rogers
rose and asked the court to compel Harrington to face the
jury while testifying. The court so ordered the witness. Then
Rogers quietly took his place near the end of the rail before
the jury box. He stood there silently, his eyes fixed on the
witness and never wavering for an instant. Harrington started
to falter in his replies.

Realizing that his witness was in a bad way, Ford rose
and demanded that Rogers be made to stop trying to hypnotize the witness. The court ruled that the request was not in
order as hypnotism was a science not recognized in his juris-
diction. Harrington's testimony was eventually expunged

from the record on a showing by Rogers that it was inadmissible.

Rogers never let a day pass without some attack on the prosecution, or without invoking his well-known trick of putting some one other than the defendant on trial, and on one occasion he so enraged Ford in the midst of a motion to the court, that the prosecutor tried to hurl a heavy ink bottle at Rogers.

Commenting editorially on the expertness of Rogers in goading an opposition counsel, the *Fresno Republican* of July 12, contrasted this incident with Rogers' performance at San Francisco:

When Heney tilted, as prosecutor, against Earl Rogers as an apologist for crime, he was the "wild man of Borneo" to the staid and more polished members of the San Francisco bar. But now that Fredericks and Ford, prosecutors of Los Angeles, lost their tempers under the goadings of this same Rogers in the Darrow case, nothing is said about the wild man of Borneo. Fredericks and Ford, unlike Heney, are recognized as the socially elect of the profession, but Heney, in the wildest excitement of the Calhoun trials, never tried to throw an ink bottle at Rogers, as Ford tried to the other day. Plainly, as a matter of social etiquette, it all depends upon whose ox Rogers gores.

Earl Rogers unquestionably reached his peak as a great criminal lawyer during this trial. Throughout it he called upon every artifice in his extensive and variegated repertory; and invented a few new ones. There had to be a trump for every trick of the prosecution, fighting a desperate battle to send Clarence Darrow to San Quentin. And he fought with Darrow also.

Time after time, behind the locked doors of Earl's office in the California Building after a court session, Darrow and Earl fought just as desperately as they battled the prosecution. Darrow had his own ideas as to how the next day's proceedings were to be conducted. These were often at variance with those of his chief counsel. On several occasions Rogers threatened to quit him flat if he persisted in some course that Earl believed was wrong.

Concerning these differences of opinion as to strategy, Rogers more than once, when the drinks were coming thick and fast, confided to intimates that he had little respect for Darrow's ability as a lawyer, attributing his success mainly to wide publicity and his wonderful gift in delivering emotional appeals to juries.

The last big argument between the two men was over the subject matter of Darrow's address to the jury which was to close the defense. Darrow had evinced a desire to make such reference to the McNamara dynamiting that might be considered as condoning the offenses of the brothers. Rogers talked him out of it, arguing that the jury would never accept any such condonation and that it would react unfavorably to the defendant. Darrow finally consented to abide by Earl's decision.

Rogers opened for the defense and confined himself to logic rather than to histrionic spellbinding. He knew that Darrow in closing would attend to the sentimental appeal as no other lawyer could. He realized also that something more substantial than an appeal to the emotions should be carried into the jury room, for tears dry very fast. To fix his points in the minds of the twelve men, Rogers had caused a huge chart to be hung from the judge's bench to the opposite wall. On it were lettered the names of the witnesses who had testified for the prosecution, classified under headings according to the nature of their testimony. This was another typical Rogers invention and a highly effective one.

As Rogers padded gracefully before the jury, he punctuated his remarks by dramatically approaching the chart with a long pointer in hand to single out the next victim of his verbal bombardment. The whole burden of his argument was conspiracy against Darrow, and in this manner he closed:

"Will you tell me how any sane, sensible man who knows anything about the law business—and this defendant has been at it for thirty-five years—could make himself go to a detective and say to him: 'Just buy all the jurors you want. I put my whole life, my whole reputation, I put everything I have into your hands. I trust you absolutely. I never knew you until two or three months ago, and I don't know very much about you now; but there you are, go to it!'"

Darrow, who had made many eloquent pleas in the years that had gone, surpassed himself. He was pleading for his own liberty now. The tremor in his voice was not simulated; the tears in his eyes were genuine. It is quite likely that no such moving argument was ever before delivered to a jury.

Wiping his streaming eyes with a handkerchief until it was a sodden ball, he finally flung it to the floor before the listening jurors. From then until he had finished he used the sleeves of his coat to mop the undiminished flow of his grief. Several of the jurymen were in tears. When Darrow reached his peroration, Ben Smith, the hard-boiled official reporter, was crying as though his heart would break, the tears falling thick and fast into his note-book as he took down the speech. Darrow himself was almost at the point of exhaustion as he took his chair. He was trembling as though with ague.

Rogers, as was his wont, had not even waited for Darrow to begin. He had, as usual, gone out in the hall and smoked a succession of cigarettes, waiting for time to listen to the court's instructions.

The instructions required something like thirty minutes. The jury retired and was out a little more than half an hour. The verdict was "not guilty."

The trial had lasted three months and three days, a record for Los Angeles. Darrow publicly acknowledged his gratitude to Rogers. During the trial he had repeatedly told reporters that Earl was by far a greater criminal lawyer than he.

The second Darrow trial was that for the bribery of Juror Bain. It was generally regarded as merely a perfunctory gesture upon the part of the district attorney's office. If with the stronger case the prosecution could not convict Darrow, the second trial seemed merely a legal contest forced upon Fredericks and his aides because of their fear of being called quitters, or perhaps the insistence of the anti-union forces was responsible. Judge Conley of Madera presided.

But Earl sickened before the second trial was well under way. He was told by his physicians that his life and reason depended upon his immediate withdrawal from the case.

Despite his physicians' insistence that he must quit the trial or die, Rogers stubbornly refused to stop until he could finish cross-examining Lockwood, who testified against Darrow in the second trial also.

"I wish to finish questioning Lockwood," he persisted, "and when I am through with him I shall decide whether I can appear again or not."

He did handle the cross-examination with his usual skill, but, rendered supersensitive by illness and piqued by that witness's ability to withstand serenely the most searing questioning, the defense attorney at times got the worst of their cross-fire of caustic repartee.

"So," sneered Earl at one point in his badgering, "you're a public-spirited citizen, who believes in running with information to the district attorney?"

"Yes, Mr. Rogers," retorted Lockwood, "I am a public-spirited citizen and I believe in the exposure of criminals, strange as it may appear to you."

Earl acknowledged this body-blow with a wry smile.

At the end of Lockwood's cross-examination, Judge Conley came down from the bench and pleaded with Rogers to quit;

but the sick lawyer still remaining obdurate, he was taken forcibly in hand by his doctors and put to bed.

The trial then proceeded with Judge Powers, a well known attorney from Salt Lake, added to counsel for the defense. Of the Rogers staff, Jerry Giesler remained throughout the second trial.

Heavy drinking had undoubtedly been a factor in Rogers' illness. Those close to Rogers, however, ascribe his withdrawal from the case chiefly to differences of opinion with Darrow, partly over finances. During the interim between the first verdict and the beginning of the second trial, Rogers also had been in court almost continuously in other cases and was in poor physical and mental condition.

Without Rogers to restrain him, Darrow did what he had wanted to do in the first trial. He attempted to condone the wholesale destruction of the *Times* employees as a social crime rather than a horrible murder. This plea in his argument to the jury caused several members, according to their story, to hold out for conviction. The jury could not agree and was discharged. It was not until the following December, ten months later, that the remaining indictment was dismissed.

CHAPTER XXV

In the interim between the two Darrow trials there occurred one of those incidents which correspondents for out-of-town newspapers were wont to classify as the sort that "could only happen in Los Angeles."

Guy Eddy, city prosecutor and an aggressive leader in the reform administration which had cleaned up Los Angeles, was arrested on a morals charge. There was nothing vague about the allegations. He was declared to have been caught actually *in flagrante delicto,* which, translated into the western vernacular from the legal Latin, would read "caught in the act."

The arrest created a sensation, both because of the prominence of Eddy and the character of the charges.

The fantastic nature of the case was accentuated by the fact that, although Eddy was charged with contributing to the delinquency of a minor, the aforementioned minor was a married woman, who admitted that she had been induced to join in a plot for the city official's ruin.

When the reform element of the western commonwealth, headed by Hiram Johnson, took over the reins of government, one of the first laws enacted was that intended to shield the young maidenhood of the Golden State. With restricted districts abolished, some sort of safeguard was needed.

But the California reformers did not want to do a halfway job of protection. So the author of the law wrote into it that it would be a felony to philander with any female person under the age of twenty-one years—married or unwed, pure as a vestal or lewd as any street hustler. Of course this was not the exact language in the law, but that's what it meant.

Eddy's reform activities and local politics were concerned in the conspiracy against him. He was being groomed by the Lincoln-Roosevelt League—the Progressives—for the office of district attorney to succeed Captain Fredericks, classified as of the old guard, which still controlled the politics of Los Angeles county. Eddy's candidacy had not been announced, but it was fairly certain that he would be a candidate. The Good Government League, which controlled the city, numbered Eddy among its stalwarts.

Eddy was the author of the rooming-house ordinance passed by the city council. Those who had been hurt by that piece of legislation were said to have been willing collaborators in the attempt forcibly to retire Mr. Eddy to something in the nature of private life.

The ordinance which Eddy wrote and sponsored prohibited a man and woman, not married to each other, from occupying a room together in any hotel or lodging-house. Thousands of arrests and convictions were obtained under this law. A system of espionage had sprung up during its enforcement and keyhole gazing had come to be a major indoor sport. There were almost as many stool pigeons as there were members of the police force and the vice squad worked in eight-hour relays.

So the many who had fallen afoul of the rooming-house ordinance, chiefly the landlords, were more than willing to participate in a bit of reprisal.

It may be stated parenthetically that both laws are still in effect. It is still a penitentiary offense in California to have intimate relations with any young lady under twenty-one though she may have been married many times, or even be the inmate of a brothel. And it is still a misdemeanor for an unmarried couple to occupy a room together even if they have gone there only for the innocent purpose of looking at some interesting stereoscopic views of Niagara Falls or the Yosemite Valley.

The woman in the Eddy case was Alice Phelps, a good-looking girl, whose beauty was compared by newspapermen to that of Evelyn Nesbit Thaw. According to the story, Alice had gone to Eddy's office in the Central Police Station by pre-arrangement with him—as well as with four officers—and had participated in "an illegal act" while the four curators of virtue peeped through gimlet holes made in the door the night before.

It seems that the zealous guardians of the law had been apprized of the forthcoming commission of the "illegal act" and had made due preparations to witness the same, perhaps so that they would be qualified to appear in court. The door to the city prosecutor's office had been removed the previous night, five holes bored in it and filled with putty. Then the door had been partially replaced on its hinges.

When the fair Alice had entered the office to keep her tryst, the quartet of officers poked the putty out of the holes and applied their eyes to the several orifices. When they judged the proper time had come for action, they broke the door from its insecure moorings and interrupted the love scene.

Eddy, of course, insisted that the whole affair was a conspiracy devised by his political enemies. But Miss Phelps herself appeared as the complaining witness, the minor whose delinquency had been contributed to; and, to make his predicament more precarious, Eddy was said to have confessed his guilt in the presence of Superior Judge Curtis D. Wilbur, who became Secretary of the Navy some years later.

The political forces behind Eddy engaged Lewis D. Works son of Senator John D. Works, and Albert Lee Stephens to defend the accused. Both are now among the leading jurists of the state. After hearing Eddy's story, they felt the necessity of reinforcements. Earl Rogers was approached, but he was engaged in preparing for the second Darrow trial. Besides, he was not at all well. But more pressure was brought to bear upon him and he agreed to take charge of the defense. He brought into the case his junior associate, Jerry Giesler, and Frank Dominguez.

For the state appeared the veteran prosecutor Frank Blair, and Asa Keyes, then one of the coming members of the district attorney's staff and later to become district attorney himself with disastrous results to his own fortunes, through trial and imprisonment for accepting bribes in the case arising from the notorious Julian oil stock-juggling.

Earl threw himself into the case with intensity. It was the sort of affair which gave him wide scope for all of his well-known devices. One of the first things Earl did was to dig up the husband of the Phelps girl.

The courtroom of Judge Fred V. Wood in the old Hall of Justice was packed when the trial opened.

The police officers were first to testify, and their description of what they had beheld through the peepholes was such that the newspapers admitted sorrowfully they could not publish it.

When Alice Phelps came to the stand she created something of a sensation. She was described by the reporters as beautiful with all the innocence of virginal youth. She was smartly garbed in a tan creation that did not fail to accentuate the pleasing lines of her figure. But despite her apparent innocence she related glibly and unblushingly all the incidents of the visit to Eddy's office before they were interrupted by the invading minions of the law.

The ever-varying technique employed by Rogers was strikingly illustrated by the contrasting methods he used in the cross-examinations of Policeman Johnson and Alice Phelps.

The attorney had not asked the officer many incisive questions before the witness showed that he was thoroughly frightened. Policemen were aware that Rogers knew all about them and dreaded being handled by him in court.

"What is your business?" asked Earl with deadly menace.

"I am a police officer," confided the witness, none too confidently.

"What!" exclaimed the lawyer. "You know you have no standing as a police officer!"

"Yes, Mr. Rogers, I am a regular officer under Chief Sebastian."

"Why, you know you're nothing but a bouncer in a Chinese café."

"I was a special officer for a while at a Chinese café; yes, sir."

Then, with Johnson scared stiff through fear of further open comment on his status as an officer, Rogers for an hour submitted him to a bombardment of rapid-fire questions concerning the size of the holes he had bored, how far vision through them could range sideways, and innumerable other repetitions that induced Johnson to contradict himself.

"Are you morally certain there were any holes in the door at all?" Earl barked at him at the close of the day's session, and the wearied Johnson hesitated so long that Rogers turned his back on him and grinned; and the jury smiled too.

"I'll have some more questions to ask you tomorrow," said the attorney as Johnson left the stand.

"All right, Earl," was the quavering reply.

But at a later session when Alice Phelps seated herself in the witness chair for the dreaded cross-examination, Rogers, garbed in a new frock coat with a white gardenia in its lapel, beamed upon her so graciously that she smiled coquettishly in return. And when he began his questioning his manner was that of a courtier in the presence of royalty. Fat and crafty Prosecutor Keyes watched the proceedings furtively, but naturally could file no objection to the defense counsel's extreme politeness. Earl's interrogations were couched in honeyed accents. He soon had the pretty witness trying to please him.

"When you first met Mr. Eddy in his office did he tell you

anything other than that you have already testified to?" purred Rogers.

"Well, let me see. Oh, yes; he told me that he loved me."

"Did you believe him when he told you that he loved you?"

"Well, I don't know as I did. No, I did not."

"And his attentions, I suppose, were very disagreeable to you?"

"Well, some of his attentions were agreeable to me and part of them were not."

He did not ask her to go into detail about the nature of the agreeable attentions and those not so pleasing, but passed on to inquire: "What did you say when Mr. Eddy said: 'I love you'?"

"I don't know. I don't remember, Mr. Rogers."

By now Earl had learned what he had been fishing for—that Alice was as dumb as she was beautiful. Whenever he interrogated her along certain lines her answers were so long coming that Judge Wood would ask her to try to be less slow; but Earl would only smile graciously at her hesitation.

"Why," he asked suavely, "did you not make an outcry when Mr. Eddy began his improper advances?"

"I was afraid."

"Afraid of what?"

After waiting several seconds for her answer Rogers asked her with a disarming smile, "Is it not true that you have a memorized story to tell and you forget every time you deviate from it?"

But before the partially hypnotized witness could agree with Earl's question Asa Keyes was on his feet, bawling objections against such "unfair insinuations," although his real object was to jar his chief witness out of the trance which Rogers had apparently thrown her into by his manner.

Earl had been waiting for a break that would aid him in his favorite ruse of putting the prosecutor on trial; but doing this with Keyes was not at all easy. Rogers more than once had said that he could get the ordinary prosecutor in an emotional tumult merely by regarding him through his lorgnette, but that big, good-natured Keyes, thoroughly grounded in the law, imperturbable under fire, was the hardest of all the district attorney's men to confuse.

Considering the time opportune, Earl now began complaining bitterly to the court that the last time the main witness for the defense, husband of Alice Phelps, had been seen was when he was going into the district attorney's office and that it was the belief of defense counsel that Phelps had been forced to leave town.

Keyes' objection to this assertion was long and grievous, and moved Rogers to sardonic laughter. He had the prosecutor on the defensive.

Despite agonized objections from Prosecutors Blair and Keyes, Earl drew from Alice an admission that she had lived with Phelps for quite some time in Milwaukee before she was married to him in a town in Illinois.

Then he showed her a certified copy of her marriage license in which her age had been given as twenty-one years on July 16, 1912, several months before the alleged contribution to her delinquency. She was confused, but stammered that she had not known what age Phelps had given to the marriage license clerk.

The prosecution put Alice's mother on the stand to bolster up her daughter's uncertainty about her age, but on cross-examination Rogers made her testimony seem as vague as Alice's had been. By persistent, deferential questioning he got out of her that the only record ever made of Alice's birth was what her father had written in an ordinary writing tablet, and that she had failed to bring that when she came to California.

The air-tight case against Eddy was beginning to show leaks.

While the spicy courtroom show was titillating the ears of

scandal lovers and eliciting guffaws from the rounders, there was injected into the extravaganza a sizzling byplay that for a day outclassed the Eddy trial itself. Alice Phelps had a rural educator arrested on a charge of having bored holes through an unused door connecting her bedroom in the Natick Hotel with that of the pedagogue.

At the police station the teacher declared that he had not bored the holes, although he admitted looking through them; and despite the fact that one witness testified he had heard the schoolmaster enlarging the holes with a pocket knife, he was finally released.

One day toward the end of the trial's second week Earl Rogers failed to turn up in court. Of course his critics surmised, audibly, that he was drunk.

But Attorney Works did not allow the good work to lag during Earl's absence. He got the leader of the peep-hole brigade, Humane Officer McLaughlin, on the witness stand and tactfully carried along the defense's motif of discrediting the prosecution's evidence by good-natured ridicule.

"Why did you allow Mrs. Phelps to go to Eddy's office and perform her part of this alleged proceeding?" Works asked McLaughlin. The witness lamely said he did not urge her to go, but that when she had agreed to go he had promised to be on hand to protect her.

"Why didn't you protect her when the alleged crime was being committed?"

After considerable thought the officer said that he had taken steps to protect her immediately after he had determined "in his own mind" that a crime had been committed, by breaking down the door.

Rogers was back the next day, palpably not suffering from after-effects of a carouse, and put a long string of witnesses on the stand to testify that they had looked through the peepholes in Eddy's door, but had been unable to see the spot where the officers said the alleged malefactors had been sitting.

Next he recalled the reluctant Policeman Johnson to the stand and began to interrogate him roughly. Johnson had first testified that Eddy said in Judge Wilbur's courtroom, where they had taken him to have a warrant issued for his arrest after raiding his office, "I am ruined." But under Earl's persistent grilling he finally admitted that what Eddy really had said was, "I am ruined whether it is true or not."

"You omitted part of what he said when you were on the stand before, testifying merely that he said, 'I am ruined,' instead of 'I am ruined whether it is true or not.' Your object was to make it sound like an admission of guilt on the defendant's part—was it not?" asked Earl.

"No, I—it just slipped my mind," floundered the witness. And then Rogers denounced the officer unmercifully, making it seem that he had falsified the facts in an attempt to convict Eddy.

But Rogers had another motive in keeping the policeman on the griddle. The attorney had recognized in one of the jurors a man who had been a striker during a recent labor war, and for that labor union member's benefit Rogers led Johnson to testify that he had been employed by the Merchants & Manufacturers Association to combat the strikers.

The next witness injected a note of drollery into the day's proceedings. She was Miss Molly Summers, who had been brought from Victorville to testify that Eddy had made improper advances to her. Miss Summers displayed considerable business acumen by having the judge sign her demand for transportation before she would testify. Then she dismayed the prosecution by her crisp evidence.

"I never saw Mr. Eddy," she declared, "except when I was slinging hash in the Hollenbeck Hotel, where I often waited on him, and he never acted out of the way toward me.

And if he had, I am thirty-six years old and I guess I could take care of myself."

While the assistant district attorneys were recovering from Miss Summers' apostasy Rogers arose and dramatically informed Judge Wood that he wished to submit some facts which the court might not consider proper evidence to place before the jury.

When the jurors had been excused Earl told the court that the defense had just discovered that someone had enlarged the peepholes in the door of Eddy's office. He had picked up the shavings made by the cuttings, he said, and found they were from the door. At this point he called to the stand a well known owner of a Los Angeles lumber yard and had him qualified as an expert in such matters. The lumber man testified that the shavings undoubtedly had been made by the enlargement of the peepholes in the door of the public prosecutor's office.

If the prosecution had intended to introduce evidence to discredit the defense witnesses who had testified that the chair alleged to have been occupied by Eddy and Alice Phelps could not be seen through the holes bored by the policemen, their chance to do so was forever gone with this new development.

Prosecutor Keyes regarded the suave Rogers darkly. Perhaps he was wondering where chief counsel for the defense had been the day before, when Asa and others had heard a rumor that Earl was drunk. "If the prosecution had enlarged those holes," growled Keyes, "they certainly would have removed the evidence of the shavings." But there was nothing to be gained by going further into the matter. Rogers had his testimony about the holes in the record and there was no way to combat it, with the original holes enlarged.

Rogers placed the defendant on the stand last, and the city prosecutor, by virtue of his legal training and familiarity with the prosecution's case, foiled every attempt to shake his story.

He injected one new bit of testimony into the now completed case—that when the officers had broken into his office one of them threatened him with a gun while another disarranged the prosecutor's clothing.

Rogers had thrown so much doubt on the arresting policemen's testimony that the jury, after three ballots, acquitted Eddy.

After the trial it was learned that Alice Phelps' estranged husband, the missing witness whose absence had been so often lamented in open court by Earl, had been in Los Angeles all through the trial, sometimes even in the courthouse corridors.

CHAPTER XXVI

These were great days for Earl Rogers so far as money making was concerned. More business came into his office than he could care for. Careless as he was about fees, the gold poured into his coffers. But it went out just as fast, for the more he made, the more he spent. Automobiles, wearing apparel, expensive parties, the needs of his family. There were now four children, two sons having been born within less than two years, the last one arriving during the Darrow trial.

The first born, Adela, was now a young lady in finishing school. Her father's devotion to her was almost fanatical. Bogart, her junior by several years, was just entering High School. His father was looking forward to the day when Bogart would succeed him.

Success, however, seemed to have a blighting effect on the domestic happiness of the erratic Earl. Family quarrels became more frequent, and despite his great affection for his children, Rogers saw less and less of them. He remained away from home for long periods and occasionally he went there considerably under the influence of liquor, with a family wrangle as the inevitable result. The names of other women were beginning to be mentioned in connection with his escapades.

Nearly every evening found Earl dining at Al Levy's, then regarded as the most famous café in the West. He craved companionship, and seldom ate alone. Usually he had champagne with his dinner. Levy's was the rendezvous for all of the theatrical crowd, race track folk, and the other bon vivants. When Levy failed, to open a new café later at Spring near Eighth Street, the old crowd followed him. Here they

[237]

were joined by the advance guard of the motion picture industry which had recently entrenched itself in Los Angeles and its suburbs.

At Levy's nearly every night could be found Charlie Chaplin, then a shy young Englishman getting the fabulous salary of $125 weekly. Charlie usually dined with Mack Sennett and Mabel Normand. But not even Mary Pickford on her occasional visits, or David Wark Griffith, even when accompanied by Lillian Gish or Blanche Sweet, attracted more attention than Earl Rogers. He was as nearly a public idol as a lawyer could possibly be. His court performances were usually far more thrilling than anything produced for the screen in those days.

Midnight frequently found Earl at the Vernon Country Club on the outskirts of the city, or the Ship Café at Venice. These resorts were not subject to the early closing laws of the morally rehabilitated Los Angeles. They were the original night clubs of the city. Before starting for either place with some congenial companions, it was Earl's wont to fill a pocket with $5 gold pieces to toss at the musicians and entertainers. Then, if he had to appear in court the following morning, the remainder of the night or early morn was spent at some handy Turkish bath. He excelled as a host. He never permitted anyone with him to pay a check. That accounted for part of his popularity with some of those who frequently accepted his hospitality, but most of those seen with him were men and women eager to shine in the reflected glory of a celebrity.

It was frequently said of Rogers by those who knew best his forensic ability: "I'd sooner have Earl Rogers drunk defending me than any other lawyer, sober." And in those days drink did not seem to impair his brilliant mental machinery.

Once while in the midst of an extended debauch he received a hurry call from Attorney Will Anderson. A client of the latter had been charged with a criminal offense and Anderson wanted Earl to defend him. He would not take a refusal, even though realizing the condition of Rogers. So Earl went down to the beach suburb of Venice where the defendant, Pete Pirotte, a policeman, was about to go on trial for assault, false arrest and perhaps several other charges.

It seems that Pete did not like a certain barber in Venice and one day while in an exuberant state, perhaps from the bracing ocean zephyrs, he took the barber by his collar and haled him to the Venice calaboose. When the tonsorialist finally got out, he caused Officer Pirotte's arrest. There didn't appear to be any defense for Pete. The fact that he didn't like the barber could not be offered in extenuation.

Rogers heard the story and asked that a number of Pete's colleagues on the police force be subpœnaed. Pete said they didn't know anything about it. Earl told him that was none of his business. The complaining witness got on the stand and told his story of Pete's alleged brutality and his own unwarranted imprisonment.

Then Earl put Pete on the stand.

"Mr. Pirotte, isn't it true that the complaining witness has a twin brother who resembles him greatly; and that this twin brother is a notorious crook for whom the police have been looking?"

There was an immediate outcry from the prosecuting attorney. He objected strenuously to the question and of course the court would not permit the defendant to answer. He was excused.

In succession, each of the policemen was called to the stand and the same question asked by Rogers, with the same result. The prosecutor fumed but there was nothing he could do. As the last policeman left the stand, Rogers arose in a dignified manner and said that he would rest his case. He had not succeeded in introducing a word of evidence, but there wasn't a man on the jury who didn't believe that the barber had a twin brother who was a fugitive from justice and nothing short of a murderer, and that Pirotte's act had been the result of mistaken identity. The jury promptly found Pete not guilty.

As they left the courtroom Lawyer Anderson said to Lawyer Rogers, as he shook his head solemnly: "Earl, sometimes I think you are inclined to be unethical."

Earl looked at him in surprise as he guided his colleague into Shaw's barroom. "Why, Will," he declared, "I don't understand what you mean."

"You knew damn' well, Earl, that barber didn't have a twin brother," said Anderson.

Earl gave him a look of pity, as he placed a silver dollar on the bar. "Why, my dear Billy," he replied, "whatever made you think I suspected the existence of a twin brother?— George, a little of that Waterfill & Frazier bourbon, with a chaser of beer."

Los Angeles at this period was the pugilistic capital of the country. The state at the time permitted twenty-round championship encounters and many titles changed hands at the old arena of the Pacific Athletic Club at Vernon, just outside the Los Angeles city limits. Boxing contests were not permitted within those sanctified precincts.

It was in the big open air Vernon arena that Jess Willard, the huge battler from Kansas, first attracted the attention of sport writers by knocking out another heavyweight, Bull Young. The feat would perhaps have caused no great comment but for the fact that Bull never recovered consciousness. Jess clipped him on the chin in the eleventh round with a terrific uppercut. The stricken man dropped to a sitting posture, then fell slowly backward. He was rushed to a hospital, where an operation was performed on his skull, and the next day he died.

A charge of manslaughter was laid against Willard. The big fighter who was later to win the world's championship from Jack Johnson at Havana, was terrified. He was sure that if he were not executed he would spend the remainder of his days in prison. Earl Rogers, as usual, had been a ringside spectator. Tom McCarey, head of the fight club, went into a huddle with the frightened Jess and the result was Rogers' employment to defend him. Earl immediately assured Sheriff Hammel that he would be responsible personally for the appearance of all those connected with the fatal bout.

Practically all of the city's clergy took official notice of the tragedy, the women's clubs insisted upon a cessation of the "so-called sport," and many of the newspapers demanded prohibitive legislation.

Unsuccessful in his first skirmish for dismissal, Rogers demanded an autopsy, and when it was performed he immediately shifted all blame from Willard's shoulders to those of the operating surgeons. The club doctor said that when he had examined the gladiators before the fight he had found them about normal; but, under Earl's questioning, he admitted that Young's heart had had a queer sound, probably because of his use of cigarettes.

Then Dr. A. D. Houghton, city councilman and stormy petrel of municipal politics generally, helped Rogers out appreciably by discovering another flaw in Bull's physical make-up. He testified that Young had been afflicted with acromegaly, a strange disease of which only one other case had been reported in this country. This disease, testified Dr. Houghton, affects certain glands and causes overgrowth. So with this proof that the late Bull Young had been addicted both to cigarettes and acromegaly the jury must have decided it served him right, as they turned loose the future champion of the world, absolved of all blame.

On the closing day of the trial Rogers sprang a surprise on his junior associate, Jerry Giesler, that was typical of the man. On the preceding day he had told Giesler that the latter would not have to open for the defense as had been planned, because Earl believed it would be more effective if he alone argued to the jury. That evening Giesler, freed of the responsibility of farther participation, went to a party and appeared in court the next morning without having gone to bed.

The opening argument of the prosecution was concluded about half an hour before time for the noon recess. All through his career Rogers had a distinct aversion to breaking up his plea to a jury. He always tried to time his arguments so that there would be no interruption. He wanted to have the unbroken attention of the jurors until he finished.

Seeing that there was only half an hour remaining, Earl, without a word to his associate, rose and addressed the court, saying:

"Your Honor, my associate, Mr. Giesler, will address the jury from now until noon and I shall begin my argument at two o'clock."

Before the gasping Giesler could get his breath, Earl had picked up his hat and cane and was half way out of the courtroom without even a glance in the direction of the young lawyer. The latter, wholly unprepared and still suffering from the loss of sleep, managed to stall through the half hour by reading from the penal code about different sorts of manslaughter.

Soon after Willard was acquitted he became the leading "white hope" and then the successor to Jack Johnson as champion. Money began pouring in and he became involved in much litigation over conflicting contracts. He sent for Earl Rogers and the latter made a trip East to extricate Jess from his legal difficulties. Later Rogers brought suit to compel Jess to pay his fee of $25,000.

Rumors of an impending divorce in the Rogers family reached the local newspaper columns in the fall of 1913. The domestic affairs of the couple came to a climax when Earl forcibly attempted to take his infant son, Thornwell, from the Rogers home in Hollywood. Earl had been very ill during the second Darrow trial and had made a sea voyage to Alaska, returning much improved. However, he began drinking again soon after his return and, after a series of domestic rows, left home and took up residence in an apartment house at Ocean Park.

The Los Angeles newspapers gave much space to the attempted abduction of his son. The story was that Earl had entered a side door of the house and passed through the dining room where Charles E. Van Loan, the noted sports editor and fiction writer, one of Earl's closest friends, was conversing with Mrs. Rogers and her children.

The attorney had his hand in his pocket as if holding a weapon. When Van Loan tried to dissuade him from his declared purpose of taking his son by force, Earl said, "I'll kill you, Charley, if you interfere in any way." Then he went upstairs to the nursery to get the child, but the nurse locked the door and refused to give up the boy, and Rogers retired from the scene vowing further trouble if Thornwell were not turned over to him forthwith.

Papers the next day stated that Mrs. Rogers had engaged E. W. Britt, a prominent lawyer, to represent her in divorce proceedings. She intimated that her request for a decree would be based upon her husband's "temperamental eccentricities."

The suit was filed some time later and Mrs. Rogers charged cruelty. It came to trial the following March and Mrs. Rogers was given a decree after a hearing lasting but twenty minutes. Rogers did not appear. Author Van Loan testified to the attempted kidnaping and a medical student who had been acting as a nurse to Earl testified that Rogers had once forcibly expelled his wife from his sickroom. Counsel for the defendant had made an effort to have the plaintiff bound by an agreement not to marry again on penalty of forfeiting alimony of $300 monthly, but Judge Monroe struck out the objectionable clause.

CHAPTER XXVII

EARLY in 1915 occurred another one of those politico-judicial rigadoons that characterized the Los Angeles of the chemically pure era. Charles E. Sebastian, the Good Government chief of police, was running for mayor backed by the reform element of the city. At the same time he was being tried before a jury of his peers on a morals charge—contributing to the delinquency of a minor.

Truly an imposing civic show was that trial. It exuded drama, was enlivened by boisterous comedy and courtroom pyrotechnics, and reeked with the political fertilizer in which it had its inception. Municipal officials and civic leaders took sides as the lively spectacle unfolded. Even Governor Hiram Johnson was almost dragged into it. Yes, it was a great show and Earl Rogers was the ringmaster, a rôle in which he excelled.

Charlie Sebastian was an easy-going product of kindly, pleasant old-time Los Angeles. He had risen from the ranks of patrolmen, had been in charge of the Chinatown squad, and was exceedingly popular, as well as a good officer. He was a handsome fellow with fine dark wavy hair, and a splendid figure which was enhanced by his natty chief's uniform. A favorite with the ladies, he responded easily to their admiration.

Sebastian had played the game of the reform element, and when it was suggested that he run for mayor he snapped at the bait eagerly. The same civic leaders who had backed the unfortunate Guy Eddy were behind him. And practically the same clique which brought about the former city prosecutor's downfall were the objectors to Sebastian's ambition to become the chief executive of their city.

Scandal being the oldest and most reliable form of political hokum ever employed to discredit a candidate, it was resorted to by the political enemies of the police chief to keep him out of the mayor's chair. Securing evidence of loose romancing against Charlie was ridiculously easy.

The charge against Sebastian was made under the same law invoked in the Eddy case. A legislative invention of the reform element of California to protect the young womanhood of the state, it was once more used as a boomerang on one of its champions.

Specifically, Sebastian and a woman named Mrs. Lillian Pratt were alleged to have corrupted the morals of a minor sister of the latter named Edith Serkin, by permitting her to be present when they met for amorous dalliance in a so-called mystery room a stone's throw from the office of the chief. The grand jury had returned indictments against the two after Miss Serkin had appeared before that body and told her story.

When the indictment became public, to an accompaniment of screaming headlines in the daily papers and frantic accusations of frame-up by the section of the press supporting the chief's mayoralty aspirations, Sebastian was temporarily suspended by the police commission. His political organization, reeling under the blow, regained its balance and redoubled its efforts. The entire city split into rival camps.

The offense charged by the indictment was punishable by a penitentiary sentence. The array of evidence looked imposing. Sebastian became panic-stricken. There was no doubt at all that he was on friendly terms with his co-defendant and that they had met in the rooming house just up the street a hundred feet from the police station. His enemies seemed to have him hopelessly entangled in their net of accusations. It was an Earl Rogers case if ever there was one.

There wasn't much chance to get a record fee out of the

case, but it promised an abundance of publicity and unlimited opportunity to bask in the spotlight. Earl needed no further inducements.

Rogers got away to a flying start by having himself indicted by the grand jury on the charge of trying to intimidate that august tribunal. He boldly declared that the grand jury was party to a disgraceful political plot to ruin the career of the police chief and prevent his election as mayor. Of course he was never called upon to answer to the indictment.

An effort was made to have Sebastian tried separately, but the judge, who was brought in from a rural section of the state, refused to allow a severance of the cases and the two defendants went to trial together.

The prosecutor was Thomas Lee Woolwine, who had been elected district attorney to succeed Captain Fredericks when the latter was elected to Congress. Woolwine was a tall, handsome fellow with raven locks, a magnetic presence and a consuming ambition to be governor of California. Well-fixed financially in his own right and married to the daughter of one of Los Angeles' wealthiest families, Tom Woolwine had sought the office of district attorney only as a stepping stone to the higher office. He came from a fine old Southern family and was a natural born crusader.

Earl Rogers was Woolwine's acknowledged bête noir. It was Earl's boast that he could "get Tom's goat" easier than that of any other courtroom opponent. He could throw Tom into an almost maniacal fury by drawing the deadly lorgnette on him.

Woolwine would have much preferred to delegate his chief deputy, Asa Keyes, to prosecute the Sebastian case, but because of its political importance he felt it imperative to head the prosecution forces himself. A victory would advance him towards his goal as those opposing Sebastian were much more powerful than those supporting his candidacy, although his cause had captured the public's fancy.

The young sister of Sebastian's alleged paramour was, of course, the chief witness, as well as the person whose morals allegedly had been affected by the behavior of the couple. Her testimony on direct examination was letter-perfect. She related how her sister had frequently visited the Arizona rooming-house at the corner of First and Hill Streets, where Chief Sebastian met her.

The girl, a pretty little thing with wide innocent eyes, coolly and calmly went into detailed description of her reserved-seat view of the amorous exhibition. Every detail of her story had the effect of another nail in the coffin of Charlie Sebastian's political ambitions. He wilted visibly as the girl proceeded with her story, making the task of his defender more difficult. To clinch the telling points of her testimony Edith gave specific dates of the love sessions.

As date followed date, Rogers turned to Woolwine and with a smile remarked audibly that there was nothing like fixing dates accurately. The prosecutor grinningly agreed. Then he turned the witness over to Earl for cross-examination, with a smile that challenged him to get what comfort he could out of the state's star witness.

After a long series of innocuous questions pleasantly propounded, during which Earl apparently stilled whatever qualms the girl had felt immediately upon being turned over to him. Rogers suddenly launched his case upon a course that disclosed the theory of his defense. Question after question was hurled at the witness which she never answered because of the violent objections of the prosecution. The crafty counsel for the defense knew that the witness would never be permitted to reply to the queries which carried the implication that two other sisters of Mrs. Pratt, heretofore unknown to the case, were willing aides of the plotters against their sister and the police chief.

Members of the jury straightened up in their chairs, reporters sharpened new pencils, and the prosecutors literally gnashed their teeth as the queries of Rogers opened his new attack. Whether true or not, Earl's questions contained the sensational inference that these sisters were dissolute characters whose motives were two-fold.

Through a series of additional unanswered questions, Rogers disclosed the amazing theory that the two women had been impelled in their allegedly nefarious undertaking by the desire to obtain possession of their young sister for immoral purposes; that failing in this, because of the protection afforded the girl by Mrs. Pratt, they had joined the political plotters against Sebastian, hoping that eventually they could enslave innocent young Edith.

This new offensive created a sensation. Rogers mentioned the names of the sisters and in his interrogations provided details of their supposedly immoral mode of living. The district attorney grew apoplectic in his hysterical efforts to prevent further questioning along these lines. His objections were invariably sustained by the court, but whether the theory of Rogers was true or not, he gave the jury plenty to think about.

There was no defense that the district attorney could employ against this sort of attack. He could not call to the stand the opposing politicians or the rival candidate for mayor, nor did he dare produce the two sisters of the witness. He could not enter a rebuttal to testimony that had not been admitted. So Woolwine sat and writhed during the days when Edith Serkin was on the stand under cross-examination, realizing that he was being made the victim of a typical Earl Rogers trick. Bitter clashes between Rogers and Woolwine occurred frequently.

One Friday afternoon, while the girl was still on the stand, Rogers and Woolwine were observed conversing in whispers in a corner of the courtroom. They were extremely pleasant and this unusual sight caused a buzz of animated comment.

Judge, jury, lawyers and spectators marveled at this strange friendliness between the bitter antagonists.

Then both attorneys approached the bench and Woolwine addressed the court.

"I understand, your Honor," declared the prosecutor, "that Mr. Rogers has a very important engagement tomorrow and I would suggest that the court declare an adjournment until Monday."

Judge Wood indicated his surprise. For some days he had been worn to a frazzle by his efforts to keep Rogers and Woolwine within the bounds of propriety. His nerves had become jumpy from listening to their rasping comment upon each other's lack of legal knowledge and fairness. And now Tom Woolwine was interceding with the court for a favor for Rogers.

The judge hemmed and hawed. He looked from Woolwine to Rogers, trying to figure it all out. Maybe these Los Angeles lawyers were trying to put something over on a guileless jurist from the unsophisticated wilds of Amador County. Also, he wanted to get this trial over. He would have held night and Sunday sessions in order to get out of this reeking mess that needed chloride of lime more than anything else.

"Isn't it possible," asked the court, "that Mr. Rogers could delegate this task to one of his associates?"

Woolwine laughed aloud. Earl turned with a tolerant smile to the judge from the hinterland.

"It's quite impossible, your Honor. It is really too important for that. And even if I could I would not allow anyone else to fill that engagement, your Honor. I am craving the indulgence of the court for—well, your Honor, for the purpose of getting married!"

"Oh, I see!" gasped the court. Then he joined sheepishly in the laughter, and to hide his further confusion declared that he would not wait until the regular time for closing the session but held court adjourned immediately until the following Monday morning.

The next day Earl Rogers and Miss Edna Landers were married by Judge William P. James. The engagement had been announced in July of the preceding year.

Edna Landers was a beautiful girl whom Earl had met while he was obtaining a divorce for her elder sister. The family came from Canada and had resided in Los Angeles only a short time when the meeting occurred. Edna was a vital young woman, warm-eyed and placid, and the possessor of a gorgeous voice. Her chief purpose in coming to Los Angeles was to perfect that voice for the concert stage. But her meeting with the lawyer ended all ambition for professional glory. With him she embarked on a career that was far more strenuous and heartbreaking than any struggle for fame could have been.

But to return to the sordid Sebastian mixup. After the usual congratulations the following Monday morning, Rogers resumed his cross-examination of the prosecution's stellar witness. With a true sense of drama he saved his heaviest guns for the climax.

Earl's manner towards the witness was even more courteous and kindly than before. Tom Woolwine turned and whispered to Asa Keyes that love was a great thing. "Just see what it's done to tough old Earl." But Tom spoke too soon.

The girl on the stand was glad to repeat for the smiling, soft-spoken defense counsel the exact days and hours of those momentous meetings at the rendezvous. She was sure of the dates because there were related circumstances, such as one occasion when it was raining and the gallant police chief had held an umbrella for her and her sister as they walked up the hill to the rooming house. Another important tryst she fixed by the fact that the following morning she had read in the newspapers of a particularly brutal murder, known as the

Bundy case. Other dates were fixed in like manner. Edith certainly knew her evidence.

Then the chief counsel for the defense opened up with deadly effect. Taking each date fixed so positively by the girl's testimony, he released a devastating attack under which the witness withered like dry grass before a prairie fire. He brought in a hotel register to prove that the chief of police was in another city at the time of the Bundy murder and for some days prior to that crime. He brought in reports from the United States weather bureau to prove that it had not rained within several days of the date which the girl had fixed so positively as the one when the chief had escorted the sisters through the rain to the setting of the illicit love-scene. Practically every other date met the same fate.

Woolwine's confusion was almost pathetic. He realized that Rogers had purposely drawn out the girl's cross-examination to interminable lengths in order to give his detectives ample opportunity to check up on every detail, so that he might confound the carefully prepared testimony of the state.

All too late Woolwine realized what had been going on in Earl's crafty brain when earlier in the case he had remarked to the prosecutor that there was nothing like fixing dates accurately. Woolwine at the time had taken his opponent's remark as a compliment on his own care in having Edith Serkin fix specific dates for all the alleged Sebastian-Pratt love scenes.

CHAPTER XXVIII

B ʊ ᴛ there was still the mayoralty to be won and Rogers redoubled his efforts.

The campaign was sizzling along, paralleling the trial and rapidly reaching its climax, the primary election. Rogers had long since entered upon a course which in reality made the trial a potent part of the campaign. It had been a more difficult task than the public or even Sebastian's cohorts had realized. Sebastian was weak. He wanted to quit under fire and Rogers was determined that he shouldn't. Time after time he pleaded with his counsel to permit him to withdraw from the political race. Nearly every afternoon in Rogers' inner office the attorney stood over the cowering shoulders of the police chief and mayoralty aspirant and cursed him for a coward. And Charlie would lift his head, throw back his shoulders and declare that he would go through with it. But his courage seldom lasted more than twenty-four hours.

Two days before the primary election as Sebastian stood in the library window of his home, two shots rang out in the night and bullets crashed through the glass.

Official reports stated that the bullets missed the chief by inches and that it was the boldest attempt at assassination in the police annals of the city.

Newspapers supporting the chief devoted lurid headlines and denunciatory editorials to "the dastards who would not balk at murder to prevent fearless Charlie Sebastian from becoming mayor of the great metropolis of the West."

Papers opposing Sebastian derided the deed as a shameless attempt on the part of the mayoralty candidate to create public sympathy for himself and his cause. Earl Rogers was credited by the political wiseacres with authorship of the shooting, but no originality was ascribed to him. By connoisseurs of the devious science of politics, especially as practiced in the West, an attempted assassination had always been regarded as a bit of sure-fire strategy.

The fanatical followers of the Good Government candidate honestly believed that an attempt had been made to destroy their leader and they threw themselves into the campaign with more ardor than ever.

The manner in which Los Angeles elects its municipal officials merits a word of explanation. The city and county government is non-partisan and under the city charter the two candidates for mayor polling the highest vote in the primary election become the nominees for the final election a month later. If a candidate is given a majority of all votes cast for his office he is automatically elected.

On the day of the primary election, the most exciting in the history of the city, the Sebastian trial was still in progress. A record vote was cast and before half of the ballots were counted, Sebastian's nomination was conceded. There was great joy in the chief's camp that night and the next day the trial was resumed.

Rogers was eager to let the jury learn about the defendant's success at the polls, but newspapers were kept from the jurors and they were well isolated between court sessions. The morning session had not progressed far when Earl saw his opportunity. Asa Keyes was interrogating a newspaperman regarding some investigation work he had done for the defense.

"What have you been working at lately?" asked Keyes of the witness.

Before the witness could reply, Rogers spoke up quickly.

"You may find that he has been compiling bulletins for his newspaper," declared Rogers, "showing that Sebastian won out in yesterday's primaries three to one."

Before the judge could reprimand Rogers, Woolwine was raging at the chief counsel for the defense. "Yes," he yelled, "but the big vote was due to a fake assassination!"

That was an opportunity which Rogers quickly seized. Simulating intense indignation, he had the district attorney immediately summoned to the witness stand. With lorgnette aimed at the furious prosecutor, Rogers demanded to know where the witness had obtained his information as to a "fake assassination." The infuriated district attorney would have been helpless under Rogers' deft manipulation, but, realizing Woolwine's incapacitating rage, Judge Wood would not allow him to answer Earl's questions. Rogers, however, was able to get before the jurors the inference that the prosecutor had made the accusation without having investigated the assassination attempt.

Had Woolwine been given an opportunity to collect his thoughts he might have confounded his interrogator by calling attention to the fact that had the shooting been a genuine attempt to kill, the marksman could not have missed Sebastian if the latter's story of the shots were true, as his figure almost completely filled the window which had been pierced in two places by bullets. But the lorgnette was too much for Woolwine and Rogers knew that the chance he was taking was not a long one.

The case went to the jury that day after an impassioned address by Rogers in which he bitterly denounced Sebastian's political enemies as having manufactured the entire case in order to prevent his election to the mayoralty. The jury remained out but a short time and returned with a verdict of not guilty.

Rogers issued a statement to the press saying: "This verdict is a rebuke to politicians of the slimy sort. The mud-slinging of Sebastian's political enemies has been rebuked by an honest and intelligent jury."

Sebastian was still to be elected mayor thirty days thence,

so the game had to be continued. Rogers made public letters which he had written to Governor Hiram Johnson demanding that he order an investigation of the attempted assassination of Sebastian and that the attorney general look into Woolwine's assertion that it wasn't genuine.

Nothing came of these moves, but they were effective in the campaign. The night of the chief's acquittal he was restored with great éclat to his post by the police commission. The campaign waxed hotter and hotter. Rogers became Sebastian's chief political adviser now that he had freed him. He felt that his job would not be done until the chief should have traded his gold-braided uniform for the silk hat and frock coat that were emblematic of the city's most exalted position.

Charges by the opposition that Sebastian's chief support came from the underworld were answered the night before election by an impressive automobile parade through the downtown streets of Los Angeles. Hundreds of cars were filled with women, members of the W. C. T. U., religious organizations, and civic welfare societies, each car bearing a banner containing the legend: "DO WE LOOK LIKE THE UNDERWORLD?"

That did the trick and Charlie Sebastian laid aside his gold star and natty uniform to assume the reins of government of Los Angeles.

But Sebastian's reign as mayor was short-lived. The *Record,* an evening paper which had bitterly opposed him, began publishing a series of letters which Sebastian had written Mrs. Pratt. One of the letters was penned while he was on a trip with his wife. It expressed the wish that the other woman were with him rather than his legally wedded spouse, to whom he referred as "the old haybag."

The publication of the haybag letter proved Sebastian's undoing. Always weak, he could not bear up under further notoriety. Good-natured and easy-going Charlie squirmed in abject misery at the public humiliation attending this written admission of his relations with his former co-defendant.

Then detectives employed by the civic leaders who had opposed Sebastian reported that he was spending much of his time away from his official duties, at the home of Mrs. Pratt. One night a small delegation of the erstwhile police chief's political adversaries paid a visit to the house, where Sebastian was asked to sign a resignation already typed and ready for his signature. There was no Earl Rogers at hand to stiffen that weak spine and good-natured Charlie sighed and signed. In a few days he stepped down from the mayor's chair and said farewell to public life forever.

His fair-weather friends quickly forsook him. A year or two later he was operating a filling station at a prominent Hollywood street intersection. Then a long illness left him penniless and physically helpless. The woman who had loved him and shared his shame in the public pillory was the one person who remained steadfast. For a year or more toward the close of his life, visitors to Venice, the ocean resort near Los Angeles, beheld a sad-faced woman caring for an invalid who sat motionless in a wheel-chair on the porch of a tiny dwelling, a still handsome man with white wavy hair who smilingly acknowledged greetings of occasional passersby. But there was no recognition behind his smiling eyes. Charlie Sebastian's mind was blank. When the end came, Lillian Pratt was almost alone at his grave.

No story of the Sebastian affair could be complete without an account of the party which Earl Rogers gave to the newspaper men who had covered the long trial. It was a dinner and the scene was a secluded eating resort in "Dog Town."

"Dog Town" was to old Los Angeles what the Latin Quarter is to Paris, what Greenwich Village was to New York, or Montgomery Street was to San Francisco in its days of artistic splendor. There good fellowship, true Bohemianism in all its radiant warmth, held sway. The French restaurant where Earl and his hilarious guests gathered about the festive board was on Aliso Street, adjacent to a livery stable.

Burly Frank Dominguez had assumed the rôle of toast-master and was well primed for a burst of oratorical blue fire calculated to do full honor to the occasion—and to Earl Rogers. For this epochal event Frank had supplemented his other resplendent habiliments with a gorgeous satin waistcoat of apricot fawn, star-dotted with embroidered bric-a-brac.

As the toastmaster arose to pay tribute to his chief it was noticeable to the naked eye that several of the Fourth Estate had been imbibing freely of the rare wines and liquors provided by their free-handed host. At every attempt of Frank to get his address started the scribes would cheer vociferously and handclap boisterously. The distinguished toastmaster was being razzed.

Earl regarded this unseemly behavior with a jaundiced eye. Time enough, he felt, for this gayety after the master of ceremonies had delivered his eulogy of the honored host.

After several futile attempts to make himself heard, the toastmaster was pleased by sudden quiet upon the part of the raucous crew about him, and he got well along in his bombastic beatification of their hero before he was brought up short by the realization that there was something malignant about the strange silence.

Glancing downward Dominguez perceived with a violent start that which had momentarily distracted the attention of these unappreciative guests. One of the reporters had discovered a half-grown cat prowling around the floor and had thrown him onto the table, where the kitten's hind feet had landed in the bowl of soup at Dominguez's place.

When the toastmaster's shocked gaze came to rest on the feline guest the latter was freeing his nether extremities of soup by kicking alternately backward with his hind legs, each motion registering a splotch of grease upon the beautiful vest that adorned Dominguez's generous paunch.

[257]

The toastmaster's ensuing outburst of profanity was hardly in keeping with his ceremonial duties, but his newspaper friends greeted his efforts with thunderous stamping of feet and howls of appreciation of a job well done.

At this stage of the disgraceful proceedings the host decided that he must dispense with any further introductory remarks by his apoplectic associate and rose to his feet in outraged dignity.

"Gentlemen," Rogers began, but paused in disgust as he realized that someone had just dumped a seidel of beer into the pocket of his immaculate frock coat.

"Gentlemen," he resumed in just anger—but at this moment a stalk of celery struck him on the brow and knocked his handsome Napoleonic cowlick askew. He straightened the lock of hair and drew himself up in imperial dignity.

"Gentlemen," he grated—"or at least I once thought you were gentlemen—you may eat my viands and drink my wine, but as for me, *I shall leave!*"

Seething with rage he strode from the table. But just as he reached the door a mule in the stable downstairs, perhaps disturbed by the unseemly racket, gave vent to a lusty bray. Earl, just passing through the door, thought the mule's outburst another gibe from one of his graceless guests. He turned to bestow a last glare of cold fury and unutterable contempt upon them.

"That's right, bray," he roared, "you misbegotten sons of——"

But the rest of his tirade was lost in the slam of the door.

The banquet proceeded with no further unseemly interruptions, but without the presence of a host.

CHAPTER XXIX

In the sporting-house ballad of "Frankie and Johnny," it is mournfully narrated that the redlight lady named Frankie "killed her man because he done her wrong." The lament further relates how she paid the extreme penalty for the excellent marksmanship which had eliminated Johnny from this vale of tears.

There is no doubt that, had Earl Rogers been available, Frankie would not only have been liberated, but she would probably have been enshrined as a national heroine. At least that was a favorite boast of the Los Angeles barrister. He was wont to declare, especially when the audience was one appreciative of the subject matter, that he could have gotten Frankie off without working up a sweat. It is just as well, however, for had that celebrated lady of easy virtue not gone to the gallows, musical America would have been deprived of a threnody that has been accorded a place in our native classics.

The tragedy of the original torch-song had its reality in the story of Gabrielle Darley. Incidentally this *cause célèbre* of the primrose path gave Rogers a chance to demonstrate what he might have done had the mythical Frankie sent for him instead of depending upon home talent. Unfortunately, however, most authorities contend that the Frankie and Johnny incident occurred years before Earl Rogers first saw the light of day.

The Johnny of this real life story was a good looking young fellow named Leonard Tropp. Leonard was Gabrielle's man. He was of the habitually unemployed class of that period, referred to by the crudely-spoken as pimp or macquereau,

[259]

terms reduced to the vernacular as respectively "P. I." or "mac." In newspaper stories these gay lads were usually called sweethearts or lovers.

Nearly every prostitute of that period had her mac. It is strange, but an established mental phenomenon nevertheless, that despite the commodity in which these women trafficked, they had to have some object of the opposite sex upon which to lavish their affections. Through some strange psychological or pathological alchemy, nothing in human emotions could transcend the depths of a redlight woman's devotion to her lover. She would kill for him. She would also kill *him* at the merest suspicion of infidelity.

As for the man himself, although subjected to constant scorn and indignities at the hands of gamblers, bartenders and others of higher social scale in tenderloin boundaries, he overlooked all slights in his addiction to a life of ease. He was perhaps the male forerunner of the present day gold-digger.

Gabrielle Darley was a beautiful young thing of not quite twenty. According to her own story—the one related by her *after* the trial—she had followed the life of a sporting woman since her early teens, mostly in the restricted districts of various Arizona towns. Her ambition to have a sweetheart of her own was realized when she met young Tropp. She gladly turned over to him the money she had honestly earned by her professional adeptness. Leonard, in turn, would buy her jewels and furs with her own money and Gabrielle was deeply grateful to him for these favors. They came to Los Angeles.

Soon afterward when Gabrielle, in response to a conviction that all was not well with her romance, shot him down on a busy street corner, it seemed just another case of a prostitute doing away with her man because he "done her wrong." Leonard, it seems, had been given money by Gabrielle to buy her a diamond wedding ring and in some manner, probably through the grapevine telegraph of the underworld, Gabrielle discovered that he not only intended to give the ring to another lady but was about to heap insult on injury by uniting with the other woman in the bonds of holy wedlock.

Though the affair on the face of it was just another sordid episode of the half-world, Earl Rogers transmuted the Darley trial into a tragic and beguiling melodrama that held, during its progress, the rapt attention of the community, and invoked stirring comment from pulpit and press to the exclusion of all other current subjects.

It is quite likely that Earl was spurred in his desire to make a great show of the trial because it provided the journalistic début of his young daughter Adela. Still in her teens, Adela had been assigned by the city editor of the *Evening Herald* to write a daily human interest story of the trial. That daily sob story was the most widely read literature in Southern California during the progress of the case.

When pretty, demure little Gabrielle took her seat in the courtroom at the opening session of the trial, the setting was complete for a typical Earl Rogers drama with a typical Rogers cast. The little lady of the red lights was flanked by Los Angeles women of unimpeachable social standing who had been recruited as "moral support." Foremost among them was the celebrated coloratura soprono, Ellen Beach Yaw, famous as Lark Ellen. Since taking up her residence in a Los Angeles suburb she had devoted herself assiduously to welfare work among young people.

So that those present, particularly the members of the jury, should know the identity of the distinguished visitor, Rogers took occasion before court convened to introduce Lark Ellen to the judge and to the prosecutor, Assistant District Attorney W. J. Doran. Doran tried to move away from earshot of the jury when Earl approached with the noted songbird of the concert stage, but he was too late. Having studied law under Rogers, the prosecutor knew at once what the game was. Of course, every juror knew a moment later that the beautiful lady who sat with her arm across the slender shoulders of the defendant was the famous Ellen Beach Yaw.

There were two witnesses who had seen Gabrielle shoot down her sweetheart and, in behalf of the prosecution, they testified that they had heard the shot and had seen the girl standing with smoking revolver over the fallen man.

Rogers had no choice but to place the defendant on the stand. His only chance to free her was to make the jury believe that she had performed a public service when she did away with Tropp. Under the skillful questioning of her counsel, Gabrielle told a touching story of male depravity and betrayal. She had been a waitress in a boarding house in Arizona, testified Gabrielle, when she met Tropp. She fell in love with him and he had promised to marry her. In fact she had given him money to buy the wedding ring and she burst into tears as she told in detail of his duplicity. He had bought the ring, but for another girl.

When Doran took over the dewy-eyed defendant for cross-examination, he made a determined assault on her past. Gabrielle showed no little skill in parrying attempts to have her specify by name and date all the eating-places which had employed her. Nettled by her vague replies the prosecutor forgot the old Rogers precept never to get rough with women on the witness stand. He declared with some degree of certainty that Gabrielle might have worked in houses other than of the hash-dispensing sort.

Gabrielle burst into tears and Rogers sprang forward to the rescue. In a boiling fury of indignation Earl characterized the behavior of the prosecutor as "a contemptible effort to influence the jury at the price of humiliating a pitiful young woman already bowed down by the weight of a terrible load of misfortune."

The society leaders present scowled at the prosecutor and even members of the gallant dozen in the jury box cast unfriendly eyes in the direction of Bill Doran.

Shaking with suppressed emotion, Rogers continued his denunciation. "And we object," he declaimed, "to any further use of such innuendo as that contained in the prosecutor's question when he asked this defenseless little girl where Tropp 'picked her up.'"

Doran was at a decided disadvantage when he was permitted to resume his cross-questioning of the defendant. But he had created more than a reasonable doubt in the minds of the jurors that Gabrielle had been an innocent young thing before she came to Los Angeles.

Compelled to change tactics without more than a moment's consideration, Rogers on redirect examination undertook a bold stroke. He induced satisfactory replies from Gabrielle to questions as to her fear of bodily harm from Tropp. She told how he had upbraided her only that day for not bringing him more money. It was because of her fear of violence at his hands that she had concealed a pistol in her muff when she went out.

According to her original story, which she now repeated, the revolver had gone off accidentally while Leonard was mauling her about on the sidewalk after their meeting; she had chided him about the other woman and he had struck at her; he had seized her roughly as she attempted to defend herself, and from then until she was told she had killed him, "everything was blurred."

To support the girl's testimony that the lethal shot was fired while the gun was inside the muff, the latter was introduced as an exhibit. There was a hole in it that Rogers declared was made by the bullet that pierced the heart of Leonard Tropp.

The prosecutor was vehement in his assertion that it wasn't a bullet hole at all. "If that isn't a moth hole," Doran declared hotly, "I'll eat the muff!"

Rogers, with serious mien, interrupted Doran. Addressing

the court he asked that the prosecutor's remark be stricken from the record.

"If the court please," solemnly declared counsel for the defense, "I object to the statement for the reason that Mr. Doran has failed to lay any foundation of evidence to show that he ever actually ate a muff."

The court ignored the objection. The jurors smiled. The spectators tittered. The prosecutor scowled.

The girl's own story, entirely unsupported by corroborative testimony, was all there was to the case of the defense. It was up to Rogers to convince the jury by force of argument and eloquence that there before them in the guise of a pretty little girl of the streets sat the only original and authentic Mary Magdalene.

Wiping an occasional furtive tear from his eye, Rogers plunged into the most ardent and eloquent appeal to the emotions. He quoted from the Scriptures. "Let him who is without sin cast the first stone," he intoned reverently and slowly enough to take in with his roving glance each of the twelve men who sat spellbound by his eloquence.

Until the lovely Gabrielle in the first flower of girlhood met the traducer Leonard Tropp, she had been as pure as the snow atop Mount Wilson, was the impressive assertion of the defender. As proof of his declaration he pointed majestically out of the window in the direction of Mount Wilson. He again told the story of the girl as given by her on the stand, but with eloquent embellishments of drama and heart interest. The women surrounding Gabrielle as she sat with downcast eyes, wept unashamedly as they heard again how her betrayer had lured the soul-starved little waitress from a railroad eating house in Arizona to Los Angeles under promise of marriage; how he had then induced her to lead a life of shame that they might get the money to assure their future happiness; how pretty little, sorely deluded Gabrielle had given this dastard the money with which to buy the wedding ring, money earned at the price of her honor; and how then, instead of giving her the ring, he had purchased it for another woman.

No twelve chivalrous Western gentlemen could resist such arguments. Before the tears had dried on their cheeks they had voted a verdict of acquittal and Gabrielle Darley stood before the world absolved of her crime. Had they been permitted, the jury would undoubtedly have voted her some token of appreciation for having rid the world of such a monster.

There was little money in the way of fees in the Darley case for Earl Rogers, but he would have taken it and paid the costs himself just for the opportunity to stage a vivid drama and to display his own histrionism. But the case paid him better in a pecuniary way than he had expected. A few days before the trial began, a quiet little woman of something more than middle age appeared at his offices and asked to see Mr. Rogers.

When the attorney appeared the little old lady told him in an embarrassed, halting manner that she had read of the case of Gabrielle and expressed a wish to help the girl. She said that in her youth she had had a similar experience; that she had been in sporting houses and had risen to the high estate of a Madame. She said this rather proudly. But that was a long time ago, she explained regretfully, and she was now a respected member of society. Earl kindly thanked her but said he didn't see how she could help.

Then the little old lady brought out a package which she had kept concealed beneath her cape. "I no longer have much money," she said with a wistful smile, "but perhaps you can raise some on these." She handed Rogers the parcel and disappeared before he could recover from his surprise. Unwrapping her offering he found it to be a cigar box containing a large number of unset gems. A hasty visit to a pawnbroker brought something like $3,000 into the Rogers office cash-box. The mysterious contributor to Gabrielle's defense was never again heard from by anyone connected with the Darley case.

There is a sequel to the incident of little Gabrielle that seems no less a fabrication of some clever plot-weaver than the fantastic story of her liberation.

Not many years after the trial Adela Rogers St. Johns emerged from her sob-sister chrysalis as an author and playwright of national reputation. One of her minor literary works was a short story called "The Red Kimono." It was the real life story of Gabrielle Darley without any attempt to fictionize it. Real names were used, as was the custom of the magazine publishing it. Then followed an interesting chain of events.

One of the author's closest friends was Dorothy Reid, widow of Wallace Reid, film idol of yesterday. Some time after Reid's death, his wife determined to become a picture producer. The first story she purchased was "The Red Kimono." The motion picture followed the story in its most minute details. Many years had passed since the trial of Gabrielle.

"The Red Kimono" went into the theaters in the summer of 1927 and in June, 1928, almost thirteen years to the day after her trial, the erstwhile Gabrielle Darley emerged from long oblivion to bring suit against Mrs. Reid and her picture company. She asked for damages on the ground that her right of privacy had been invaded and her property rights in the incidents in her past life appropriated.

The complaint was a sensational document and an unusual one. Brought in the name of Gabrielle Darley Melvin, the plaintiff admitted that prior to 1915 she had led a depraved life, but while it was true that this was so and that she had been tried for murder, she had since rehabilitated herself in the eyes of society. She had married and in the Arizona town in which she and her husband lived she had been respected by her new friends, and had been "treated by them as a lady of culture and refinement."

Then one evening in a motion picture theater her startled eyes beheld moving across the screen the long buried events of her blighted girlhood. With a shock she realized that with her name thus blazoned nightly before the gaze of countless beholders everywhere, concealment of her life tragedy was no longer possible. Before those whose friendly regard and respect she had enjoyed during her years of regeneration, she now stood shamed, stripped of her hard-won reputation as an exemplary matron, revealed to all in the light of a murderess and a prostitute.

"As a result of the showing of the picture, 'The Red Kimono,'" read her complaint, "the plaintiff has become and is now exposed to obloquy, contempt and ridicule, and has grievously suffered in mind and body and been made sick to her damage in the sum of $50,000."

The suit aroused widespread interest among members of the bar as well as with the general public, for its legal aspect was without precedent. Never before had a petition involving such association of law and facts come before a court. Dorothy Reid could not deny any of the plaintiff's allegations as to the invasion of her rights of privacy; but the defense maintained that no such right of privacy was covered by the California code, and the Superior Court upheld that contention.

Upon the plaintiff's appeal from that ruling the state's Appellate Court reversed the decision of the Superior judge, remanding the case back for trial.

The decision was of far-reaching importance to the motion picture industry as well as to the legal profession. The court held that although the law of privacy was of recent origin and not clearly defined as to doctrine, some states had recognized it as "the right to live one's life in seclusion without being subjected to unwarranted and undesired publicity."

As to this right of privacy the court, although recognizing the non-existence of any specific law covering the case, held that a certain protection is provided under the California state constitution which provides that all men "have certain inalienable rights, among which are those of defending life and liberty, . . . pursuing and obtaining safety and happiness."

The action of the picture producer in using the true name of the woman, the court further declared, "was unnecessary and indelicate and a willful and wanton disregard of that charity which should actuate us in our social intercourse and which should keep us from unnecessarily holding up another to the scorn and contempt of upright members of society . . . Whether called 'right of privacy' or by any other name is immaterial because it is a right guaranteed by the constitution."

But as to that part of her complaint claiming property rights in the use of her name and her past as plot and theme for the motion picture, the higher court held that the use of her maiden name and the incidents of her life did not infringe on any property rights.

Commenting upon this phase of the case the decision recognized the contention of the defense that "there can be no privacy in that which is already public"; also that the use of the incidents was not actionable "because they were a matter of public record."

This decision was handed down early in the spring of 1931. Taken from there on further appeal by the defense to the Supreme Court, the highest state tribunal declined to interfere with the judgment of the Court of Appeals and the case, at the time this is written, still awaits trial in the Superior Court of Los Angeles County.

When Earl Rogers pulled out the emotional stops at the Darley murder trial and inspired his daughter by his vivid dramatization of Gabrielle's tragic story he set in motion a succession of melodramatic events destined to outlast the longest serial ever conceived in the brain of scenarist or director.

A decade after his passing back into cosmic dust, seventeen years after his legal craft and histrionic art had freed Gabrielle Darley from the gallows' menace, her bizarre romance still flickers upon the screen of life.*

* The suit of Mrs. Melvin was dismissed upon motion of the plaintiff early in 1933.

CHAPTER XXX

MUCH has been written recently in glorification of the criminal lawyer of today. Magazine articles and books have extolled his cleverness, based upon the number of acquittals obtained in murder trials. Individual scores are cited as proof of consummate skill in the courtroom. Yet, the "not guilty" verdict was infinitely more difficult to obtain in the preceding generation than in these days of racketeer domination, gangster vengeance, and the corruption of law enforcement agencies generally.

A further contribution to the loss of confidence in public officials has been provided by the methods employed by the police to obtain convictions. Juries are immediately distrustful upon the vaguest hint of violence in extracting confessions from accused persons. The third degree and like expedients have come to be regarded as the usual way of inspiring an admission of guilt.

This hostile spirit toward those engaged on the side of the law has become an invaluable aid to the defender of criminals, particularly so within the past fifteen years. Before the birth of that distrust the mere accusation formally made by a prosecutor was sufficient to cause prejudice against the defendant and provide a serious obstacle for his counsel to overcome.

Regardless of the ancient legal axiom that a man is innocent until proved guilty, there can be no argument against the theory that the mere bringing of an indictment constitutes a difficult hurdle for the defending lawyer. Juries may be cautioned to disregard an indictment as evidence of guilt, but it is contrary to human nature to regard it otherwise.

But the most serious hindrance to successful prosecution nowadays in the large cities—and, by the same token, the greatest aid to a successful defense—is the natural trepidation of the juror with respect to the gangster influence. Most of the imposing records made by the criminal lawyers under discussion have had to do with the liberation of men charged with racketeer murders.

In these cases no especial legal dexterity or courtroom wizardry is required. The man on the jury realizes that gangster vengeance is not a mythical or fancied danger. Fear of racketeer reprisals has been much more effective than forensic skill in causing jurors to vote "not guilty." After all, it is not so much of a strain on a juror's conscience to vote that way when he gives consideration to the fact that the person or persons dispensed with by the defendant could easily be spared by society.

To overcome the greater handicaps presented in his day Earl Rogers was forced to devise many expedients. As pointed out previously, in practically every big murder case he was compelled by circumstance to create some new device which inevitably found its way into the repertory of his emulators. But few of his more ingenious inventions were ever very useful tools in the hands of less gifted workmen.

The Gabrielle Darley case was the last great murder trial in Earl's career; that is, great in his own exacting estimate of the adjective.

True, the case was followed by his appearance in a long succession of court battles in which, with few exceptions, Rogers continued to secure acquittals of obviously guilty clients, thus keeping alive the popular tradition that he freed murderers by some sort of magic. But the trial of Gabrielle was the last one characterized by full opportunity for that spectacular publicity and dramatization that was Earl's leading passion. Without such stimulus he could not bring out all the rare craft and histrionic art that clamored within him for expression. For full play of his genius he had to have an adequate dramatic vehicle and an appropriate stage setting.

However, Los Angeles was getting too big for such shows. The criminal court calendars were becoming crowded and judges were trying their best to dispose of the multitude of cases. Also, it had become more difficult to secure newspaper publicity because of the World War then in progress.

Yet despite the absence of spectacular cases these were the most productive years financially of Earl's life. The four or five years following the Darrow trial found the Rogers income exceeding the $100,000 mark annually. Members of his staff were given whatever the whim of the moment prompted. At times it was little enough; at others Earl's generosity astonished his aides. But those in the office were well satisfied as a rule. Association with the bar's leading criminal lawyer meant prestige and also brought in considerable private business.

At times, though, the line dividing private legal business of individuals of the Rogers entourage, and that which might be rated as accruing to the firm as a whole, was uncertain. One incident of that nature turned out to be intensely amusing to all who were familiar with it, except Frank Dominguez, who still shared offices with Rogers.

Dominguez had secured a case from a wealthy woman by extolling the supposed infallible virtue of his associate although he knew at the time that Rogers was at the full tide of one of his magnificent drunks. Certain of winning the case, Dominguez had the client deposit the fee of $2,500 in a bank, to be delivered to him if her suit were successful. He expected to finish the trial and collect the money before Earl would have finished his engagement with the demon rum.

Rogers did not appear at all during the trial of the suit, which his associate won. Dominguez had no reason to believe that Rogers knew anything about it, but as the twelve men filed in from the jury room with their verdict Earl slipped quietly into the courtroom, sober, faultlessly attired, serene and debonair as if he had never in his life touched a drop of liquor. And while the beaming Dominguez was being kept busy acknowledging the congratulations of court officials and fellow attorneys, Rogers without ostentation escorted the victorious client to a taxicab.

On the way to the bank, by a few adroit queries Earl learned how much she had agreed to pay the firm if successful in her litigation, and while she was still glowing from her triumph he induced her to raise the fee to $4,000. As the whole argument in persuading her to retain Dominguez had been based upon Earl Rogers' great reputation and ability, the lady showed no hesitation in turning the money over to the latter, who kept every dollar of it, much to the dismay of the protesting Dominguez.

A prolific source of income to Rogers was provided during this period by the less spectacular forms of law practice, such as contested wills. His handling of the Talent case had resulted in Rogers becoming considered a master in such litigation. His fees were unusually large in any will contest that he would undertake, and his services of this character were applied in the same year to cases as widely separated as San Diego and the state of Maine.

There was no cessation of the murder cases brought to the Rogers office. Some he accepted and others he turned down. The latter were usually hopeless ones, the sure losers. Some that he took apparently were hopeless, but with him a loser was one that was hopeless to Earl Rogers only, for his overweening ego inspired in him the belief that he could discern elements upon which to predicate a successful defense in many instances where nothing of the kind was apparent to the average attorney. And the outcome of such cases almost invariably bore out his arrogant self-appraisal.

Hard cases nearly always meant guilty clients and in more

[273]

than one instance Rogers would have lost but for the friendship of the local police. In numerous instances Earl had
defended peace officers charged with various offenses, some
serious and others trivial, without exacting a fee. There was
a strong bond of sympathy between the men who upheld the
law and the man who led all others in rescuing important
offenders from the justice they deserved.

From the time, years before, when he had obtained the
liberation of the detective trio in the Choisser killing, there
seemed to be an unwritten law among the principals of the
police department that Rogers was to get all the breaks. Just
as Earl would defend a member of the force without cost,
so would any of the law officers lend him a helping hand
without any thought of pecuniary reward. That meant great
help in actually preparing a case as well as in other respects.

It was during this period, when his financial returns were
the richest of his career, when he was seemingly at his peak,
that the decline of Earl Rogers began.

Mere flesh and blood could not stand the strain that was
placed upon Earl by the mass of work that piled into the
office and his efforts to relieve that strain by the old method.
At this critical period came to him a crushing blow in the loss
of his first murder trial. Whether this defeat was directly
caused by the weakening of his physical and mental powers
or whether this blow to his professional pride speeded his
descent has always been a moot question among his close
friends. It is difficult to judge between them; and both are
probably right, in a measure.

The blow was in reality a double one as defeat came to
the Rogers banner in two successive trials, one of which resulted in the first sentence of hanging to an Earl Rogers
client. In reality, however, neither, strictly speaking, was his
own case and had he been permitted to follow the dictates of
his own policy he would have rejected both of them. In one of
them, the Bundy case, Earl was induced by Frank Dominguez

to come to the latter's aid. Once in it he regarded it as his own
case, and failure to save Bundy from the gallows was looked
upon by him as a personal disaster. His imperious nature and
supreme ego could not brook defeat. In the second of these
defeats, the Tugwell murder case, he took over the defense
after a first trial in which the defendant had been convicted.

The murder committed by young Charles Bundy was of
an unusually revolting nature. Early one evening he telephoned to a drug store in the neighborhood in which he
lived, asking that a bottle of perfume be delivered at a certain
street number in the vicinity. He requested that the messenger
bring change for twenty dollars. As the delivery boy, Frank
Zeese, passed a lonely spot Bundy sprang out of the darkness,
seized the boy and choked him into insensibility. Then he
dragged him into the deeper shadows, killed him with a club,
and robbed him of the twenty dollars.

The killer, not more than eighteen years old, had no defense
to offer, stolidly admitting that he had committed the crime
to purchase a gift for a girl friend who had written him that
she would arrive in Los Angeles from Santa Barbara late
that evening. He was broke and wanted to buy the girl a
purse.

Quite unexpectedly, to the prosecution, Rogers put young
Bundy on the stand and the nature of his direct examination
created a sensation. The prosecution had strained to make
the crime appear as brutal as it possibly could. With the defendant himself on the stand, Rogers, rather than attempt to
mitigate the nature of the crime, drew from the boy even
more harrowing details. He had him enlarge upon the brutal
phases of the murder until Dominguez sought to protest and
the prosecutors gasped in amazement.

There was nothing to be gained by the state in cross-
examining Bundy, for Rogers had induced the witness to
testify to such horrifying phases of his act that no questioning
could have made his admissions more terrible.

It was only when Rogers swung into his final argument to the jury that the opposition came to a full realization of his strategy: that he had made of the case a revolting record of inhuman brutality in an attempt to convince the jury that no sane person could have committed such an atrocious crime. It was a desperate expedient, and it failed. Bundy was found guilty and sentenced to hang, the first verdict of the kind ever returned by a jury that had listened to Earl Rogers.

Rogers made a heroic effort to overcome the judgment. He abhorred retrials. His policy had always been to win his case before a jury. He realized that in the first trial he had always disclosed the full strength of his case. Armed with this knowledge, the prosecution in a retrial could anticipate his every move. It was always difficult to bring in new witnesses because evidence not used in the original hearing is generally regarded with suspicion. It looked pretty black for Rogers because he was really considering the case from his own personal perspective. True, young Bundy was the man who might swing on the gallows, but to his defender the great, overwhelming tragedy was that, contrary to all precedents, a client of Earl Rogers had been convicted and sentenced to death.

The oral argument of Rogers before the California Supreme Court in behalf of young Bundy is to this day regarded by criminal pleaders of the state as something of a classic. His plea was based on the theory that the defendant was insane. He argued also that Bundy, in being required to answer the questions of state alienists before the trial, had been deprived of his constitutional rights by being compelled to testify against himself. This contention by Rogers was a unique twisting of the law.

A still further argument was based on the ground that Judge Willis had erred in instructing the jury when he warned them against a defense of insanity.

"The jury was told," Rogers declared, "that moral insanity

is no defense, but we had not made a claim of moral insanity. I am not asking for anything but the safety of society, and ask that this boy be sent to the penitentiary for life, for I believe he is incurably insane."

"If you believe he is insane," asked Justice Crenshaw, deeply interested in Earl's concise but erudite plea, "why do you wish him sent to the penitentiary?"

"Because so many of those sent to asylums are prematurely released. I believe this defendant presents a typical case of sadism or congenital insanity, added to by traumatism, and I do not believe he should be hanged. His insanity is permanent. That is why I ask that he be sent to the penitentiary for life, the only logical and humane course for this honorable tribunal to pursue."

The oral plea to the higher court was so convincing that it resulted in a difference of opinion among the learned judges, but the majority upheld the verdict. Bundy was hanged.

CHAPTER XXXI

THE Tugwell case was similar in many respects to the Bundy case. Young Percy Tugwell was accused of having lured the mother of his chum into a vacant lot where he murdered her. The victim, Mrs. Maude Kennedy, had been found strangled as the result of an attempt to chloroform her. When arrested in San Francisco several days later young Tugwell had in his possession a diamond which was identified as one of those owned by the slain woman.

Tugwell was brought to Los Angeles, tried and convicted of murder in the first degree, with punishment fixed at life imprisonment. His defense was based on the testimony of his young wife, who insisted that the diamond belonged to her and that she had given it to him to obtain a new setting after the ring had been stepped upon and crushed. She had produced in support of her story a setting, the prongs of which were bent.

This evidence and a sentimental appeal based upon the fact that the young wife was approaching motherhood saved young Tugwell from the gallows.

Then Rogers was brought into the case. After going over the transcript he at first unhesitatingly rejected it, declaring that Tugwell was lucky to get off with a life sentence. But those who invoked his aid were insistent, and against his better judgment Earl assumed the burden of getting young Tugwell out of his predicament.

An appeal carried to the Supreme Court was based on the refusal of the lower court to admit into evidence the repudiation of a confession made by the accused man shortly after his arrest. Earl also made a showing that the defendant had not been properly represented by counsel in his first trial.

Desperate as the case was in the first instance, it was rendered a far more difficult ordeal for the defense by unexpected and disastrous developments just before the second trial opened.

Rogers was again opposed by William C. Doran, chief deputy district attorney, his adversary in the Darley case. Convinced that the story of the young wife was false, Doran by clever detective work discovered where the damaged setting had been purchased after the diamond had been found in Tugwell's possession. In addition he obtained, by means of a search warrant, a score of letters written by members of the Tugwell family during the first trial, that were said to contain even more damaging evidence of Tugwell's guilt. A detective employed by Rogers to do some "fishing" in the vicinity of the district attorney's office brought back the staggering information regarding the ring and the letters.

Now even the flimsy evidence upon which the defense was founded in the first trial was completely swept away. Knowing that the ring testimony could not again be brought into the case without inviting disastrous consequences, Earl decided not to put on the stand a single witness who had testified at the first trial.

Without a shred of evidence left upon which to reorganize his defense, Rogers determined to fight it out without regard to the advice of his associates to seek a compromise with the district attorney's office. Even a life sentence looked good to them at that juncture.

But Earl doggedly insisted that he would not only save Tugwell from the gallows, but would get him complete freedom. For the first time his associates questioned his judgment. Now they were pretty sure that Rogers was slipping.

The trial proceeded, the prosecutor certain of a conviction

with the extreme penalty, Rogers fighting with his back to the wall.

As never before in a career filled with desperate cases he had to resort to all those indefinable psychological tricks of which he alone was master. He kept the prosecution continually on trial with never-ending pretexts, confused their witnesses hopelessly by his rapier-like cross-examination, constantly created doubt in the jurors' minds by his gift of insidious suggestion; and, as always when driven to desperate measures, wound up his whirlwind defense by trying the case during his argument before the twelve men in the box.

Despite his loss of every iota of evidence upon which the first defense lawyer had done no better than barely save his client from hanging, Earl once again accomplished the seeming impossible—got the defendant off with only a sentence of seven years for manslaughter.

Yet he regarded it as a humiliating defeat, so towering was his estimate of his own ability as a pleader. There followed the usual debauch and a lengthy period of mental depression. Soon thereafter came the first break in the personnel of his highly efficient office staff.

Rogers and his associates were defending a physician charged with malpractice. Earl was examining an especially difficult witness and as a last resort he drew out the deadly lorgnette with a view of disconcerting the man on the stand. He snapped open the "specs on a stick," as the court habitués called it, and bringing his face as close to the witness as he could, he held the glasses to his eyes and peered at his intended victim as he would at a loathsome insect. The witness drew back and the court interrupted to ask the man being interrogated if the counsel's action annoyed him.

"No, your Honor," replied the man on the stand, "he amuses me."

One of the jurors laughed aloud.

Rogers flushed. Silently he closed the lorgnette and returned it to the breast pocket of his coat. He turned to the court and declared that his usefulness to his client had been destroyed, that he was withdrawing from the case. He bowed in dignified manner and started to leave the courtroom. Harry Dehm, who was associated with him in the case, protested. Earl was adamant.

That night Harry Dehm and Frank Dominguez withdrew from the firm and opened an office on another floor of the same building. Jerry Giesler and Milton Cohen remained with Rogers. The former had been with him ten years. He looked upon Earl not only as a mentor but as a benefactor. He had gone to Rogers' office more than ten years previously as a young law student making his way through college as a collection agent. Earl had been lax in paying for some law books he had purchased and young Giesler had been assigned the job of getting the money. Whether he did is not of record, but he did get the offer of a job in Rogers' office, which he accepted eagerly.

Milton Cohen had come to Rogers shortly after the Darrow trial and Earl ascribed much of his financial success to the ability of the young Philadelphian in handling the fixing and collecting of his fees.

The desertion of Dehm and Dominguez was really the beginning of the end of the remarkable career of Earl Rogers. But his ego would not permit him even to consider the thought that he himself was slipping. He insisted that the profession was degenerating. His oldest son, Bogart, was then attending college at Stanford, preparing to follow in his father's footsteps. Earl wrote him that the legal profession was falling from its lofty standing and advised him to give it up. He declared there was no future in it and that any other profession was preferable. Soon after this incident Bogart left school and went to Canada, where he joined the Royal Flying Corps to rise to the rank of a captaincy in the World War.

One of the arguments which Earl offered his son in his effort to wean him from his chosen course was a paper he had written while in this depressed mood. It deplored the condition of the profession and foretold its end as an honorable career. It had been intended for publication in a magazine, but for some reason or other had never been submitted by the author. Years later it was dug out of a lot of dustcovered files for the purpose of publishing it in this volume. It follows, just as written by Earl Rogers, an amazing and accurate prophecy which if read carefully today must astound any thinking persons with the completeness of its fulfillment:

THE DESTRUCTION OF A PROFESSION

It was not many years ago that the minister was the foremost citizen of any locality. Uusually, he was the general adviser in matters spiritual and material of the entire community. Frequently, he was the only man well enough informed to be competent to advise.

A little later the legal profession came into prominence. The lawyer was regarded as something apart from the ordinary run of people. His education and familiarity with business concerns made him the mentor of most of the people of his vicinity, and he had the respect and deference which always is paid to superior intellectuality.

The preacher lost his preferment through no fault of his own, but because of conditions. The lawyer is threatened with extinction for much the same reasons. I venture the assertion that the time is not a great way ahead when what the profession knows as the good lawyer will be eliminated from communal life. Even a young man can remember when, in the ordinary community, the principal lawyer was regarded as the foremost citizen. Respect and deference were paid to him, largely because of his intellectual superiority. He has not only lost his position at the head of things, but he is about to lose his professional life.

The legal profession is about to be disposed of and relegated to the limbo of things unneeded. This is not altogether so because of the general dissemination of knowledge, nor because the average man of today is quite as well educated as is the attorney or counsellor, whom he formerly looked up to.

The conditions of modern business life have eliminated the lawyer. He has gone as much as the horse has disappeared from our city streets. He is no longer needed.

A large part of the business of the lawyer of a quarter of a century ago was in the advising and carrying through real estate transactions. An abstract of title was submitted to him, which consisted of copies of all deeds and records affecting the ownership of the property; his opinion was asked as to the legality of all previous transfers, and upon his direction and advice the property was bought or sold. When I commenced the practice of law my first few years were spent in examining large black books of copies of records, out of which I deduced the ownership of the property. I drew the deeds and conveyance necessary to a proper and legal transfer; I was paid according to the amount involved and the labor required.

Today in every well-regulated community there is an abstract and title insurance company which employs clerks, a few lawyers or many, which gives certificates of title, which insures the validity and rectitude of such titles. The purchaser deposits his money in escrow with this company and it is delivered to the seller upon the discovery by that company that it can issue a certificate of clear title to the purchaser. No lawyer is consulted, and no lawyer's opinion is asked. No lawyer's activities are deemed necessary. This one system has filched from the profession fully a quarter of its business.

The old-time lawyer was called upon, in the event of an accident or a catastrophe of any sort, either to bring suits for those injured or to defend those from whom damages were sought. Today every automobile owner, every proprietor of a business establishment, either insures himself with a guaranty company against accident and loss by collision, accident, and what not, or else, if the establishment be large enough, there is a bureau of small lawyers kept for the purpose of defending or adjusting the claims.

Whenever there is an accident in the ordinary city there descends upon the scene a swarm of "ambulance-chasers," so-called "claim adjusters," who, not being lawyers themselves, solicit—this an exceedingly mild word to express the performance—the cases of all those injured, promising recoveries and no expense to the unfortunates, there being paid to the claim adjuster a commission for his valuable services in securing payment for such injuries as may exist. No reputable lawyer will employ these men, but I am safe in saying that ninety percent of the prosecution of damage cases is committed to these claims agencies, who employ some few cheap attorneys to handle them. The ethical lawyer declines to compete.

So the defense and prosecution of accident cases has largely been eliminated from the lawyer's business.

In the matter of estates of deceased persons, there is even a greater destruction of professional activity. Only a few years ago, every man went to his lawyer and had his last will and testament drawn and prepared for submission to the court after his death, usually appointing his wife or some near relative as executor and relying upon his attorney for advice as to the disposition of his affairs and concerns after his death. Today, in practically every city in the country, whether large or small, every trust company, every bank, advertises to draw wills without compensation for such drafting, providing the trust company is named executor of the estate. No reputable lawyer will advertise in such a way, but these companies announce themselves ready to draw wills without cost to the testator. If they are named as executors the companies will furnish the required bonds and generally carry on the affairs of the estate in such a way as to require no advice or service from a member of the legal profession. These companies employ some few lawyers on a salary. These counsellors appear in court for the company. All of the accounting, the disposition of property and such matters as are required in the closing up of the estate, are done by clerks in the office of the bank or trust company. I venture to say that ninety percent of the probate business of the United States today is being done by trust companies, banks, and corporations of that nature.

Physicians and surgeons always have been the prey of dissatisfied patients who expected a physician or a surgeon to restore them to absolute health and entire physical perfection. Because of the failure of the medical profession to accomplish the impossible, thousands of malpractice suits are brought every year by patients who claim lack of skill or improper treatment on the part of their medical attendants. Formerly the defense of doctors against such exactions constituted a portion of a lawyer's practice by no means to be overlooked. Today every doctor carries an insurance against such attempts to secure money from him. These insurance companies defend these cases and pay such judgments as, perchance, may be procured—they are rare—and these companies hire a lawyer for a very small salary, sometimes even maintaining lawyers who have no other business or concern. The average lawyer gets no malpractice case unless he chooses to bring suits of this sort, which, as a rule, a reputable lawyer hesitates to assume.

Every corporation maintains its legal bureau; all of the business of any corporation of considerable extent is done by a few men hired at a most inconsiderable salary. The day when the so-called corporation lawyer was able to obtain large fees from syndicates and corporations for legal services has long passed, and it is indeed rare that it is necessary for one of these concerns to consult outside counsel.

Even in the criminal practice there is small consolation for the ethical practitioner. True, there is occasionally a criminal case of notoriety, and, it might be said, distinction. These cases go only to men of wide reputation. The lawyers of the country who can try important criminal cases are very few, and the business is a monopoly in their hands. Most lawyers never get a criminal case of consequence. The ordinary man who is arrested and taken to jail forthwith is importuned by the arresting officer, the jailer, or some other individual who interviews him, and he is urged to give his case to some disreputable legal harpy who pays a commission, divides his fee, with the officer or other person who "steers" the arrested man to his office.

It is only the lawyer of wide acquaintance and a great reputation for successful defenses who, today, gets any business in the criminal courts without paying—as no decent lawyer will—a commission to sheriff, policeman, jailer, or other person of that ilk.

As a member of the faculty of a law school, I look over the thousand or so young men who are struggling to enter upon the legal profession, and I wonder what they are going to do to make a living. I know that not one lawyer in fifty is making money in the honorable and legitimate practice of his profession. I know that only a small percentage of them are making a living, and that the remainder are either stealing or starving to death.

No lawyer can advertise, yet trust companies and all such organizations advertise to do the work of the lawyer. If a lawyer should advertise, forthwith he should be disbarred, and yet we hear of no effort on the part of the profession to prevent legal business from being monopolized by these concerns.

There remains to the ethical lawyer today but a small portion of the practice he could expect a few years ago. About all a self-respecting attorney can do today is to take what is left over after these other concerns get through taking the best of everything. The profession stands by and watches its business being filched from it—and does nothing. Courts which promptly would disbar an advertising lawyer, smile a welcome upon the clerk who appears for a powerful trust company in a probate matter.

All that is left to the honorable attorney who declines to take a salary from a corporation and lend his license and learning to their emolument is divorce cases and such unimportant litigation as chances to come his way, unless, perchance, he is a man of great reputation.

Taken in all, I think it may safely be said that the day is not far distant when the lawyer, in the old sense of the word, will be confined exclusively to small towns, small business, and to unimportant litigation.

We have had men of reputation, educated under the old system who, by reason of past performances, are sought after, even by these great corporations. But there are no new men coming up; there are no young lawyers acquiring reputations, because they cannot get the business which enables them to display their ability and learning. The young lawyer of today must enter into employment as a clerk—for he is nothing else—of these syndicates who conduct the practice of law, if he desires any business whatsoever.

Where are our judges to come from? How are lawyers to develop themselves? When the present generation of big men dies off, where are their successors to be educated? Only in the offices of these concerns. Deterioration of the profession is one of the astounding things of today. Its elimination is not far off.

CHAPTER XXXII

Just one more of those fantastic murder cases that inevitably found their way into his offices fell to the lot of Earl Rogers before the complete disintegration of what remained of his staff of legal associates. Despite the knowledge of those closest to him that he was rapidly losing his grip, the general public for a long time was wholly unaware of his impending downfall. To all outward appearances he was the same debonair boulevardier, faultless in dress and deportment and the complete master of his opponents within the railing of the courtroom.

Notwithstanding the spirit of weariness and discontent gnawing within him, he continued to be the same graceful figure before the jury, his diction perfect, his manner courteous as that of the old-time gentleman. But no one knew better than Earl himself that his days as a leader in criminal practice were numbered.

It was in the midst of this era of spiritual turbulence, of rebellion against life, profession and self, that Earl was drawn into the Barrett case. Its high notes of grotesque drama and ghoulish humor must have seemed raucously attuned to the turmoil of his own soul. It gave him a chance to wallow in the uncanny and delve into the occult without stint. It was a holiday for him, perhaps the last murder case that he really enjoyed trying.

Benton L. Barrett, a retired Indiana farmer, sixty-four years old, lived at Santa Monica with a recently married spouse nearly thirty years his junior, and the latter's sixteen-year-old son, Raymond Wright. The marriage was said to have been brought about through the medium of a matrimonial agency. In October, 1916, Mrs. Barrett and the boy disappeared.

Several days later Barrett entered the office of his attorney, Ona Morton, in Los Angeles, and astounded the latter by stating quite casually that he had slain his wife and her son and buried their bodies. His story was vague as to details. Barrett said that his memory was rather poor and he could not think of just how he killed them, but that he was praying continuously for restoration of his mislaid mental faculties.

His attorney was convinced that Barrett was insane, but, realizing that it was a case for the district attorney, took his client immediately to Woolwine's office. The prosecutor had him held for murder and Rogers was engaged to defend him. Jerry Giesler was associated with him in the defense. He had been with Rogers in perhaps two score murder trials and Earl had often declared that he would not try an important case without his aid. His great value to Earl, the latter frequently said, was that he had an uncanny intuition in anticipating every move that might be made by the prosecution. While aiding in the preparation of his own case, Giesler would simultaneously prepare his version of the state's case; so his help was always invaluable.

Rogers could get little out of Barrett. The self-accused man had a very well developed religious complex and he was always praying for guidance, but when it came to giving facts about his crime he was uncertain of everything. He stated that before the killing there had been a family row following his discovery of evidence of infidelity on the part of his wife, her alleged paramour being a husky young blacksmith. He declared that she had not denied his accusations and had belligerently ordered him out of the kitchen where the interview took place. As he was leaving, he said, he picked up a saucer from which a kitten had been drinking milk, whereupon his spouse chided him with the query: "Do you think you are running this kitchen, you old sonofabitch?"

Barrett gave some time to thought and managed to remember a few more details. Later that same day, he asserted, he had gone to the barn to feed the family mule, when his wife and her son entered and attacked him, whereupon he killed both, either with a club or an iron bar. He could not remember which. Then, declared Barrett, he had burned their bodies in a brush pile in the yard. Later, because he did not want the bones lying around, he gathered them in a pail and tossed them into a cesspool in the yard.

Before the preliminary hearing and the subsequent Superior Court action came the usual trial by newspaper. Not a sun set without the addition of some new detail. There was an almost daily discovery of new bones which the state alleged were human and the defense as earnestly insisted belonged to some inferior species.

Detectives employed by the defense learned that prior to Barrett's confession he had been given a remarkable examination by a small coterie of neighbors who had constituted themselves special investigators to discover the whereabouts of the missing couple. The personnel of the volunteer probers was fantastic, to say the least. One was a woman credited with hypnotic powers, another had a son attending a medical college, a third was a male spiritualistic medium. A Holy Roller and a palm reader were also said to be in the group.

As a result of this development of bizarre facts, Rogers maintained that Barrett had been hypnotized by his neighboring probers into believing that he had committed the double murder. A friendly reporter gave the crime a new appellation. It became "The Mental Murder." Theretofore it had been headlined as "The Bonfire Murder."

This was the cue for other volunteer experts to get into the case. Earl with cynical humor encouraged them to do their worst, favoring especially a self-styled scientist who was particularly efficient in the use of the divining rod. This man said that he had discovered innumerable wells with the aid of his hazel branch, sometimes known as the doodle-bug. His theory was that as the human body contained eighty-five percent water his twig would disclose the spot where the bodies were buried. After scouring the Santa Monica hills for days the doodle-bug expert vanished from the scene, without finding a single corpse.

The cesspool gave up a variegated assortment of bones and a gold dental filling which were identified by various experts in various ways. There was some confusion when the defense detectives and reporters brought in more bones. There seemed to be more than enough for two bodies, state and defense garnering a grand total that would start any fair-sized graveyard in business.

An expert from a Los Angeles crematory was called in by the defense and avowed that it was a physical impossibility for Barrett to have burned the bodies in a brush fire. A horde of alienists, engaged by the defense, after examining the accused solemnly declared that the prisoner was suffering from hypnotism and autohypnosis; that his confession had been brought about through malign occult influence. This clinched the theory of a "mental murder."

The case was further involved by rumors and published reports that the supposedly murdered Mrs. Barrett and her son had been seen in San Diego, or Texas, or Kansas. These reports were printed in the newspapers while the trial was in progress and served to help confuse the issue until everyone concerned was running around in circles. It was intimated that the defense counsel had something to do with these beclouding rumors.

Throughout it all Barrett remained calm and unexcited. He showed worry but once. That was when, on a visit to his home, a newspaper photographer took some flashlight pictures in the parlor. He was afraid that the lace curtains might have been blackened by the flash. On the stand, after a rather strenuous cross-examination by the state, Rogers had the defendant admit that he didn't have any distinct memory of any phase of the entire mess.

Rogers argued for the liberation of his client on two grounds, the non-existence of a *corpus delicti,* and insanity. That is, there was no tangible evidence that Barrett had killed the missing mother and son, but, if he had, he was mentally deranged.

The jury had its doubts about the bone exhibit, and brought in a verdict of insanity. Barrett was committed to an institution where he remained for some years. He was eventually liberated and returned to Indiana.

The case took its place in Los Angeles criminal annals as an unsolved crime, some of those who worked on the case still insisting on a theory that the mother and son had themselves manufactured the evidence of murder before disappearing.

Earl's downward progress was accelerated at about this time. He began to show his deterioration in his personal appearance. He appeared frequently at his office unshaven and with bedraggled apparel. Whatever money came into the office was squandered without thought of his patient assistants and his domestic obligations. His retrogression professionally was fully as marked. He began to accept cases for the money only. He still boasted of his efficient preparation for court contests, but his professional abilities could not but be seriously impaired by his mental and physical degeneration. Hope that his love for beautiful Teddy Landers would bring about complete rehabilitation was short-lived.

At a family council it was decided to have Rogers sent to a sanitarium. He was haled into the court which dealt with psychopathic cases, on a complaint signed by a sister. It was agreed that he be kept in a private institution at Glendale, a Los Angeles suburb, Rogers finally assenting to the plan. But he never again spoke to, or of, his sister, so bitterly did he resent this move. He referred to it as the crowning disgrace of his long career, despite the fact that there was no publicity in connection with his confinement.

Upon being discharged, Earl made another effort to restore himself. He was afforded an opportunity in a sensational libel suit against a Los Angeles newspaper, the last civil case in which he appeared. Joseph Scott, an eminent Los Angeles lawyer who had been associated with the McNamara defense and who was a power in Republican politics, was the plaintiff and the *Los Angeles Record* the defendant. Scott asked a large sum in damages because of an allegedly libelous story with reference to his withdrawal from a lawsuit. Rogers was employed as chief counsel for the defense. His associate was a young attorney, Leon Yankwich, now a prominent California jurist.

Earl pulled himself together for the trial of this suit because he believed that with the publicity involved it would reinstate him professionally in public esteem. Throughout the case he conducted himself in much of the old, brilliant manner. His mind was apparently as keen as in his palmiest days, his cunning in cross-examination unimpaired, his resourcefulness in general tactics as masterful as ever. The case attracted much attention and resulted in a defeat, if an award of $1 damages could be regarded as such.

"They never come back," Earl used to repeat the famous saying of Charley Van Loan regarding erstwhile pugilistic champions. He knew in his heart that this "comeback" was merely a brief respite, a pause of the toboggan in his headlong plunge down the slide.

The next day Earl was picked up in the street helplessly drunk and taken to the French Hospital. An hour or two later, Paul Schenck, an old friend and former legal associate, received a telephone message from Earl that he was dying and wanted to see him at once. Schenck had witnessed previous "death bed" scenes in which Earl had played the star rôle, but, realizing something of the pace at which the other had been traveling, he feared that this one might be genuine.

As Schenck entered the room he affected a gay air and demanded to know what Rogers meant by saying he was going to die.

"Going to die?" dramatically queried the white-faced Rogers. "I've already died!"

"Well, you're a pretty live-looking corpse," vouchsafed his former colleague.

"Nevertheless," declared Earl doggedly, "I was dead when they got to me in that gutter."

Then he went into a detailed story of his sensations as life had left him; the comments of the police who had picked him up as a dead man. Despite the fact that the end had come, his detached consciousness or soul hovered near and he could recall everything that occurred about his lifeless clay and every word that was uttered. It was all very complimentary to the supposed decedent and highly dramatic. Even the first physician called to his side had failed to find any semblance of pulse. The great Earl Rogers was really dead. "There will never be another like him," he quoted one of the police who were bearing the body.

Yet, despite his demise, a mysterious manifestation of Providence had allowed him to come back to life. There were things to be done; and only Paul, his old friend, could be entrusted with these last services.

"But," he continued solemnly, "in a half hour I shall die again and that passing will be final. That's why I sent for you in such a hurry. Now—"

"Just a minute, Earl," interrupted the lawyer. "Before we go into this, how would you like to have a drink?"

Earl sat upright in bed.

"Got one on you?" he demanded eagerly.

"Sure," declared Schenck, as he pulled out a small flask. He had armed himself previously.

Earl grasped it and took a long pull.

Then he handed back the almost emptied flask and started to slide out of bed.

"How the hell did I get in here, Paul?" he complained. He began to dress himself. "Come on over to the office, I've got some stuff there that's a little better than the rotgut you drink."

CHAPTER XXXIII

ORDINARILY Earl Rogers would not have undertaken the defense of young Harold Denman. It was a sure loser on the very face of it. Only a miracle could save him from the gallows, and Earl knew that miracles did not occur in the course of a criminal trial. Only the pressing need of money with which to buy liquor could have induced him to take it. He had dropped so far in the professional scale that he now had to depend on sporadic minor cases to provide him with the necessaries of life.

Harold Denman, just twenty-one years old in 1918, was a soldier at Camp Kearney, near San Diego. While on furlough in Los Angeles with two other companions the trio got drunk and attempted to rob a small grocery store to get money for more liquor. During the holdup Denman shot and killed Philip Metz, owner of the store.

After hearing every angle of the story Rogers was impressed with the futility of trying to save his client through any of the usual trial methods. He went to the district attorney and offered a plea of guilty to murder in the second degree. The offer was rejected. He offered a plea of guilty of murder in the first degree if the state would agree to a sentence of life imprisonment. This also was turned down.

Rogers buckled on his armor and went to trial with little hope in his heart, but determined to do his best to save the young doughboy from the gallows. He had a deep feeling for the accused youth; realizing better than anyone else the impulse under which the boy slew the man he was attempting to rob. No one knew better than Earl Rogers what alcohol would do to a young fellow of Denman's type.

The only evidence that could be introduced by the defense was that of fellow soldiers who testified to Denman's drinking habits. According to them he was a confirmed alcoholic and had also used marahuana, the frenzy-producing weed of the Mexicans. Of course Earl tried his old trick of putting the prosecution and state witnesses on trial, as well as his other familiar stratagems. But, somehow or other, the old devices seemed weak and futile. Each day convinced Earl that his client would wind up at the end of the thirteen steps in San Quentin's death house.

On the last day of the pleas to the jury, Rogers, at the final moment, determined to stake all on a bold stroke. He had always taken chances, with his own life as well as with the lives of others, and had almost invariably won.

Rogers began his argument by tracing the history of the young soldier since he joined the army. The defendant, said Earl, was not a man of strong mental powers, but rather a weakling, who fell an easy prey to the habits of his most vicious companions and within a short time was enslaved by alcohol.

Soon thereafter his craving was unsatisfied by ordinary whisky. Lemon and other flavoring extracts, paregoric and like fluids containing either alcohol or the more insidious drugs, were consumed regularly by soldiers, according to counsel for the defense, who went on to describe how the smoking of marahuana, which Denman had learned from companions who had been on the Mexican border, produced a state similar to insanity, rendering him unaccountable for his deeds.

Just enough fact had been adduced from the defense's witnesses to give Earl's specious plea a color of logic and sincerity. There were indications that the jurors were reacting favorably to the Rogers' treatment. He felt encouraged to launch the desperate stroke upon which the life of his client depended. He told of the departure of the trio for Los Angeles on leave from the strenuous military training; how Denman and his merry-making companions realized they were soon to go "over there," perhaps to give their lives for their country; and that, exhilarated by the sense of temporary freedom from restraint and obsessed with the coming ordeal, they had drunk some of the poisonous concoctions that were always available to soldiers if they had the price.

"Then gentlemen, what happened?" Rogers impressively asked the twelve men who were intently taking in every word that fell from his lips. "Is it necessary for me to recount it? Have you not already surmised what that vicious chain of circumstance was? When this boy's brain was inflamed by alcohol, when he was no longer responsible, only a human automaton, he did what for a whole cruel year had been ground into his consciousness, what his government had taught him to do—he *killed!*"

Judge Craig half rose in his chair. Lawyers sitting within the rail gasped. With patriotic fervor at its highest pitch since the United States had entered the war, a statement of similar import made on the street would have been regarded as treason. But the jury was obviously impressed.

Rogers wiped his pallid brow. He was shaking as if with ague as he dropped heavily into his chair. However, he turned a look of triumph in the direction of the row of state's counsel. Then he threw an arm about the shoulders of young Harold Denman and patted him encouragingly.

The final argument of the prosecution was the customary stereotyped plea for hanging. It was concluded just as the noon hour struck and the usual recess was declared. As lawyers, jury, courtroom attachés and spectators emerged from the Hall of Justice pandemonium greeted them. Flags were waving, whistles blowing. Newsboys were shrieking: "Americans in Great Victory!" "Hindenburg Line Finally Broken!"

We were at last actually in the War, killing our enemies, driving them back to their own soil. Our warlike preparations for the past year, stern training of our young soldiers, were justified—were bearing fruit in death and destruction of the hated Hun.

Rogers paused on the uppermost of the steps. He gazed at the yelling newsboys, then at the twelve jurors as they marched in double file to the nearby café for lunch. Earl knew that before they would get there each of the twelve would know what had happened, that they too would be fired by the general exaltation, that the temporary revulsion against militarism created by his address would go glimmering.

He shrugged his shoulders in a gesture of hopeless resignation and started for what remained of his office suite. There was sure to be a drink around there somewhere.

Twenty minutes after the jury retired that afternoon a verdict was brought in. Denman was found guilty of murder in the first degree and his punishment fixed at death on the gallows.

It was Earl Rogers' last murder case. In his time he had freed four score or more from the dangling noose, most of them guilty. It was an ironic prank of fate that in his last defense of a murderer, the supreme penalty should have been invoked.

But it was even more than that, more than justice finally meted out to a criminal. The discouraged lawyer knew its full portent. He realized that it was his own death sentence, the verdict that sounded the knell of his own career.

Yet before Earl Rogers passed into the outer shades he was given an opportunity to make one final dramatic appearance in a courtroom, a chance to make one last inspired plea before an earthly judge before the drawing of the curtain on the stage he loved to tread. He was at the gloomy evening of his career. Excesses had burned him out until he was only a despairing shadow of the once incomparable counsellor.

Earl's law practice had wholly disappeared. Former friends shunned him because of the tragedy of an encounter. His hitherto immaculate dress had become the bedraggled and wrinkled attire of the outcast. His once proud shoulders drooped. His hair was white despite the fact that he was not yet fifty. Eyes that had hypnotized courtrooms were now sunken and lack-lustre.

No one knows just why Earl Rogers should have been employed to defend the young son of a well-to-do Hollywood family, who had been indicted by the Federal grand jury on a charge of attempting to evade the draft. He no longer had an office, although his name appeared on the door of an obscure attorney. Those ten letters still stood for something in the eyes of those who were not conversant with his degeneration, and any number of young lawyers, or older and more unscrupulous ones, were willing to keep Earl in liquor and food for the privilege of having his name over their own on an office door. It was always easy to say: "Sorry, but Mr. Rogers is busy in court and will be occupied for some days with an important trial. I am his partner and perhaps I can serve you." Nearly always it worked.

Unquestionably it was the former glory of Earl Rogers that sent the relatives of young Joseph Leroy, Jr., to him. Leroy was indicted for conspiracy to evade the draft and he had as co-defendants an optometrist named Howenstine and a nurse named Mrs. Kennedy. The scheme had unusual features, it being alleged by the government that Leroy had been induced to pay $1,000 for a pair of spectacles which would affect his eyes in such manner that he would be rejected for the army because of defective vision. The nurse's part in the plot was bringing prospective draft evaders to the doctor's office. The three defendants were denied separate trials and each went into court represented by separate counsel.

Realizing Earl's desperate condition, strenuous efforts were made to keep him out of the courtroom. It was feared he might jeopardize not only the liberty of his own client, but that of the other defendants. Just a glance at him was sufficient to justify their qualms. One of the other attorneys went to Rogers and told him he would appear gratuitously in his behalf. Earl stubbornly refused to listen.

Then an appeal was made to his own family to intercede. It was considered possible that his very appearance in the United States court might result in his disbarment and the ending of his career in professional disgrace. But when his own kinfolk called upon him in the squalid room of a cheap rooming house near the Federal building and pleaded with him to withdraw from the case, he gave the same answer:

"I have accepted a fee from Joseph Leroy and when the time comes for him to appear I shall be in court to defend him."

Rogers came into court in tow of a young law graduate who had just been admitted to the bar. He was unkempt. His clothes were dirty and rumpled, his linen and necktie frayed and soiled. He had not shaved for days and the heavy white stubble of his beard accentuated the lines graven deep in his features by dissipation.

Rogers was still obviously drunk, but quiet and unobtrusive in his abject misery. As the trial began Earl slept intermittently, head bowed forward on his chest. At times his embarrassed young companion prodded him awake, but he took no apparent interest in the proceedings. His client's case seemed anything but hopeful.

Only once during the early stages of the trial did Rogers evince any animation. He had risen to mutter a request that certain character witnesses be allowed to testify for his client, but upon immediate objection from the prosecution the court had promptly ruled against the motion.

The following day, however, Rogers lurched to his feet and reopened the question. As he did so, the other attorneys on his side started up in alarm, as if to restrain him, but Judge Bledsoe indicated his desire that Rogers continue. He and Earl had been boyhood chums and associated in several cases during their early days of practice.

Swaying slightly, Earl Rogers began addressing the court in husky accents. But gradually his voice cleared. In a few moments judge and attorneys were listening intently; for this burnt-out legal derelict once again, through some strange mental process, was accurately and subtly interpreting the rules of evidence, once more his touch on law was sure, his logic irrefutable.

When he had concluded, his wracked frame quivering from the intensity of his effort, Judge Bledsoe knew—every lawyer in the courtroom knew—that Rogers was right. And the Judge created what the daily papers called a precedent in Federal jurisprudence by reversing himself, changing his ruling of the previous day, and permitting counsel for the defense to introduce several witnesses to testify to the good character of Rogers' client.

Against this unexpected ruling the prosecution protested vigorously. "It is Mr. Rogers' purpose," bitterly declared Assistant U. S. Attorney Palmer, "to bring here people of wealth and fashion from Hollywood—neighbors of the Leroys—to awe members of the jury by the majesty of money."

As the prosecutor linked Rogers' name with the "people of wealth and fashion" Earl smiled for the first time during the trial. He gazed ironically at his rumpled clothes, ran his shaking fingers over the white stubble on his chin, and his smile broadened to a sardonic grin. Then he sat down and closed his eyes again.

With the exception of a few intervals of wakefulness marked by barely discernible interest in the courtroom's activities Rogers continued to doze drunkenly through the draft evasion trial. Finally the other attorneys for the defense were done, their arguments to the jury concluded. Judge Bledsoe, the jurors, lawyers and spectators were nervous and ill at ease as the time for Earl's address to the jury approached. Pityingly, they feared it would be a lamentable spectacle, this shabby ghost of the once brilliant Earl Rogers exhibiting itself before an embarrassed tribunal.

But the Rogers who swung into action for his client on that last day of the trial was no longer the wretched outcast who had sat hunched in his chair throughout the case. Somewhere, somehow, he had secured one of the fine suits worn by him in former days; probably he had retrieved it from some pawn shop. It was immaculately clean and freshly pressed. His linen was spotless. He was freshly shaven.

Rogers was apparently sober for the first time in months, although the sudden abstention from alcohol had left him shaking like a leaf. But as he spoke his quivering gradually ceased, his sunken cheeks took on a faint glow, and before his pleasantly modulated voice had been cutting through the room's silence many moments his auditors realized that Earl Rogers' dead spirit had risen miraculously from the graveyard of forgotten things, that here before them was another resurrection.

His somber eyes glowed anew with the flame of genius. Once more his incisive accents thrilled every hearer. His clean-cut summation of the evidence had the graceful flow of a poem. Again he spoke with the tongue of men and of angels. Here was a resurgence of the master intellect which had freed Clarence Darrow, Patrick Calhoun, and countless others from the law's remorseless clutch.

After a concise discussion of the evidence against young Leroy, skillfully obscuring many damaging points with his wily sophistries, he began to speak of himself and his forbears. He told of the Rogers men who had fought for the flag in the American Revolution and in the War of 1812. He related the patriotic service of his clan in the Mexican War and in the struggle between the North and the South. He brought his story down to the present.

"And in this present world cataclysm wherein the very salvation of humanity is at stake," he intoned, "this generation of my family are living up to the glorious traditions of the Rogers breed. My oldest son, like all of us patriotic to the core, knowing that I would rather see him make the supreme sacrifice than that a link in our patriotic service be broken, did not wait to be drafted. No, he went across to Canada and joined the British Royal Flying Corps that he might lose no precious time entering the service of the allies. My daughter Adela was one of the first to enlist for war work although she had a nursing babe at her breast at the time.

"And I, too old to be accepted into the ranks, warned by my physician that I have but a short time to live, too broken in health to be of use to my country in any other way, have devoted what remaining strength and powers of persuasion have been left me to beseeching my countrymen all over California to buy the Liberty Bonds which are arming and feeding our soldier boys in their gallant battle for the right."

As he approached the end of his address to the jury he paused in his pacing so that he stood beneath the Stars and Stripes draped high on the courtroom wall. Then, his mellifluous voice vibrant with a depth of feeling no juror would doubt, he delivered his peroration:

"Do you think that with the American traditions of the Rogers family behind me I could stand in this courtroom, beneath that American flag, and ask for the acquittal of this boy if I knew not in my heart he were innocent?"

Almost in a state of collapse, Earl falteringly found his way to his chair.

Late that afternoon the jury returned to the courtroom with its verdict. Howenstine and Mrs. Kennedy were found guilty as charged in the indictment; Rogers' client, young Joseph Leroy alone, was found not guilty. His two co-defendants went to Federal prison for long terms, and young Leroy went into the army, to serve an honorable enlistment.

In some respects Earl Rogers' plea in behalf of his client was the most spectacular effort of his brilliant and troubled life. True, it was festooned with all the burning emotional appeal and self-dramatization which he had so often found to be his most effective weapon; but the underlying force and shrewdness of his final argument before a jury left it memorable in the history of criminal pleading.

So what mattered it that Earl Rogers had never even thought of asking anyone to buy a Liberty bond, or that he was such a rank and outspoken pacifist that his exasperated family feared constantly that he would be arrested for seditious utterances when patriotic enthusiasm was at its highest point?

CHAPTER XXXIV

"ALL the world's a stage," wrote the greatest of all drama-
tists, but behind the footlights of real life the rules of dramatic construction are often ignored. Seldom indeed does
reality's curtain fall when the drama's climax has been
reached. The greatest tragedy in the life of Earl Rogers was
that the curtain did not fall upon his mortal span when it
was rung down on his professional career.

In her novel and play, "A Free Soul," Adela Rogers St.
Johns followed the accepted formula of the stage. Stephen
Ashe, the fictitious Earl Rogers, fell dead in the courtroom
at the conclusion of his great plea for the life of Ace Wil-
fong. Earl's talented daughter attempted in her story to make
up for the mistake which fate had committed in prolonging a
life that had ended. It was the right place for him to die.

If Earl's heart had stopped as did Stephen Ashe's at the
conclusion of his final plea, as provided by the rules of dramatic art, he would have escaped untold suffering; his relatives and friends would have been spared the lengthening of
a tragedy that was alternately fraught with faint hope and
deep despair.

Even had there been any hope of salvaging what remained
of that once fine body and brilliant mind, the last vestige of
any such hope vanished with the untimely death of his young
wife. Teddy Landers Rogers died during the national epidemic of influenza several months after Earl's farewell appearance in a court of law in behalf of a client. His only
other appearances thereafter were in his own defense.

There was no doubt of Earl Rogers' adoration of his young
and beautiful wife. He worshiped her with all the capacity

of his deeply emotional nature, even though his great love could not pull him out of the quicksands of dissipation which had been steadily sucking him under.

Teddy's life ended on the evening of February 22, 1919. Earl was being cared for at the time by his daughter in a little apartment at Ocean Park. A hard drinking bout had recently ended and he was suffering from a mild attack of the prevailing epidemic. Adela had just put him to bed when the telephone rang. It was Teddy's sister who said that the invalid had suddenly taken a turn for the worse and had been given up by the doctors. Adela did not tell her father that Teddy was dying, but when the car she had hired was stalled en route by a blowout half way to Los Angeles, Earl was told the truth. It was with difficulty that he was restrained from going the remaining miles afoot. He had been told that Teddy was waiting for him. When he finally reached her bedside, life was extinct. Teddy knew that Earl was rushing to her side but there was no waiting.

Months later Earl encountered a group of newspapermen in a café at one of the beach resorts which still permitted the sale of liquor. Invited to have a drink with the scribes, he condescended to join in a libation.

In the midst of his drink, he suddenly burst into tears. A boisterous slap on the back was accompanied by the admonition to "cheer up!" He said that he couldn't because, no matter how much he drank, he could not drive from his mind the sight of his wife as he had last seen her. Then he related a dramatic story of his race across the city to her deathbed.

"As I entered the room," he declared, "the nurse came towards me with a gesture that told me it was all over. I could not be restrained. I dashed to the bedside of my beloved and dropped to my knees. I was horrified by the sight of that dear face; her pain-distorted features were a reproach to me for my tardiness. I implored her to give me one last message, to tell me that I was forgiven. I caressed her face.

Gradually her strained features became softly composed, her dead lips relaxed into a smile of calm, ineffable peace. I knew that I was forgiven and that our love would never die."

There was silence broken only by the soft gurgle of liquid emanating from a bottle. Earl gulped down the drink and then rose. "Well, boys, got to say *adios*. Working on an important brief. Glad to have seen you all again."

He bowed, and with an airy wave of his hand departed. The newspapermen looked after him until the doors closed behind his still graceful figure.

"Well, I'll be damned!" exploded the local correspondent who was playing host.

The hard-boiled old police reporter tossed off one that never even hit the inside of his mouth. He drew a deep breath.

"Do you believe that yarn?" demanded one of the younger scribes.

"Sure I do," replied the old-timer, indignant that there should be any question about it; "every damn word of it!"

By some strange whim of that destiny which had played on him so many fantastic tricks, the existence of Earl Rogers was prolonged just exactly three years to the day beyond that of his wife. At her death he plunged more deeply than ever into the slough of forgetfulness which drink provided. Barely fifty years had he lived, yet he was a broken old man by the spring of 1919. Members of his family made repeated efforts to get him to enter a private institution, wherein his rehabilitation could be attempted. And a number of times, realizing that his health was failing rapidly, he went. But he would never stay more than a few days, or he would soon win his way with the people around the hospital and be allowed to do exactly what he pleased. Out he would come, temporarily benefited, and refuse to consider any further treatment. As always, he would never admit to anyone that he needed help.

[308]

At last, in desperation, his family decided to have him committed involuntarily to a state hospital, whose superintendent was an old family friend. His son Bogart signed the complaint and his daughter Adela, fearful that disgrace and disbarment stared her father in the face, agreed to appear against him.

Notified that a warrant had been issued for him to appear before the psychopathic court, Earl was so enraged that he armed himself, and when a deputy sheriff sought to arrest him, he plunged the revolver into the officer's abdomen and pulled the trigger. The deputy saved his life and Rogers from a felon's cell by thrusting his thumb under the hammer as it fell.

Panic-stricken by the closeness of this disaster, convinced now that unless he had a much needed rest and proper care he might do something that would cause him lasting woe and shame, the family united to put through the commitment order. Rogers was finally brought into court before Judge Louis Meyers.

Everything had previously been arranged. The newspapers, out of friendship and respect for what Earl once had been, agreed not to use the story at all. Dr. Riley, at the state institution at Patton, had made arrangements to give him special care. Everything had been attended to, and the doctors who were to sign the commitment, had known of the condition which made this drastic step necessary.

Once again Rogers rallied his shattered mental forces. He was determined not to permit his commitment on a psychopathic charge. With but little opportunity to prepare a defense, he waged a battle so sensational in its cleverness and eloquence that all of the Los Angeles newspapers gave it front page chronicling. It is doubtful if any lawyer had ever before been placed in the unique position of cross-examining his own children. He quickly nullified the testimony given by his son Bogart by a series of quick, incisive queries. But his whole manner changed when he approached Adela. She had testified that everything possible had been done for her father without avail and expressed the hope that he could be committed to an institution where he would receive every attention and consideration, as the only way to save him from himself.

At the sign that her direct examination was concluded, Earl walked slowly to the witness-stand. As he reached the side of his daughter he leaned over and kissed her on the forehead. Then, looking at her with reproachful eyes, he asked softly: "You don't think I'm crazy, do you, honey?" Adela burst into tears and vigorously shook her head. She could not speak. Earl took her arm and tenderly led her from the witness-stand to her chair.

He turned to the court with a significant gesture. Then he made his last court argument, a plea for his own liberty, against what he bitterly declared to be an attempt to railroad him into an insane asylum. And in spite of the fact that everything had been arranged to commit him, Earl Rogers walked out of the courtroom a free man at the conclusion of his plea. He started for the doors even before the judge had announced dismissal of the charges.

A few weeks later Earl was again haled into court and ordered committed to the state hospital at Norwalk. But it was a compromise commitment, if it could be called such, Rogers finally agreeing to spend six months at the institution provided the court records show that his status was that of having committed himself. The order of the court stated that he could leave the institution after giving a week's notice.

He remained two months and one day. Then without giving any notice he merely walked out of the gate of the institution. His departure was quickly followed by a sensational exposé of the conduct of the place and Rogers found a sop to his ego in the story that he had had himself committed to the Norwalk hospital solely for the purpose of investigating charges of mismanagement. The newspapers were full of the allegations, which were listed specifically as "brutality; unsanitary conditions that are criminal; abominable food; absolute indifference upon the part of the hospital officials to the welfare or health of the inmates, whom they are paid by the State of California to care for and protect." The exposé led to an investigation which resulted in the dismissal of the management by the governor.

There was no charge that Rogers had himself suffered because of the mismanagement of the hospital, as members of his family had provided for a private room and special food for him.

Earl appeared to be in excellent shape physically and mentally and he greatly enjoyed the notoriety which accrued from his charges. He also stated with a grim smile that he had enjoyed the sojourn because of the "opportunity for communion with so many intelligent persons." One of the patients was Horace Appel, who had been associated with Earl in the defense of Clarence Darrow in 1912. Appel, son of a Jewish father and Mexican mother, had been a prominent member of the California bar for years. He had been sent to Norwalk as incurably insane. His aberration was in the nature of delusions of grandeur; he believed himself to be one of the world's wealthiest men.

"Every morning," related Earl, "Horace used to bring me a check for a million dollars. The real reason that I left there was because I found out that his bank account was slightly overdrawn."

The treatment at Norwalk and the enforced abstinence from alcoholic stimulants had done wonders for Earl mentally. The publicity which came because of his exposure of conditions at the hospital also had a beneficial effect. He felt again that he amounted to something. As a result he was intelligently receptive to a suggestion from his daughter that he should complete his regeneration by a stay at the Loma Linda sanitarium, an institution conducted by the Seventh Day Adventists.

He remained at the institution for six months despite the rigid discipline of the place. There was no "tapering off" in the regimen of Loma Linda and no smoking was permitted. Earl suffered acutely from the sudden deprivation of alcohol; cigarets too were barred. If he wanted to smoke he was compelled to walk more than a mile to get outside the grounds. That he remained there despite the hardships of the cure was attributable to his acquaintance with a beautiful woman of high social standing who had gone to Loma Linda for a rest cure. She was about forty and resided in New York. The redeemed Rogers, his charming outer self again restored, conceived for her a sincere affection which this delightful companion reciprocated. They planned marriage, but upon their return to Los Angeles relatives intervened and convinced the lady that any reformation on the part of Earl Rogers could be merely of a temporary nature.

Determined to prove that his regeneration was complete Earl, now keen-eyed and debonair as of yore, went to the ranch of a friend in the mountains to build up his bodily strength. There for two months he chopped trees, indulged daily in long hikes, ate plain and nourishing food and returned to Los Angeles alive with health and vigor, his brain apparently as clear as the snowy uplands whose clean vitality he had absorbed in mind and body.

There was still his professional comeback to be staged. Outwardly he seemed filled with irrepressible vigor, surcharged with ambition. Only to his daughter Adela did he voice the doubts which clouded his vision of the future. To her words of encouragement he shook his head with a sorrowful smile. "I'm just like a badly used auto that's been overhauled and fixed up to fool a credulous buyer," he declared. "It looks fine and will run nicely down hill or on level ground, but once let it hit a steep grade—"

Nevertheless arrangements were made for Earl's reëstablishment in practice. Many attorneys were eager to take into partnership the reclaimed criminal pleader. Decision was finally made to cast his lot with a former Federal judge who had just opened offices in Los Angeles. He desired such an associate as Earl Rogers because of the latter's wide acquaintance and reputation. The partnership seemed ideal. Earl was filled with enthusiasm. He was making his home temporarily with his daughter Adela and on the first morning of his return to actual practice plans were made at breakfast with her to help him select an apartment the following day. Earl left for his new office happier than he had been in years, and more hopeful of the future.

That night Adela was a guest at the home of a friend, a famed motion picture actress. A telephone call came for Mrs. St. Johns. A friendly policeman who had known her since she was a child told her sorrowfully that Earl had just been picked up in a Chinatown gutter, paralyzed drunk.

There was no further attempt at a comeback. In a moment of relative sobriety Earl had confided to his daughter that his task now was to drink himself to death as rapidly as possible. "I don't want to live long enough to hear them say, 'There goes poor old Earl Rogers,'" he declared. He even voiced his estimate of another year as the probable duration of his life.

The fall of 1921 brought Earl a final chance to regain his standing as a lawyer. Roscoe Arbuckle, the "Fatty" of the films, had become involved in a serious difficulty in San Francisco. Powerful friends of the comedian, realizing that he was in danger of a long prison sentence despite their belief in his innocence, endeavored to induce Earl to undertake his defense.

"Not a chance," said Rogers. "I'm through."

The year 1922 dawned bleakly for the once matchless advocate. He knew that the end was near. Money which his daughter provided him for food and the other necessaries was spent for the Jamaica ginger which had become his one tipple. He declared that he "couldn't get a kick" out of anything milder than that deadly compound.

When finally adversity in its most dire form had overtaken him, Rogers sedulously held aloof from all those who had known him in his days of affluence. Instead he prowled, for human companionship, among the members of the half-world, through Chinatown, along the byways where lurked folk of strange races, criminals whom he had saved from the law, human shadows inaccessible to those with whom he had formerly associated. But there had never been any reason for him to suffer from lack of life's ordinary comforts. His children saw to that to the best of their ability.

At noon of February 23, 1922, a law clerk named George Ellis left his firm's offices for the lodging house where of late Earl Rogers had sat glooming in his room. Earl used to give the young attorney many suggestions that proved invaluable short-cuts to otherwise remote points in the wilderness of law.

Ellis ascended the steps of the lodging-house and knocked at Rogers' door. Receiving no answer to his rap he repeated it more loudly. He called, and still got no response. Knowing that Earl had been ill for several weeks, Ellis became mildly apprehensive and pounded heavily on the wooden panel, shouting the inmate's name so noisily that the landlady came down the hall to remonstrate with him.

But by now the law clerk was alarmed, certain that something was amiss with the occupant of the room. He quickly convinced the landlady that the door should be forced and with her consent drove it open with his shoulder.

A man's form lay full length upon the floor, head toward the wash-bowl fixture against the wall opposite the bed. The body was cold. Death had come some time in the night of the twenty-second, suddenly, but not without warning. The mute gesture of the outstretched arm told as plainly as any words how in his last agony Earl had arisen from his couch and tried to reach the water faucet above the basin.

So alone, in the still night, passed one of the most brilliant masters of advocacy who ever graced a courtroom. And, whether it be mere coincidence or something ordered by a power beyond human understanding, he died exactly three years to the day—perhaps even to the very hour—after the passing of Teddy Landers.

A further striking example of the mystic law of coincidence is that the towering building wherein today Superior Court judges sit in judgment, where the public prosecutor and his horde of assistants busy themselves with their official duties, rests upon the former site of the humble lodging-house in which Earl Rogers passed his last days and died. Los Angeles' magnificent Hall of Justice appropriately has been erected on that spot—a stately cenotaph to the memory of the man whose vivid career is imperishably woven into the judicial history of the Pacific metropolis.